ОКТЯБРЯ·1967·
ПОЧТА
СССР
4 к
AF372097

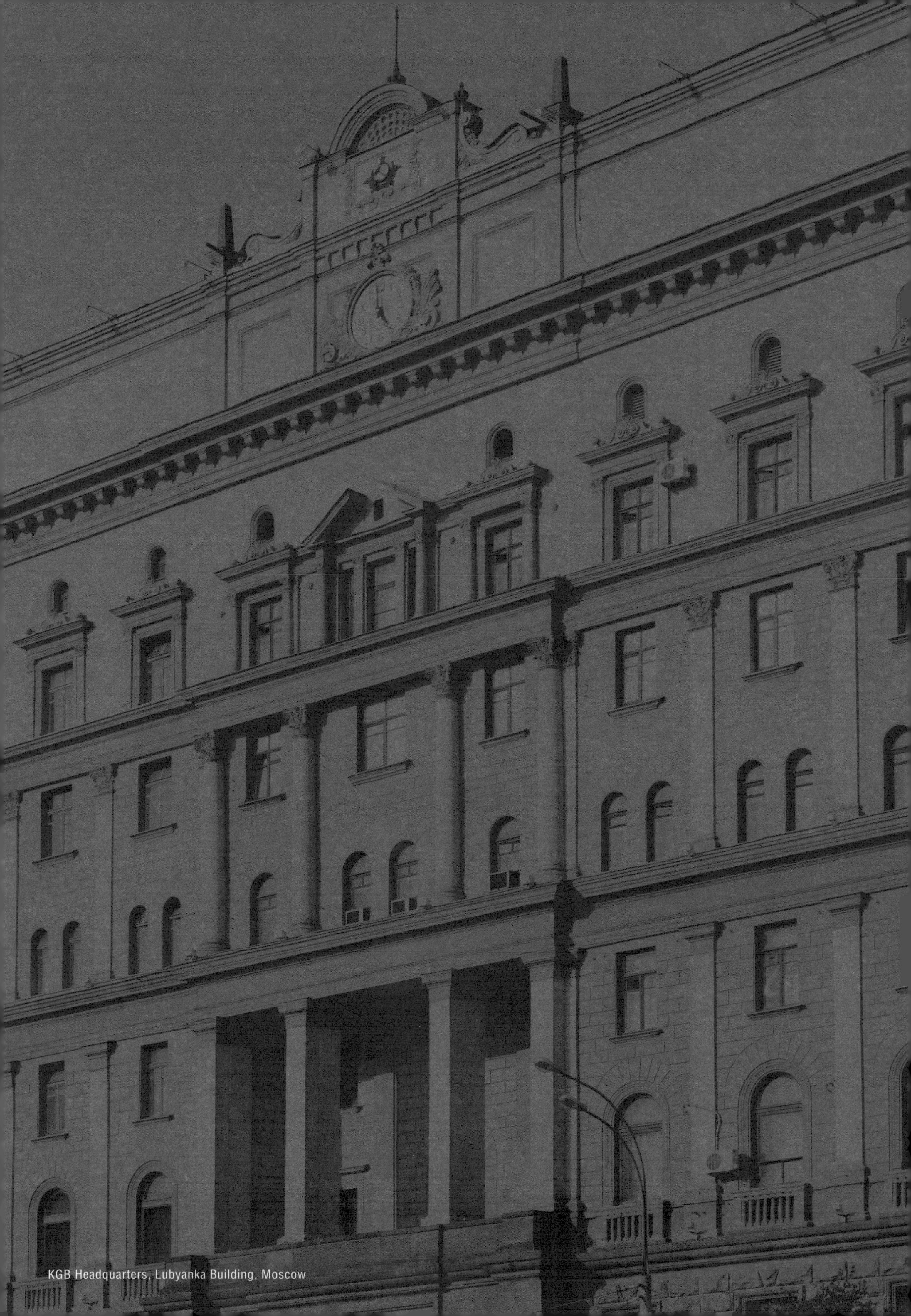

KGB Headquarters, Lubyanka Building, Moscow

"GAIETY IS THE MOST OUTSTANDING FEATURE OF THE SOVIET UNION"

JOSEF STALIN

ART FROM RUSSIA   SAATCHI GALLERY

IN ART WE TRUST

DIMITRI OZERKOV

Art never was very active in Moscow and St.Petersburg; its history consisted of bright revolutions and dark ages. Modernism in its Russian version became famous because of utopian leaders that proclaimed 'Victory over the Sun', as expressed by Malevich and Kruchenykh. It was some 100 years ago that the Russian avant-garde attempted to change the world. Is there something crucial in Russian art that is happening now and must not be missed at the beginning of our century? Everybody in Russia is thrilled to see what Charles Saatchi has selected from the country's contemporary art scene. To my knowledge, many artists wanted to be part of this exhibition.

Russian history used to be future-oriented. Artists are doomed to the legacy of the avant-garde, which means essentially pushing onward only. Local art history of the 20th century is going around in circles: the struggle to build a new future always turns out to be an inevitable fiasco. Over the last twenty years, art from Russia was manifested in all possible marginal forms. The West has seen its criminal tattoos and Cyrillic letters, its magic reflections on abstractionism and photography of the poorest people, its images of protest activities and ornamental variants on peasant motifs. Recently several new art strategies have become simply political movements which has made them less interesting to the international art viewer. It must be added that much of our national art is still being created in an artistic language only comprehensible to Russian art consumers. This visual language is so specific and enclosed that it works as a tool for communication only among locals. We are all trying to make this aspect of Russian art more appealing to an international audience but both the export of art and the local art market are still very far from being the most flourishing elements of the country's economy.

To western eyes having a Russian surname or conforming to stereotypes is enough to be identified as Russian. Being Russian now often means having parents who were born in the former USSR. Ukrainians, Georgians, citizens of Baltic countries, and people from all other ex-Soviet republics living around the world qualify as Russians in the west. This exhibition provides many examples.

Unfortunately during the Soviet Era an important part of culture was lost: people's custom of living with contemporary art. Artists became either senseless elements of the system, or invisible underground gurus. After the collapse of the avant-garde they were never publicly present as frank and candid judges of society. And we quickly forgot that they must be present. This is why Moscow and St. Petersburg have only now started to love and enjoy art again. People are rediscovering or learning for the first time about important Russian artists of the 1980-90s such as Ilya Kabakov, Dmitri Prigov, Erik Bulatov and Andrei Monastyrsky. It is only now that their work has begun to be shown in the Russian Pavilion at the Venice Biennale, for example.

This is why young artists are so important. We want them to become strong enough to represent Russian art internationally in the future. Their art — presented in this show — is multifocal and transcendent, poetic and hypocritical, politicized and romantic. It is probably the most global art in the world but still very much connected to its origins. We want them to change the world again. Tomorrow.

"WINTER'S GONE, SUMMER'S HERE, THANKS TO THE PARTY FOR THAT"

GOSHA OSTRETSOV

I am a Russian artist who lived in France for ten years in the 1990s. It was an invaluable experience. It taught me that to be able to develop as an artist and do something worthwhile I had to abandon my identity and become a French artist. The choice was unacceptable. I decided not to waste my life on absurdity, because life is short as it is, and returned to Moscow where I could contribute to the development of my homeland's culture.

The country I left in 1989, the Soviet Union, was dramatically different from the country to which I returned in 1999. I saw that the new Russian authorities did not appreciate the national culture and did nothing to help develop it. The Russia of old was a country of Rublyov's Trinity as the icon of a Christian empire and Malevich's Black Square as the anti-icon of the industrialization era. Everything else was the varnished art of the bourgeoisie or art as the servant of state ideology as exemplified by greasy spoon cafes. In the new Russia, where the party bosses have joined hands with criminals, the dominant art was the art of marketing.

This inspired me to launch the New Government project about a government whose five members always wear masks and can be replaced without the people being aware of any change.

More than two decades after the beginning of perestroika, we have a strong authority, but the carving up of budgets and embezzlement of funds is not the right background for the art. There are no reliable criteria for assessing the art, with museums long turned into private money laundering businesses and the galleries that opened at the dawn of New Russia closing down. This is the era of individualism, when artists can only develop their artistic taste independently. This is the time of the New Individualist Artist whose art has broken free from the grip of the collective unconscious and become unpredictable. It is also the era of the Consumer who has rejected mainstream galleries and is finding his own bearings in the world of art.

Unfortunately, both the powers-that-be and the private capital with vested interests in contemporary arts want to enjoy exhibitions without assuming the obligation to help artists between such projects. But I have good connections in the New Government's cabinet, which is why I have succeeded where state art centres and foundations failed: I have created an art centre with an exhibition hall and living quarters. It is the New Government that has been providing me with new contracts all these years. The London branch of the New Government has chosen to exhibit the works of six out of the 12 artists who routinely present their work in our art centre in Moscow.

Long live corruption!

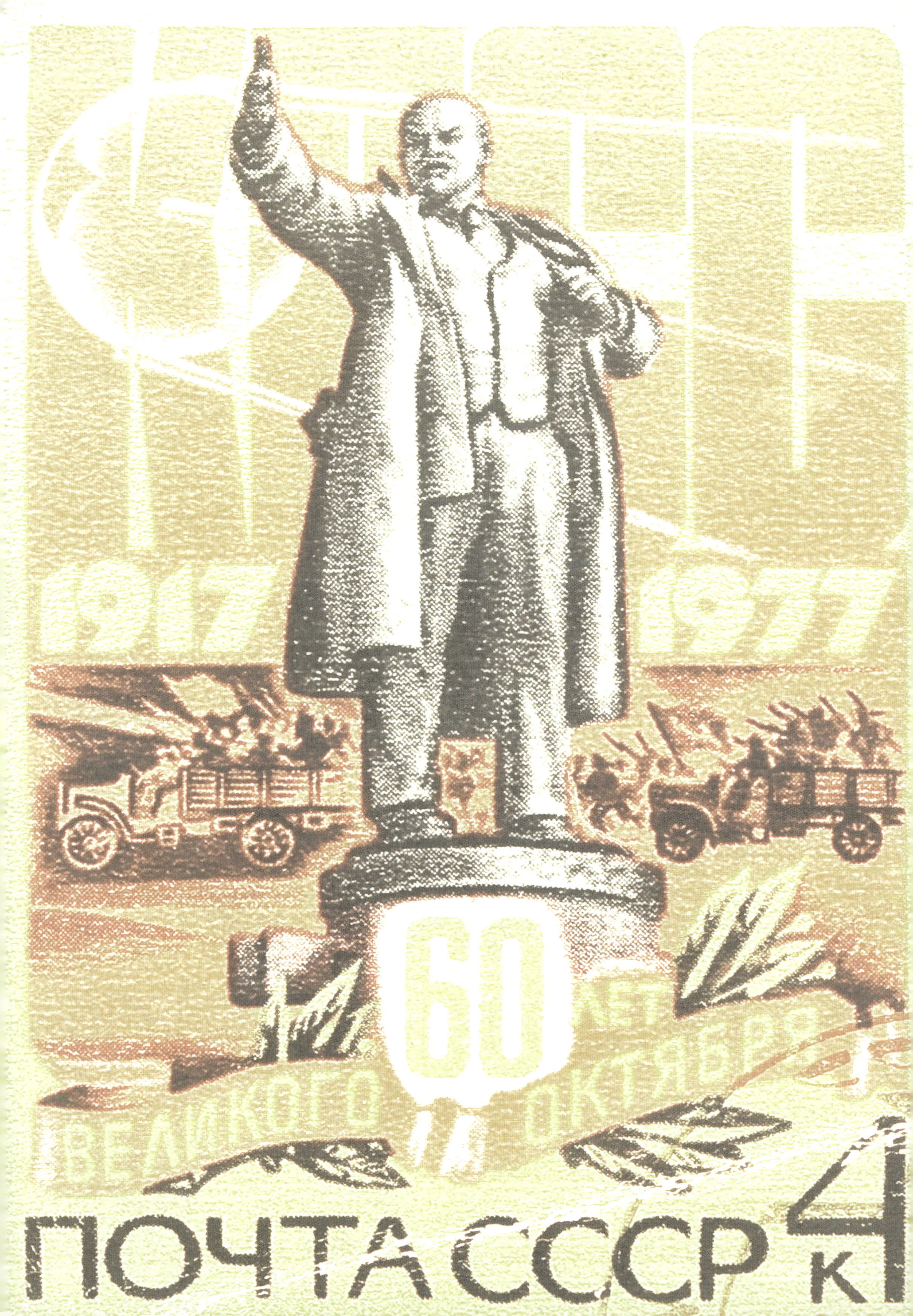

1917
1977
60
лет
ВЕЛИКОГО
ОКТЯБРЯ
ПОЧТА СССР
4 к

JANIS AVOTINS

DANIEL BRAGIN

DASHA FURSEY

LIUDMILA KONSTANTINOVA

IRINA KORINA

VALERY KOSHLYAKOV

DARIA KROTOVA

BORIS MIKHAILOV

NIKA NEELOVA

VIKENTI NILIN

GOSHA OSTRETSOV

SERGEY PAKHOMOV

ANNA PARKINA

YELENA POPOVA

ROMAN SAVCHENKO

DASHA SHISHKIN

TAMUNA SIRBILADZE

SERGEI VASILIEV

JANIS AVOTINS

With their ghostly, alienated faces and figures reminiscent of Soviet-era photography, Janis Avotins thinly painted canvases draw us into a fragile, elliptic world haunted by collective memory.

In one of Avotins' series, photographs of the heads of two sombre-looking Cold War-era bureaucrats are stripped of their original context and reappear within a dark emptiness. Their studied features look crudely eroded, as if rubbed onto, or rubbed out of, a temporary blackboard.

Two gossamer-like female figures – another solemn and almost faceless pair – appear to be walking out of a background of darkness. Their poses, soft silhouettes and the bright illumination on their bodies recall the long-exposure and bleached out feel of early photography, so often showing shapes similarly eked out of an enveloping darkness. They are beautiful, bleak and memorable, all at once.

Often using a minimalistic, monochromatic aesthetic reminiscent of fellow Latvian artist Vija Celmins, Avotins' virtuosic imprimatura washes and technique blur and erase the specificity of his subjects, imbuing his images with an air of mystery, rather than nostalgia. They playfully engage with the relationships between analogue photography, the way history can edit and turn individuals anonymous, and with our own collective memory-making – impressions fading in and out of existence.

In one work, a ghostly, isolated right hand is placed exactly in the middle of a canvas, becoming the mysterious central focus within an overwhelming nothingness. In other works, singled out yet unrecognizable figures appear framed by a similar vacuum, soaked in washes accompanied by the symbolic material presence of the canvas's grain. Recent compositions include architectural elements, but figures remain phantom-like, in a state of tension somewhere between sketchily existing and melting into the background.

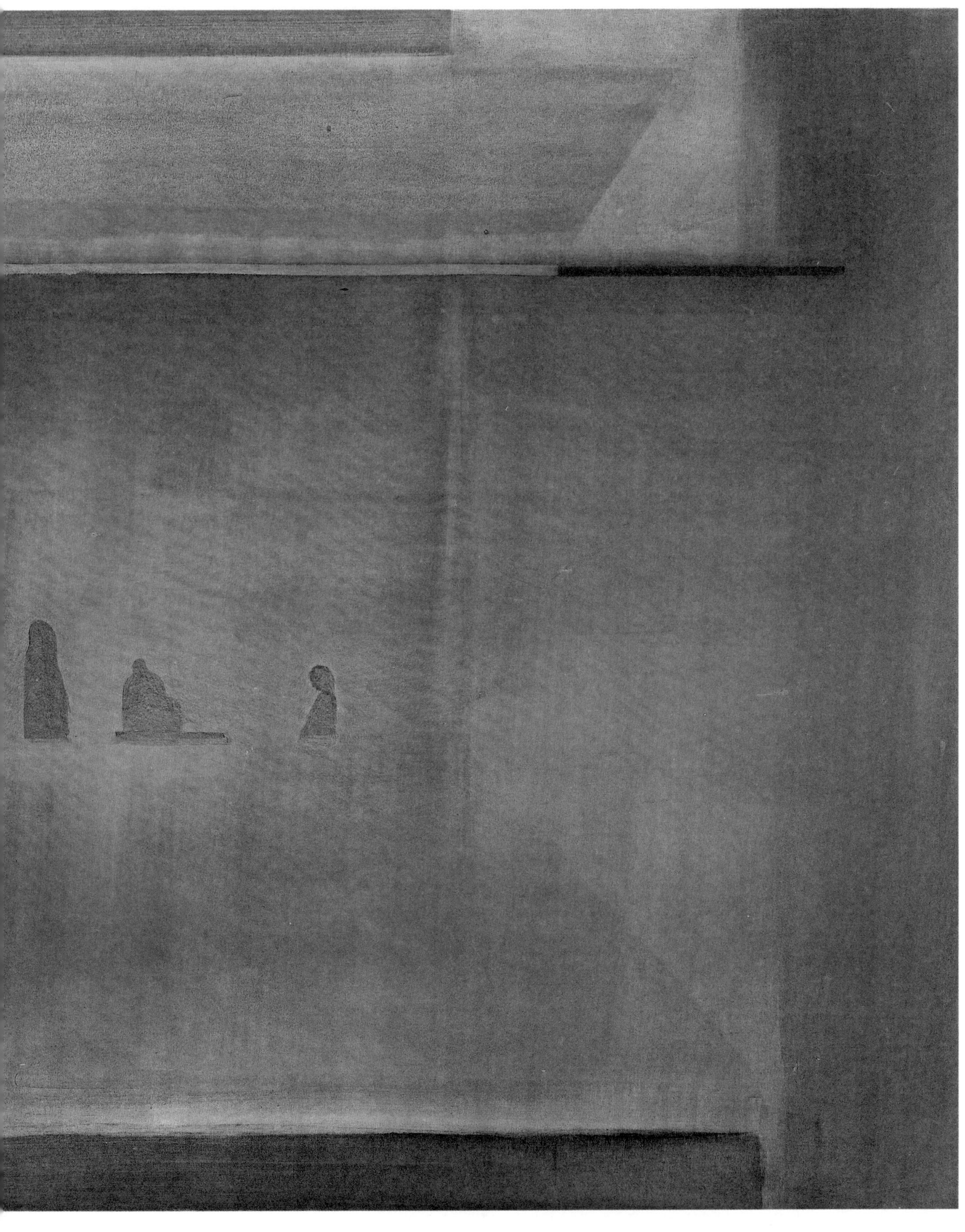

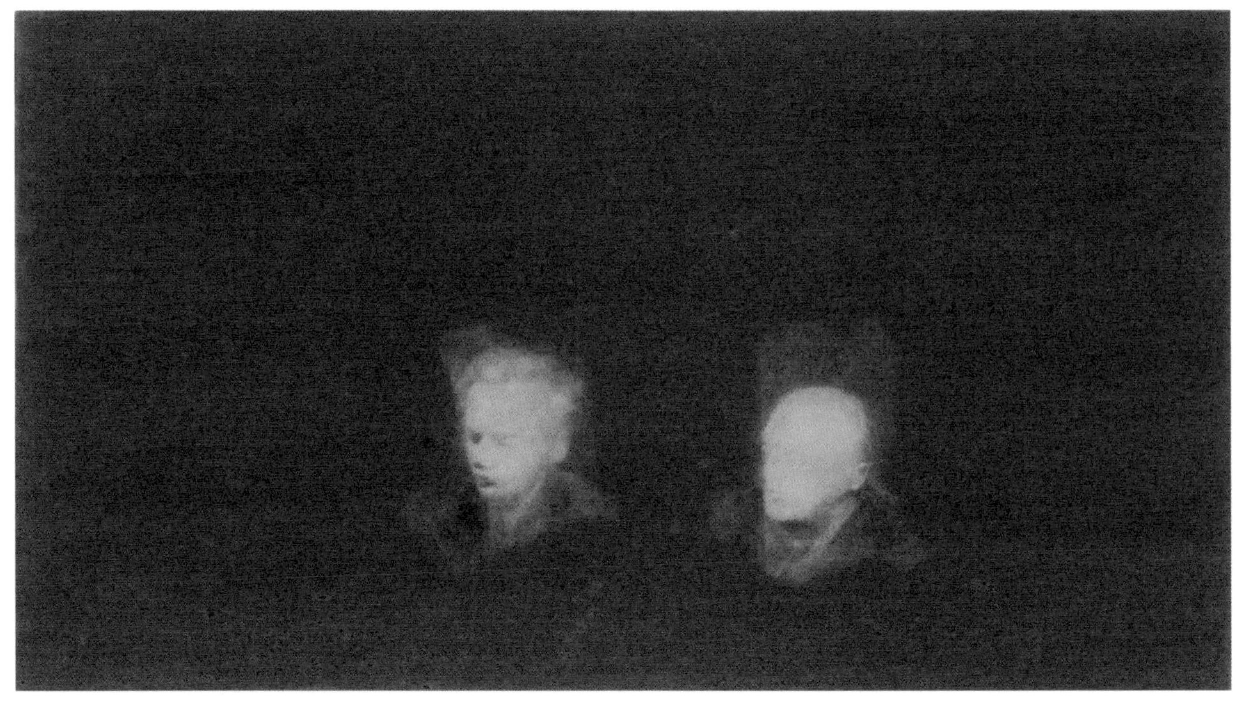

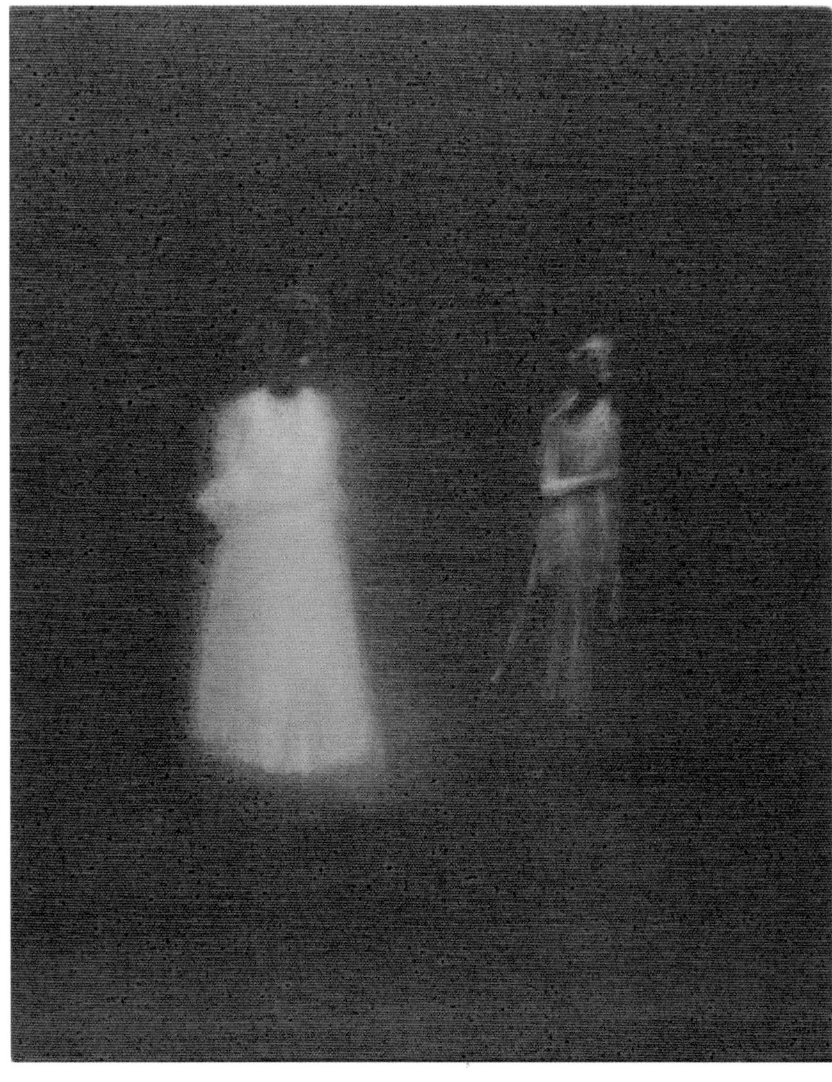

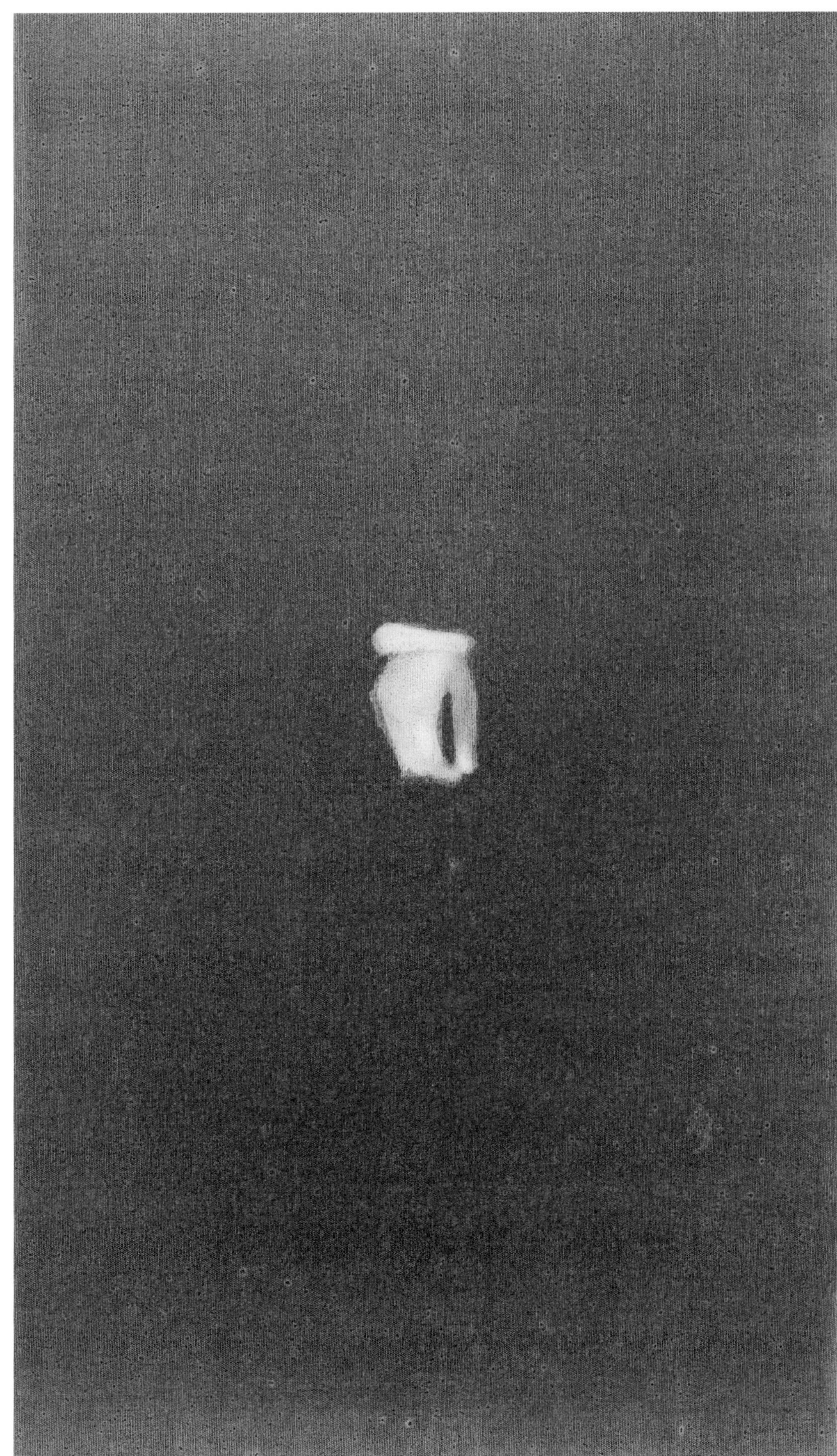

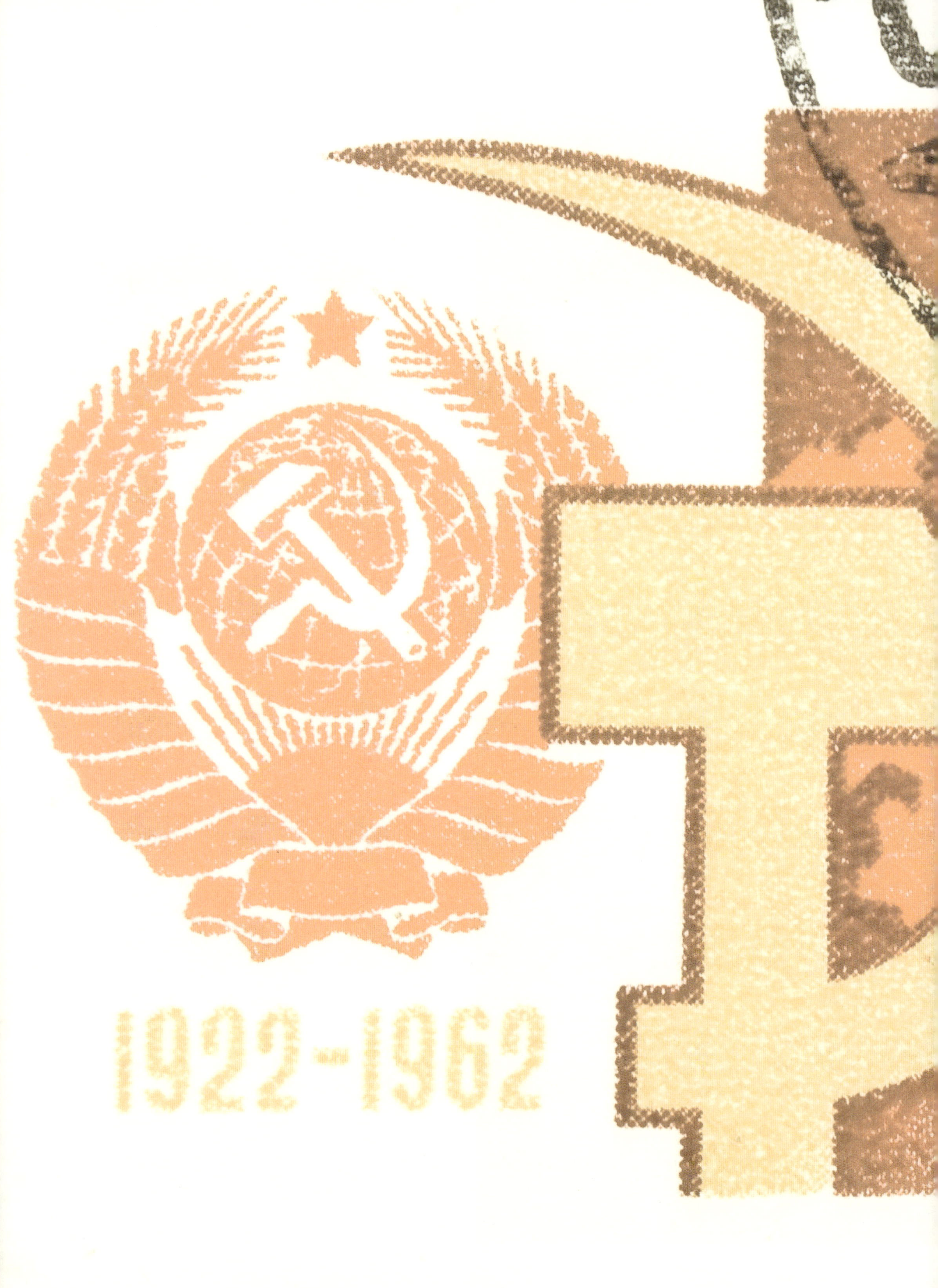

1922—1962

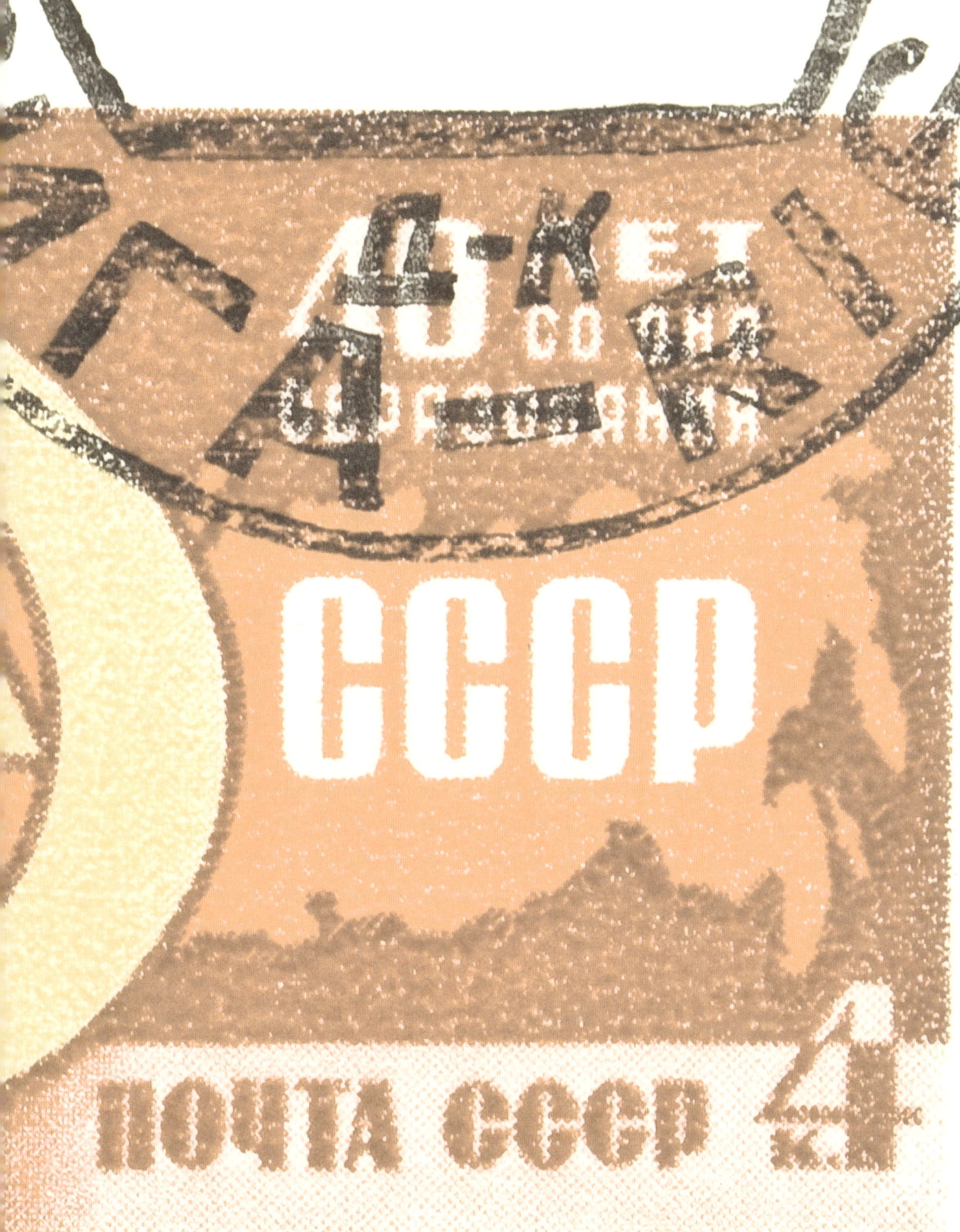
45-ЛЕТ
СОЮЗА
ССР
СССР
ПОЧТА СССР 4

DANIEL BRAGIN

In his sculptures Daniel Bragin creates unpredictable, awkward material juxtapositions; conveying an utterly deadpan economy of means, they also stand as slightly tongue-in-cheek objects celebrating a child-like joy in making.

The windshield glass and PVC strings that compose *Bedtime Story* (2012) are almost opposites in the artist's view. We associate shattered glass with car accidents, violence against shops and social riots, but here, sheets of it have uncannily been patched and finished off with candy-coloured plastic threads, the same kind that children use to make friendship bracelets. The resulting fusion of the two elements is a strangely innocent but uncomforting, even nightmarish, sheet or 'blanket', an alluring visual oxymoron "leaving a trace of cold gaiety, perhaps even in the eyes of the child".

"I enjoy putting mundane objects and commonplace materials to use," the artist explains. "The fine-tuning of each visual element and the selection/combination of details allows the familiarity to remain, whilst creating a strikingly new metaphorical interpretation."

The sagging body of his life-size *The Lady* (2010) is made out of PVC filled with sand, but its black shiny surface could suggest something like tar or mercury, shifting shapes according to gravity. Displayed in various positions – on the floor, recumbent on stairs – "it is forced to take the shape of the given surface, meekly adapting to the circumstances." Another slightly sinister, hybrid silhouette, like the piled up folds of *Bedtime Story*, it is an object that can be read on several narrative levels at once, despite its seeming initial simplicity.

DB-01 **DB-02**

THE LADY, 2010   BEDTIME STORY, 2012
PVC filled with sand   Glass and PVC strings
25 x 60 x 180 cm   Approx: 25 x 240 x 210 cm

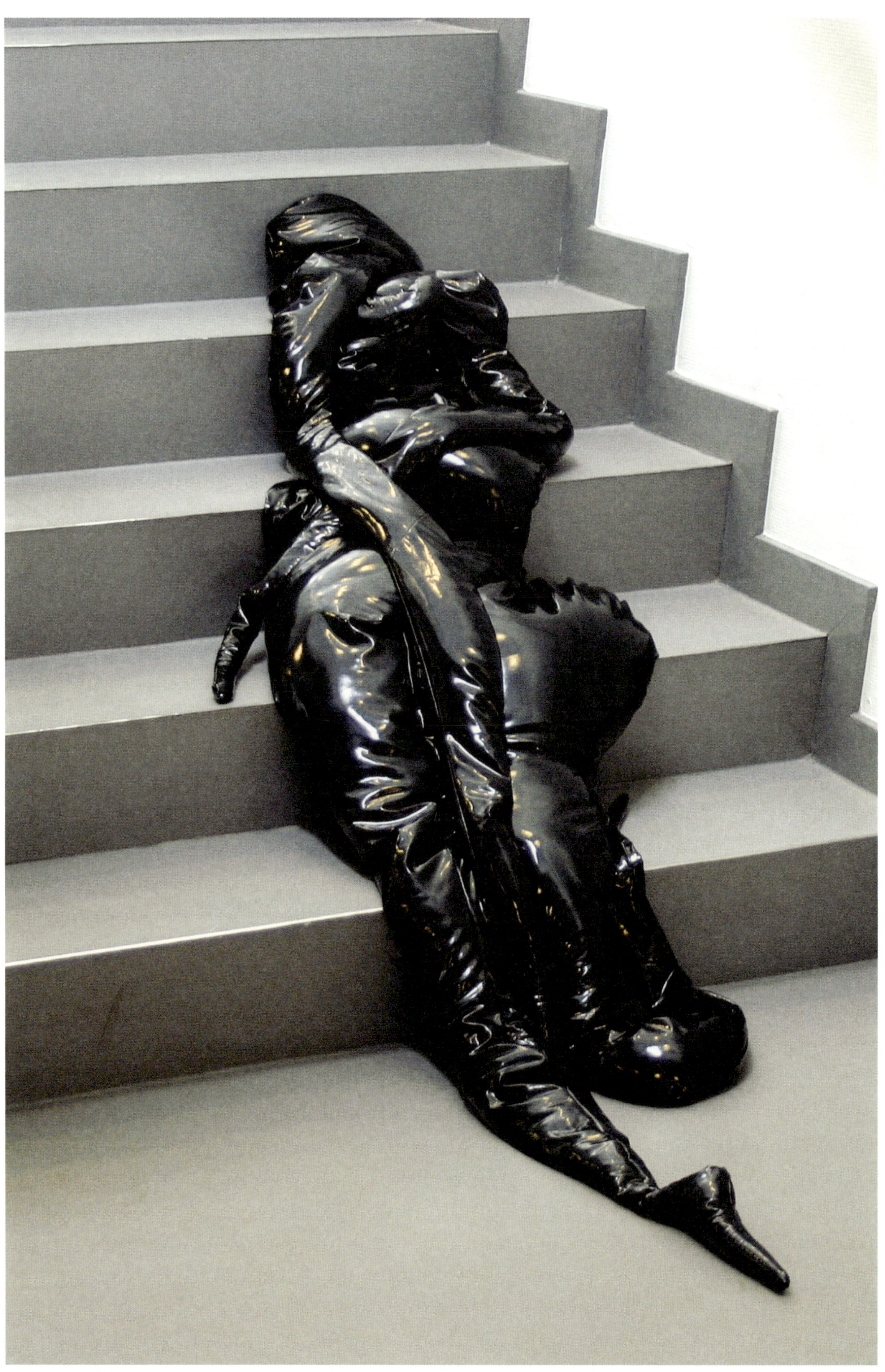

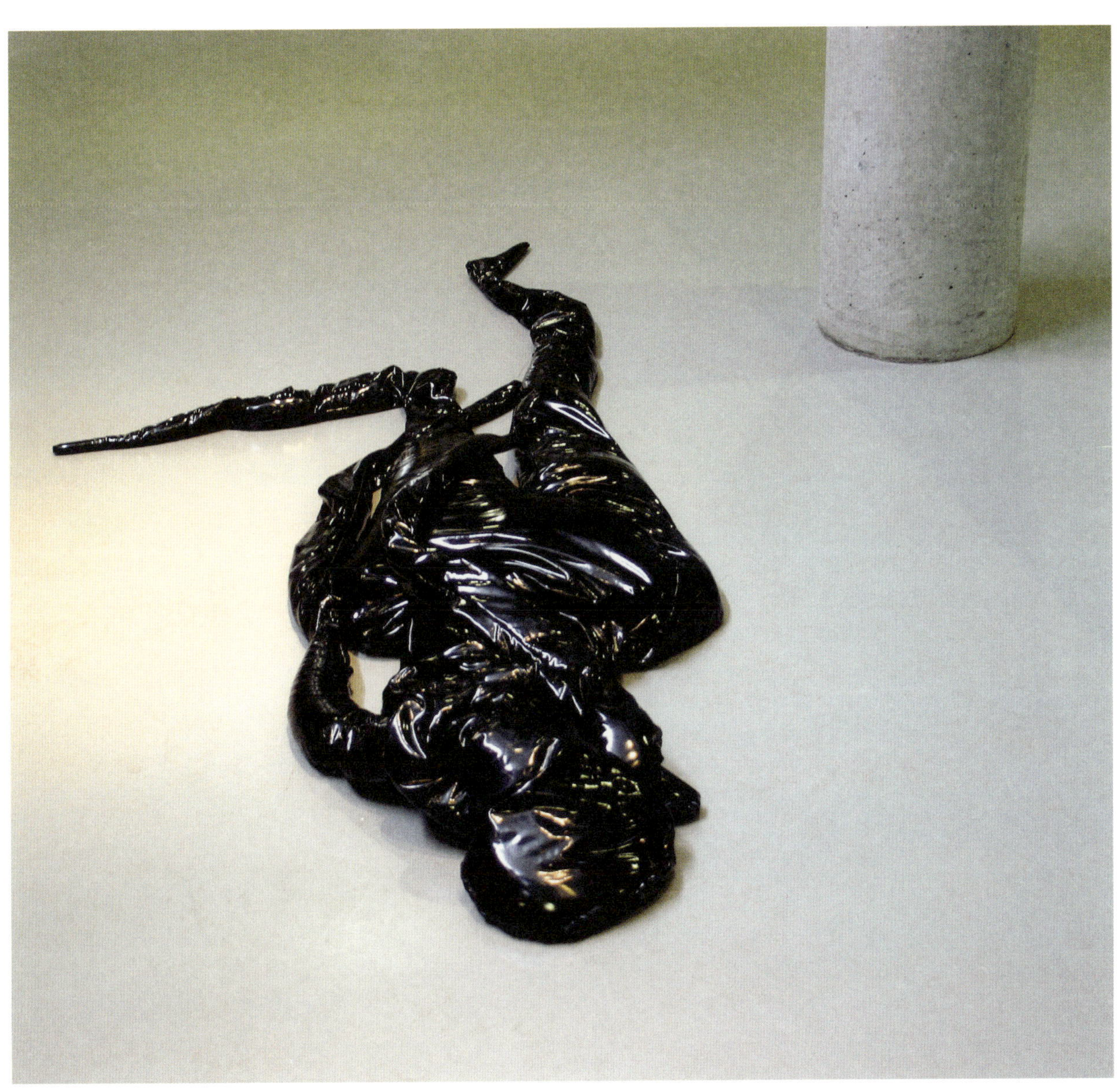

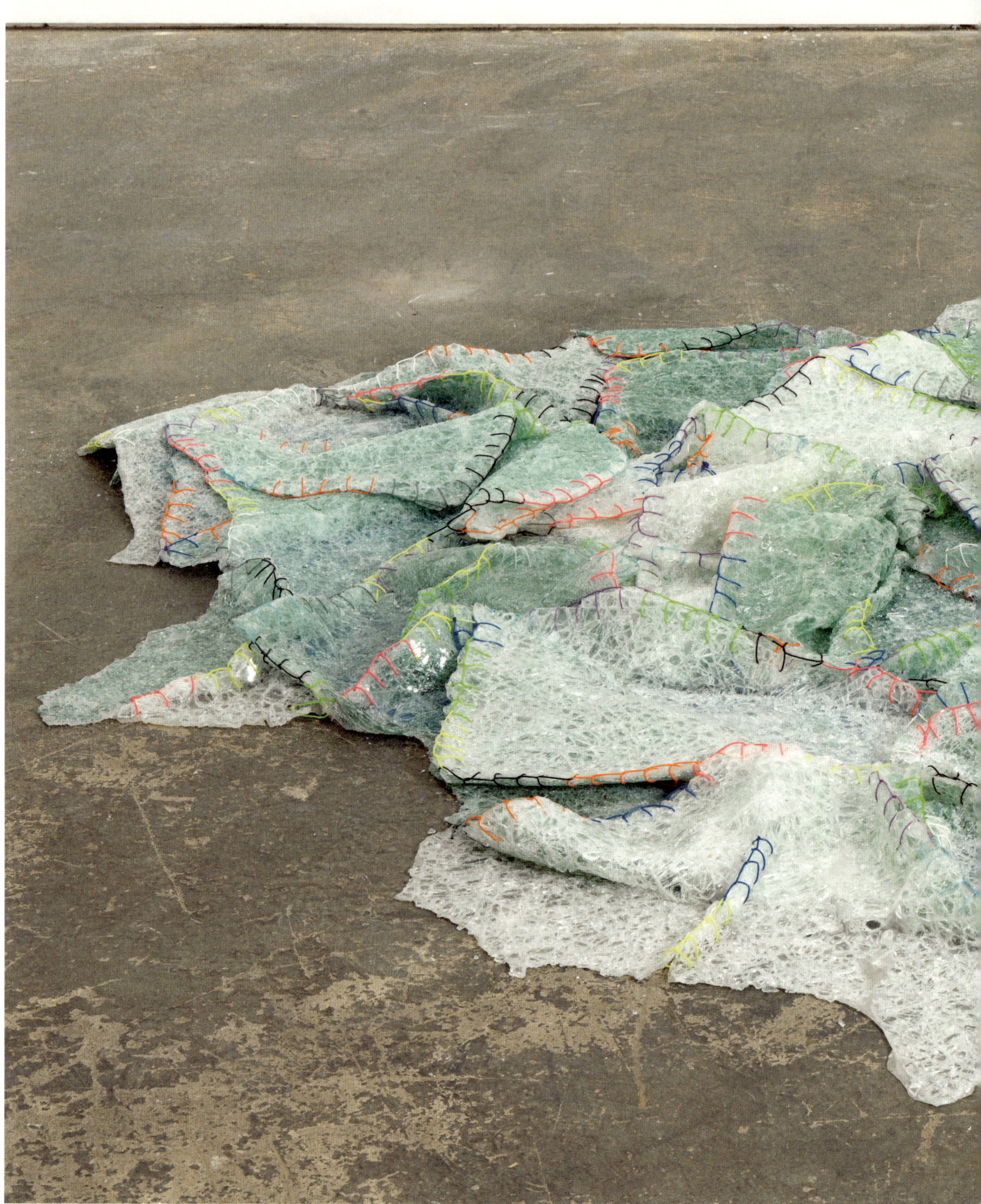

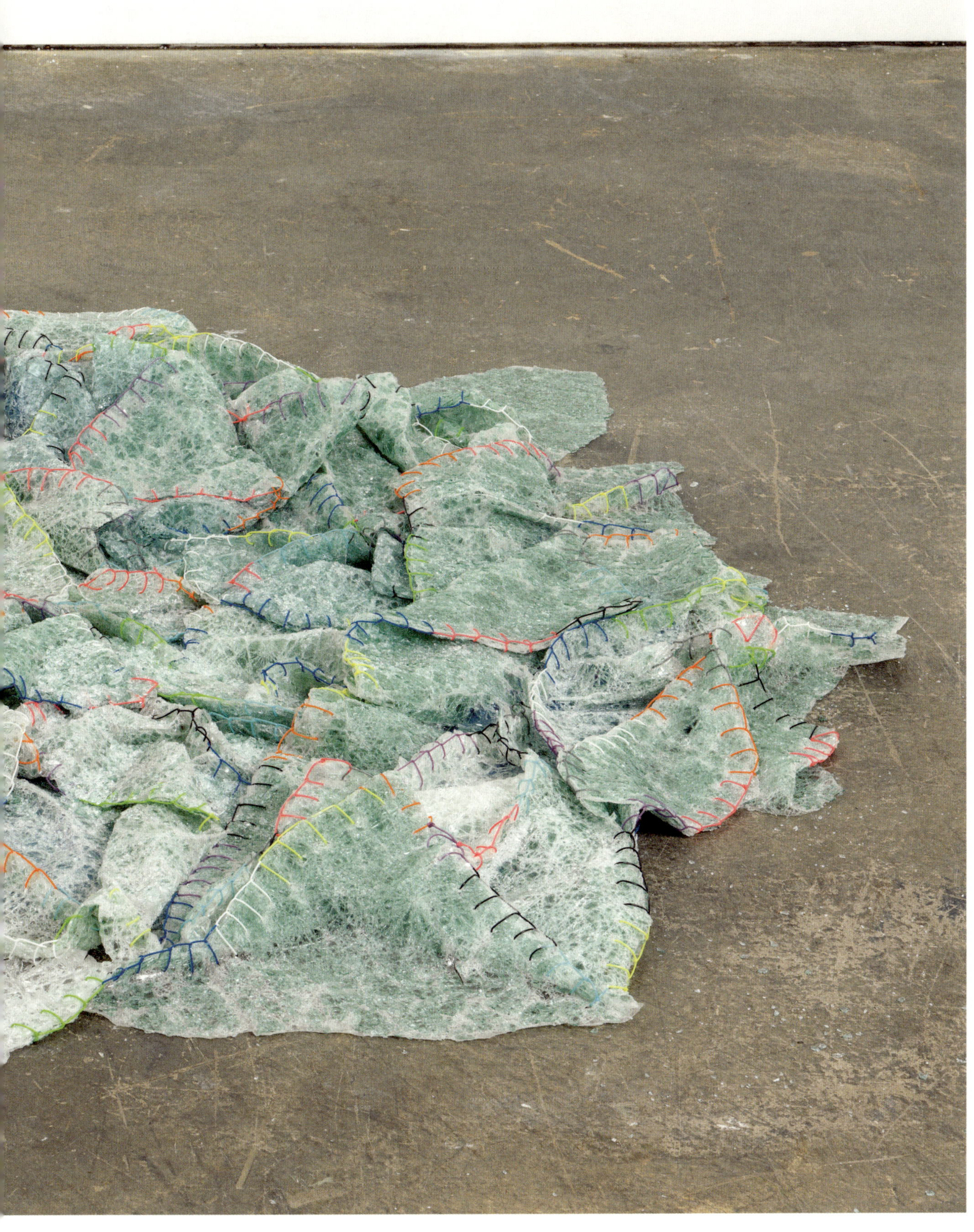

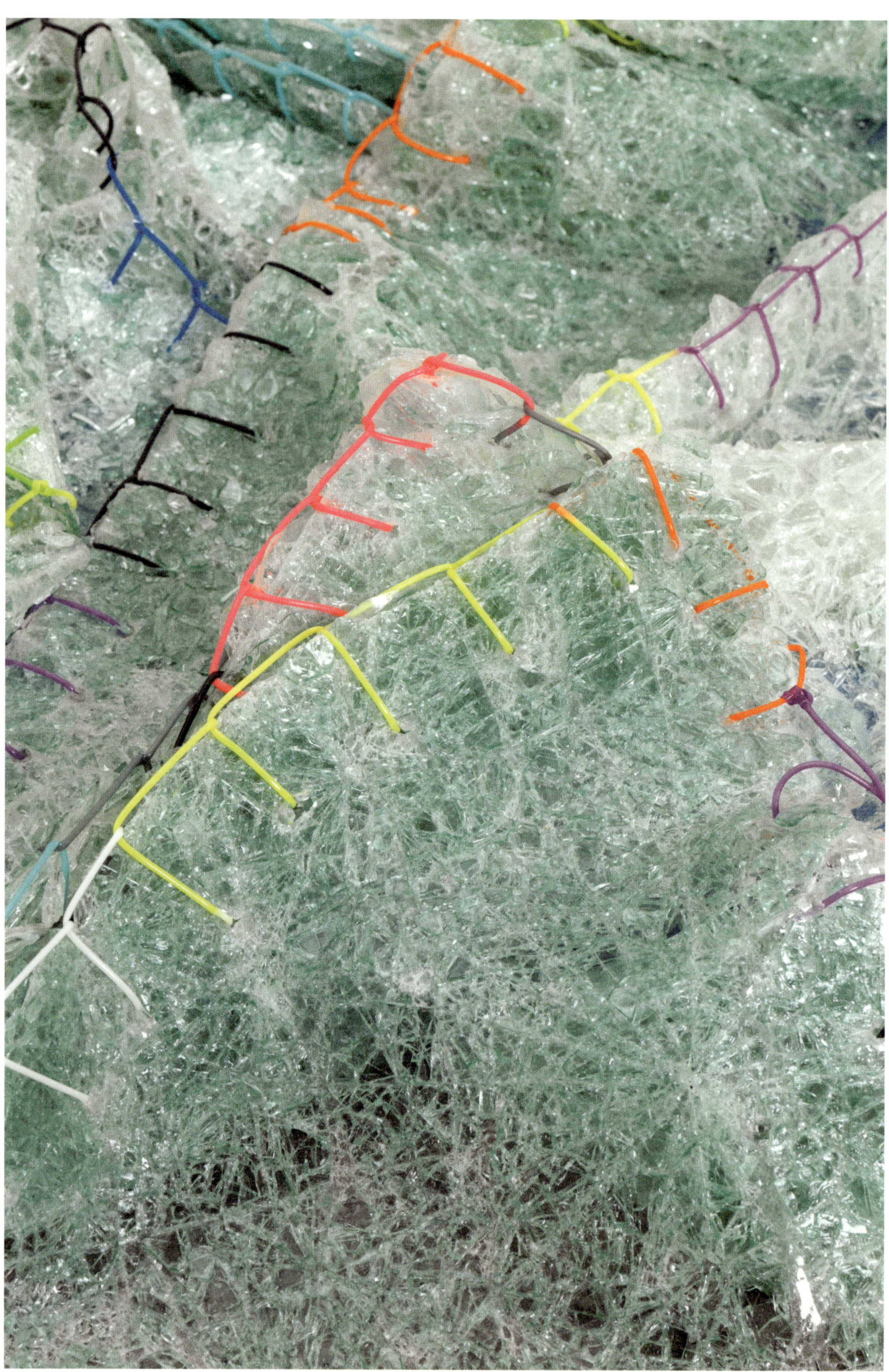

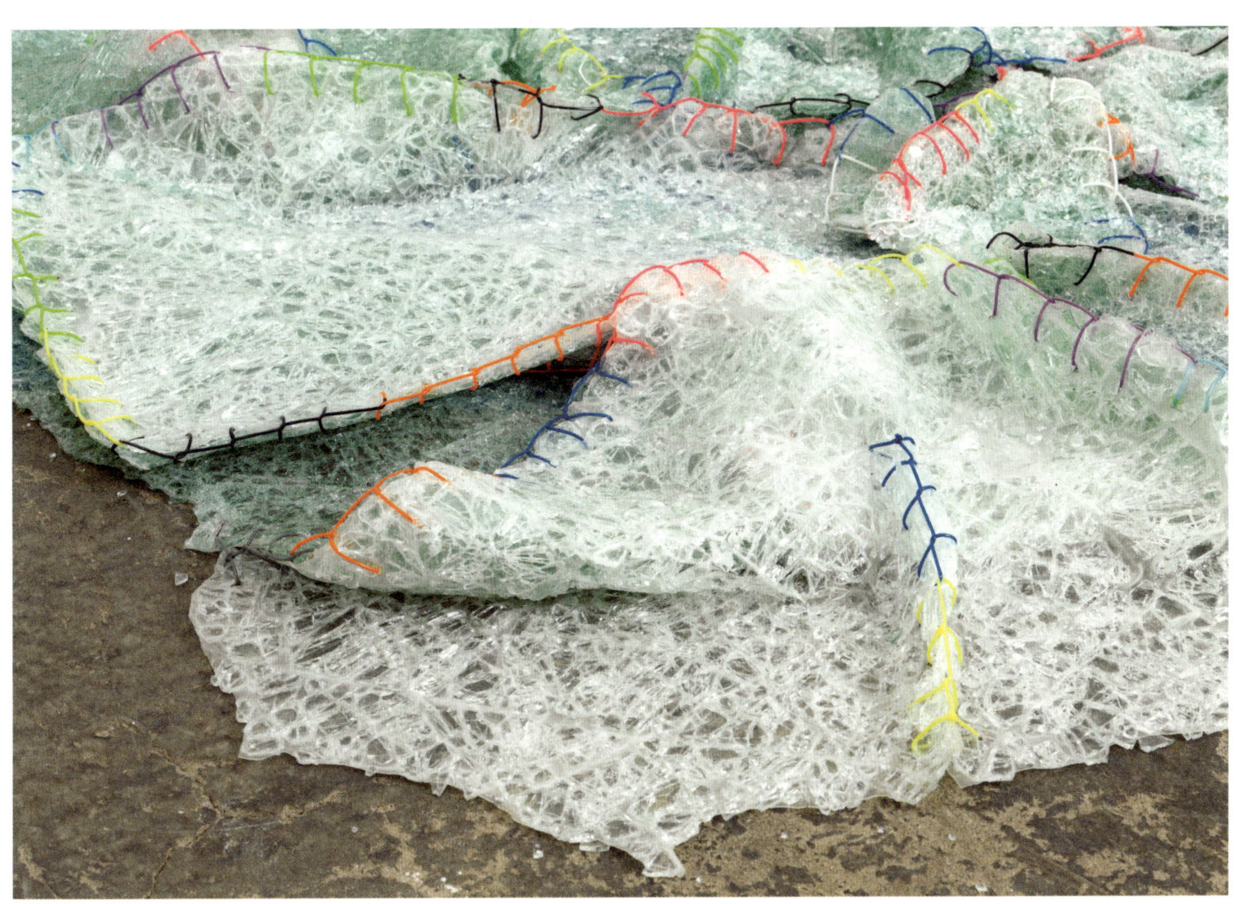

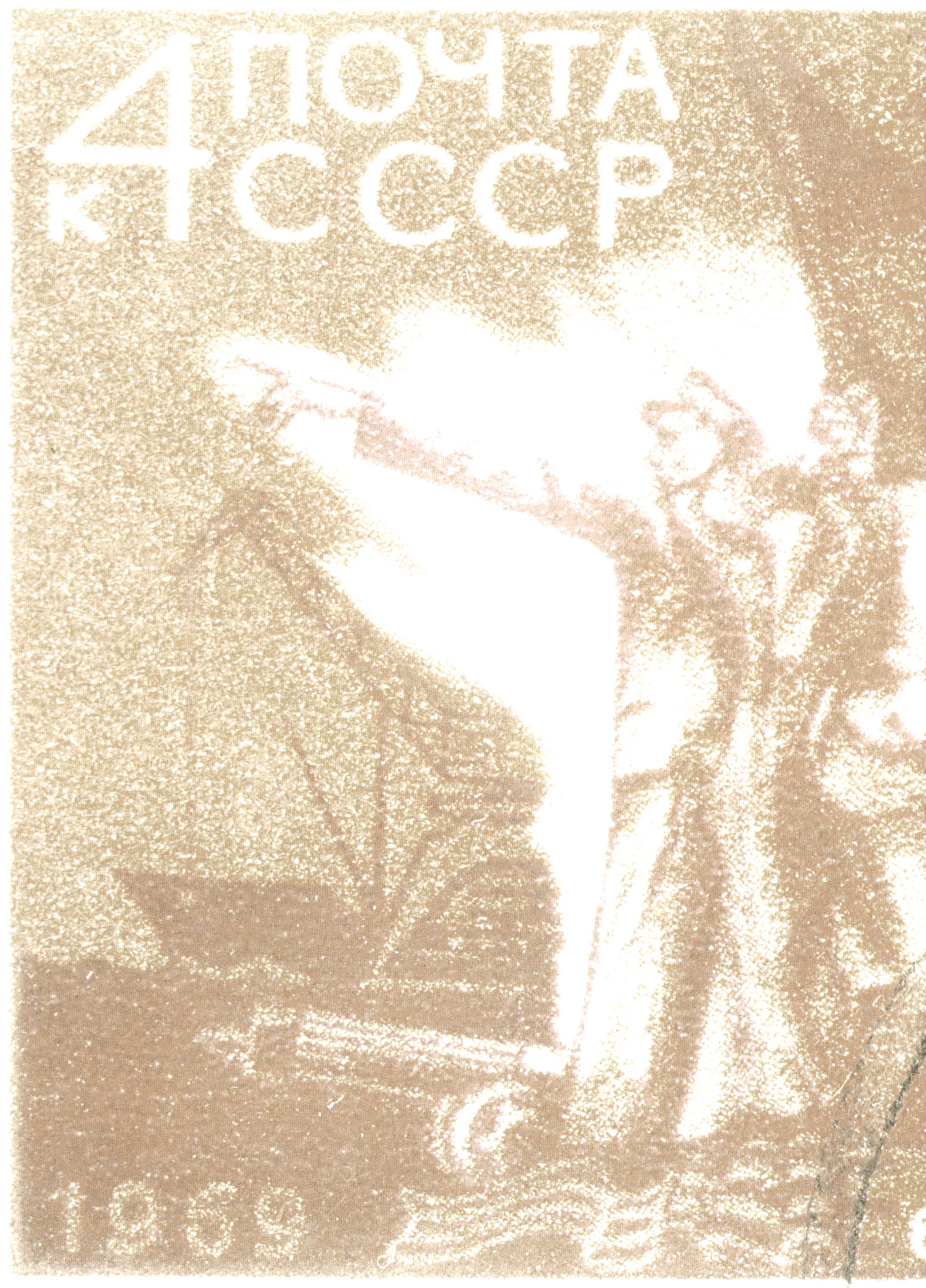
ПОЧТА СССР
4 к
1909

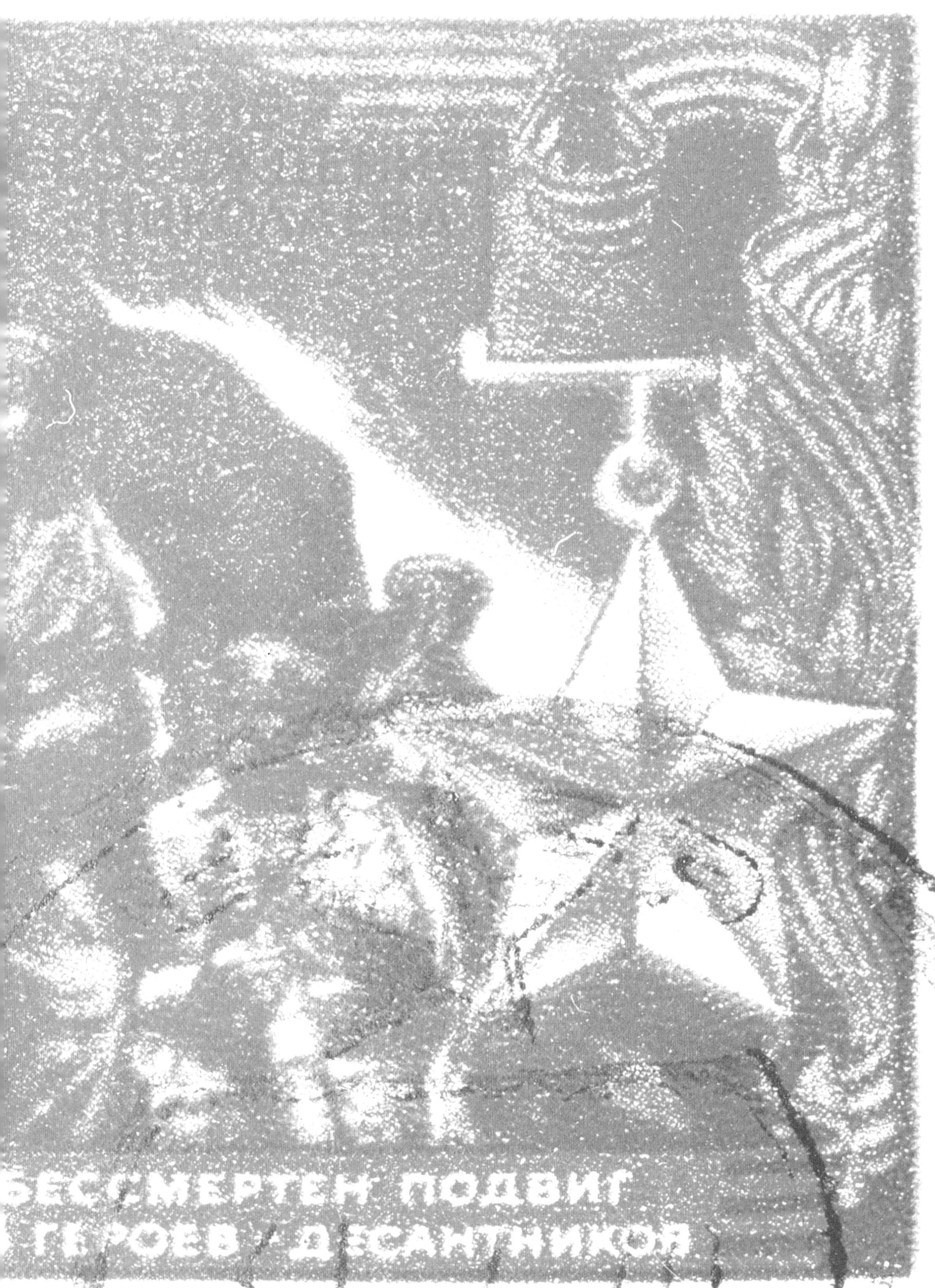
БЕССМЕРТЕН ПОДВИГ
ГЕРОЕВ-ДЕСАНТНИКОВ

DASHA FURSEY

Dasha Fursey's practice, comprising painting, video, performance and sculptural installations, repurposes cultish Soviet imagery into a fairytale-like, almost psychedelic experience.

One of her painting series depicts female Soviet Young Pioneers in scenes that take them out of iconic propaganda posters into more ambiguous contexts. The young pioneer, an alter ego for the artist, is shown romantically embracing a smiling Che; about to take a bite out of a large hallucinogenic/poisonous toadstool bearing a photographic image tagged '1917', suggestive of the Russian revolution; and also at night, out in the street, drinking tall cocktails and posing on all fours over city rooftops.

'In the mind of the young, maturing girl,' Fursey explains, 'images of the Soviet cult blend with an unconscious desire for love, unformed erotic fantasies'. Sincere utopianism and naiveté mix with an unabashed sexuality and an ironicised redefinition of feminine roles. The mushrooms unavoidably bring Alice's Adventures in Wonderland to mind; and throughout, initiation rites are symbolized through the Pioneers' red scarf tying ceremony.

Boundary Post Of A Cat Bajun (2012), a human-sized tower of glass jars containing stained-glass coloured preserves of mushrooms (again), fruit, vegetables and berries, seems precarious and uncanny, almost teetering on the brink of collapse. The preserves themselves look grubby and desperate, several steps down from Observer Food Monthly 'rustic'. One might say they're about shortage, fear of starvation, rather than indulgence, but there's also something laboratorial about their orderliness. This is no longer just food; what this fermenting, organic totem holds could be lethal, a transformative potion, or a Russian landscape preserved forever in formaldehyde.

BOUNDARY POST OF A CAT BAJUN, 2012

Glass, plastic, fruit, vegetables, mushrooms, berries

180 x 17 x 17 cm

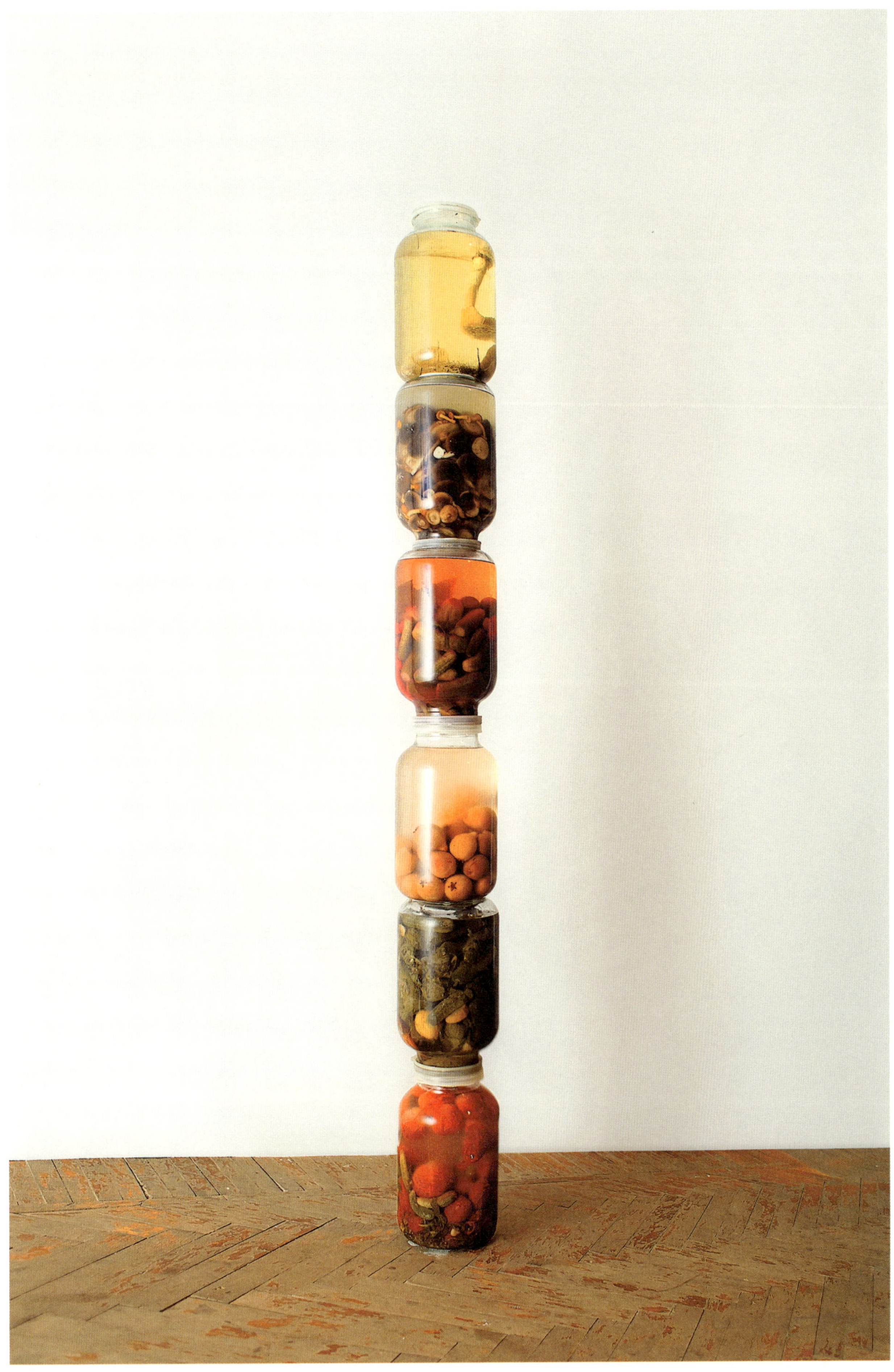

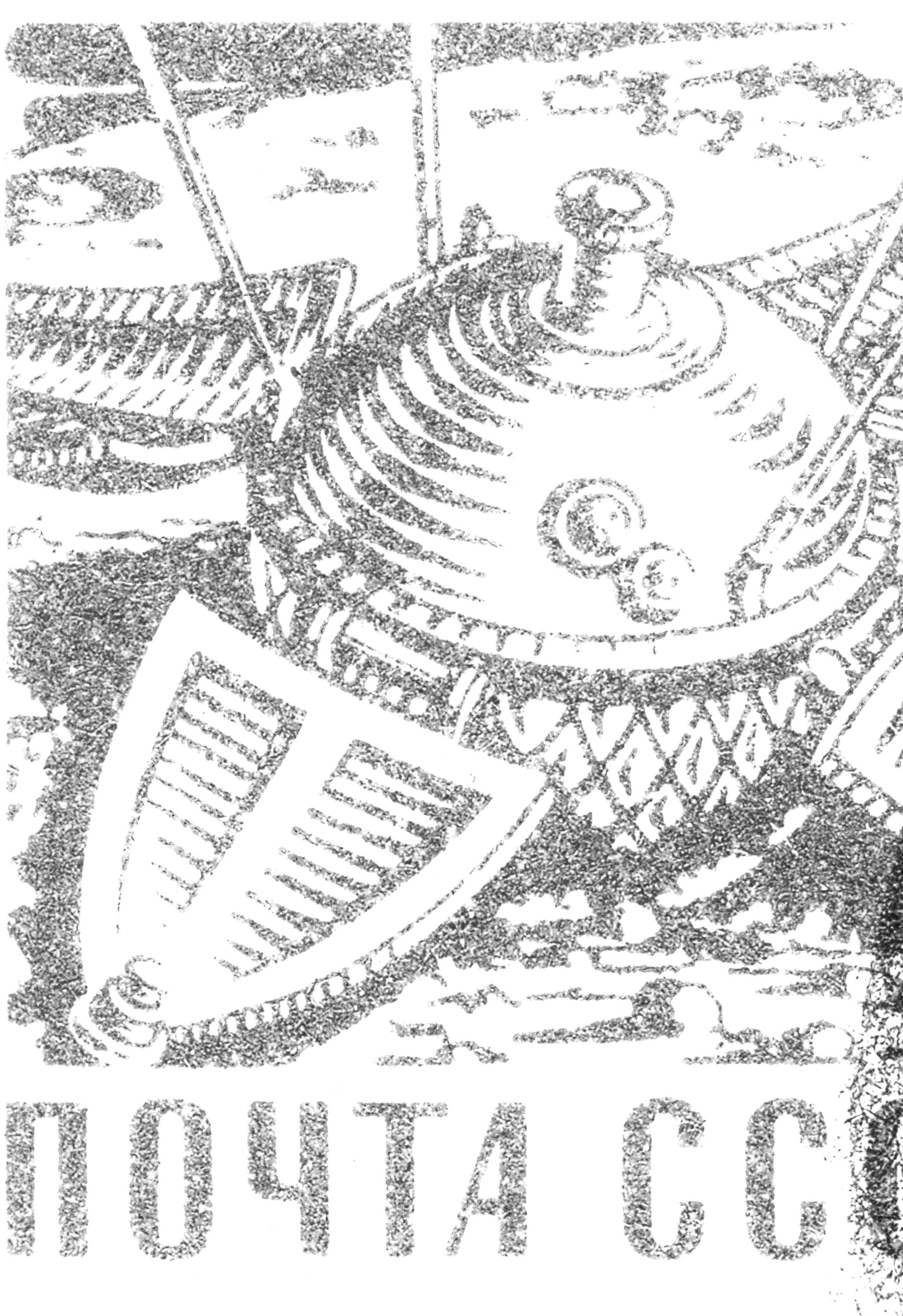

ПОЧТА СССР

1968
PEZ HOP

LIUDMILA KONSTANTINOVA

Liudmila Konstantinova's paintings raise questions about the assumed purpose and meaning of contemporary art. *Paintings for Holes* (2011) is an installation comprising 18 rectangular, monochromatic painted canvases of various sizes, hung on the gallery wall in an arrangement that at first look resembles a modernist grid. In fact, the colour block set up is reminiscent of a certain time in Soviet history – of Malevich's geometric compositions, of Russian constructivism – and of its influence on the graphic design of movements such as the Bauhaus and De Stijl.

Notably, the colours in Konstantinova's paintings, and also in her multi-coloured stalactite, *Icicle* (2012), aren't quite as strict as if they belonged in a palette of early 20th-century art – bright red sits next to olive green, which is next to canary yellow, then baby blue and puce. Like an interior decorator's colour wheel, her range is wider, less easily branded.

The artist wanted "to make a series of paintings that could be useful for different people". Catering to the lowest common denominators of acceptability – and bypassing any sticky controversial subject matter or format issues – she made canvases in all shapes, sizes and painted them in clear flat colours so that everyone could find "their own"; but crucially, they're all essentially as blank as each other.

As their title implies, the paintings were also made with another specific purpose in mind: they can be used to hide any imperfections on a wall, like cracks, paint marks or dead mosquitos. They can be arranged as desired, like modular shelving or an occasional table. Konstantinova's proposal for art today is more utilitarian chic prop than revolutionary.

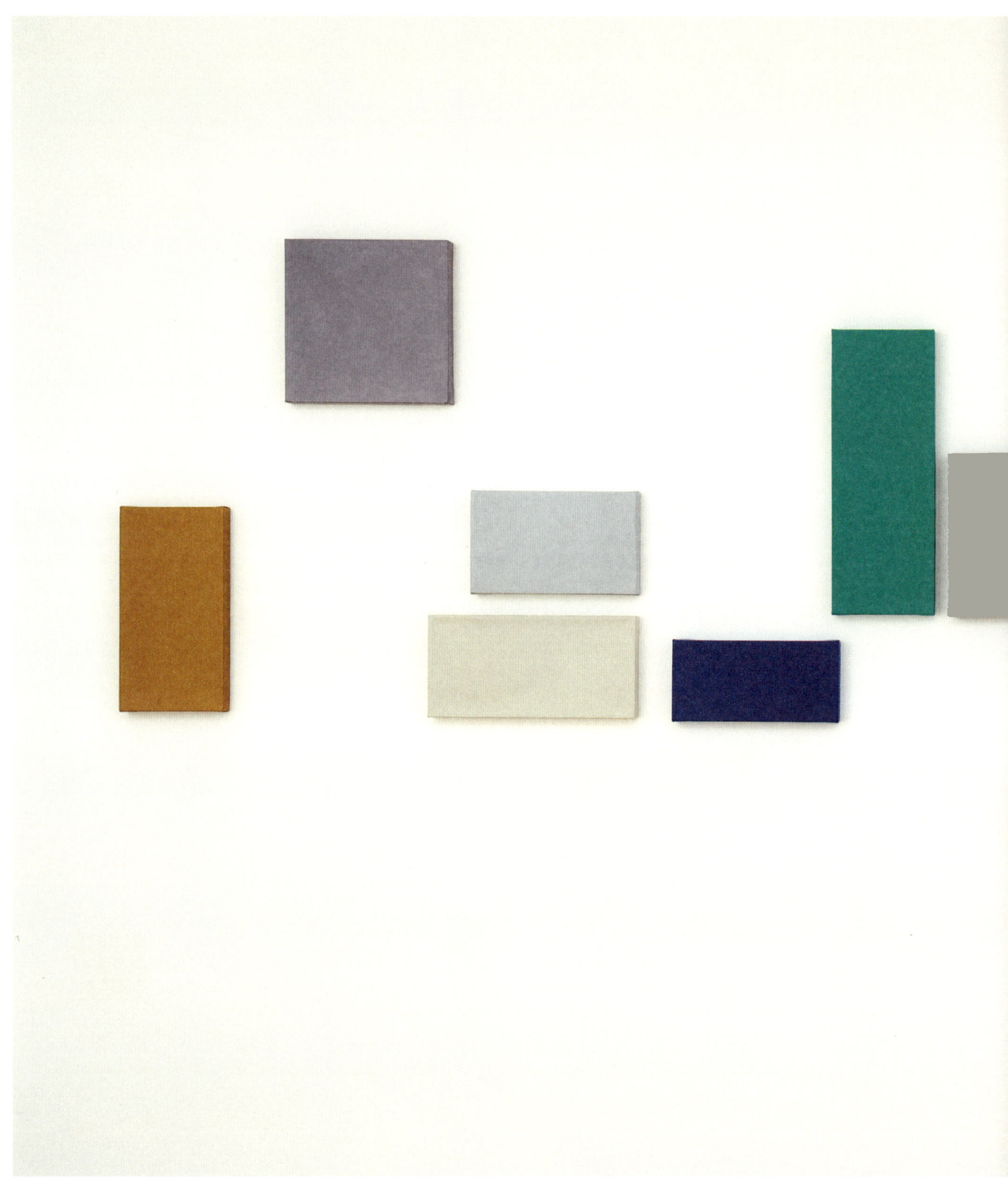

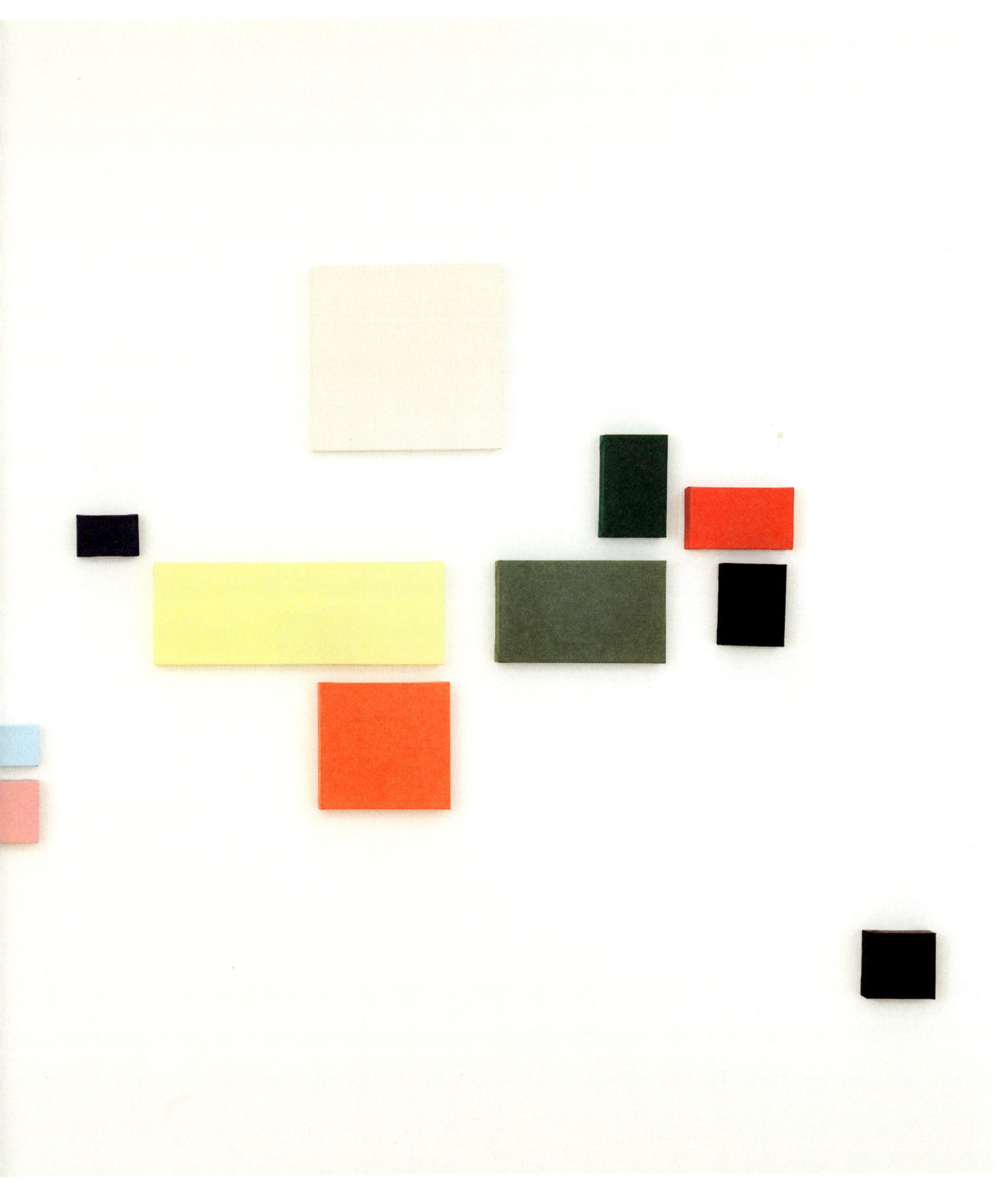

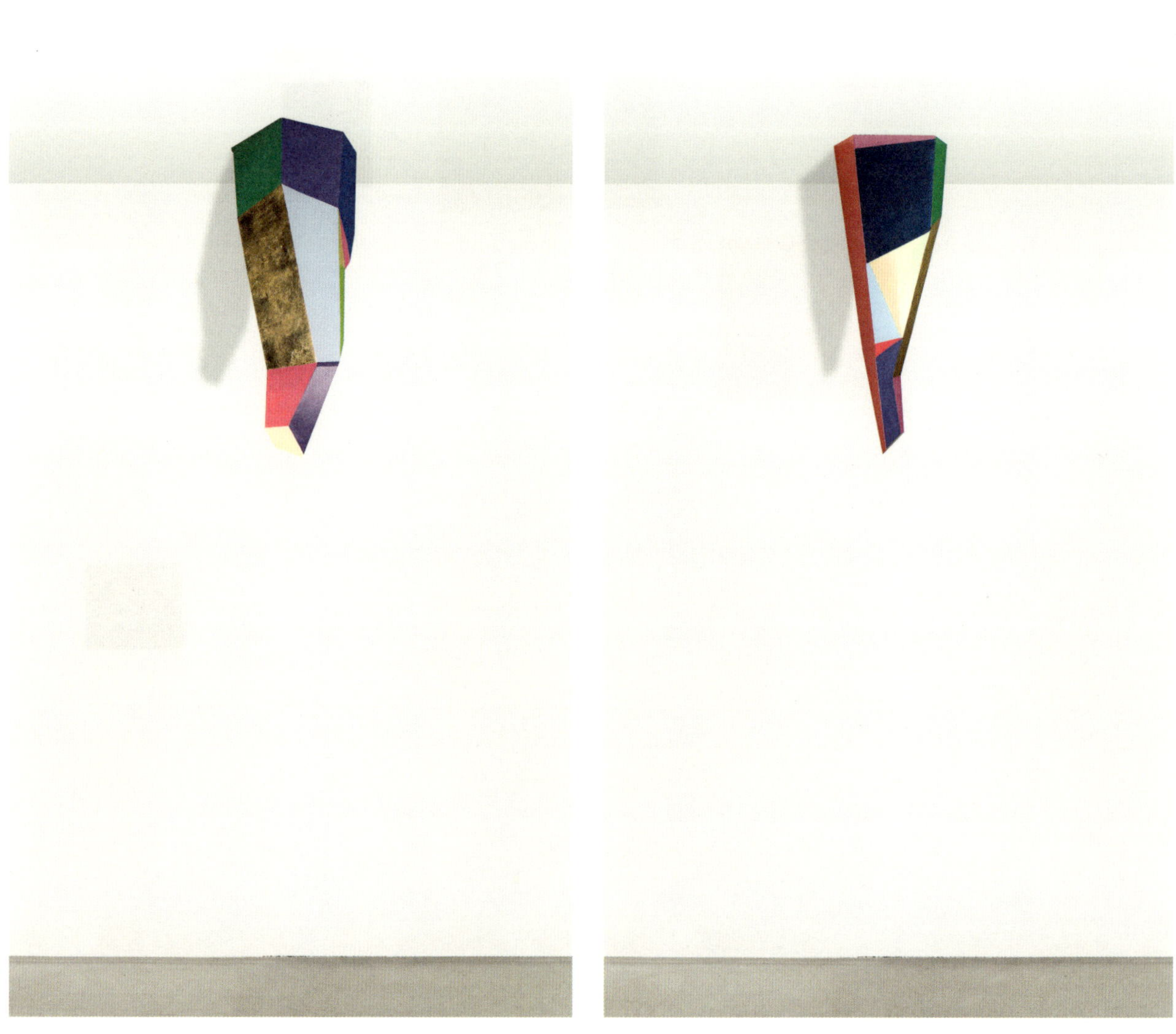

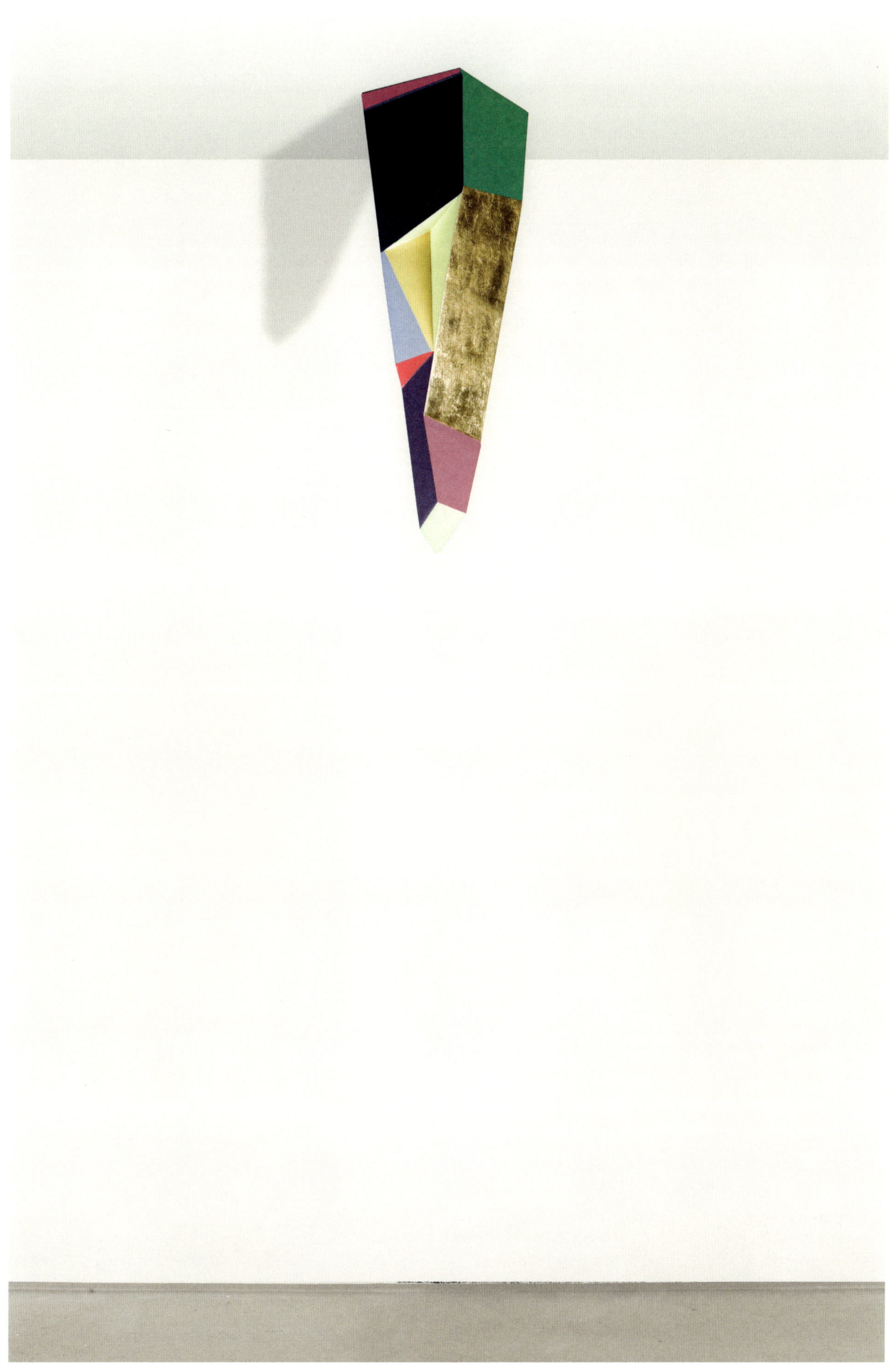

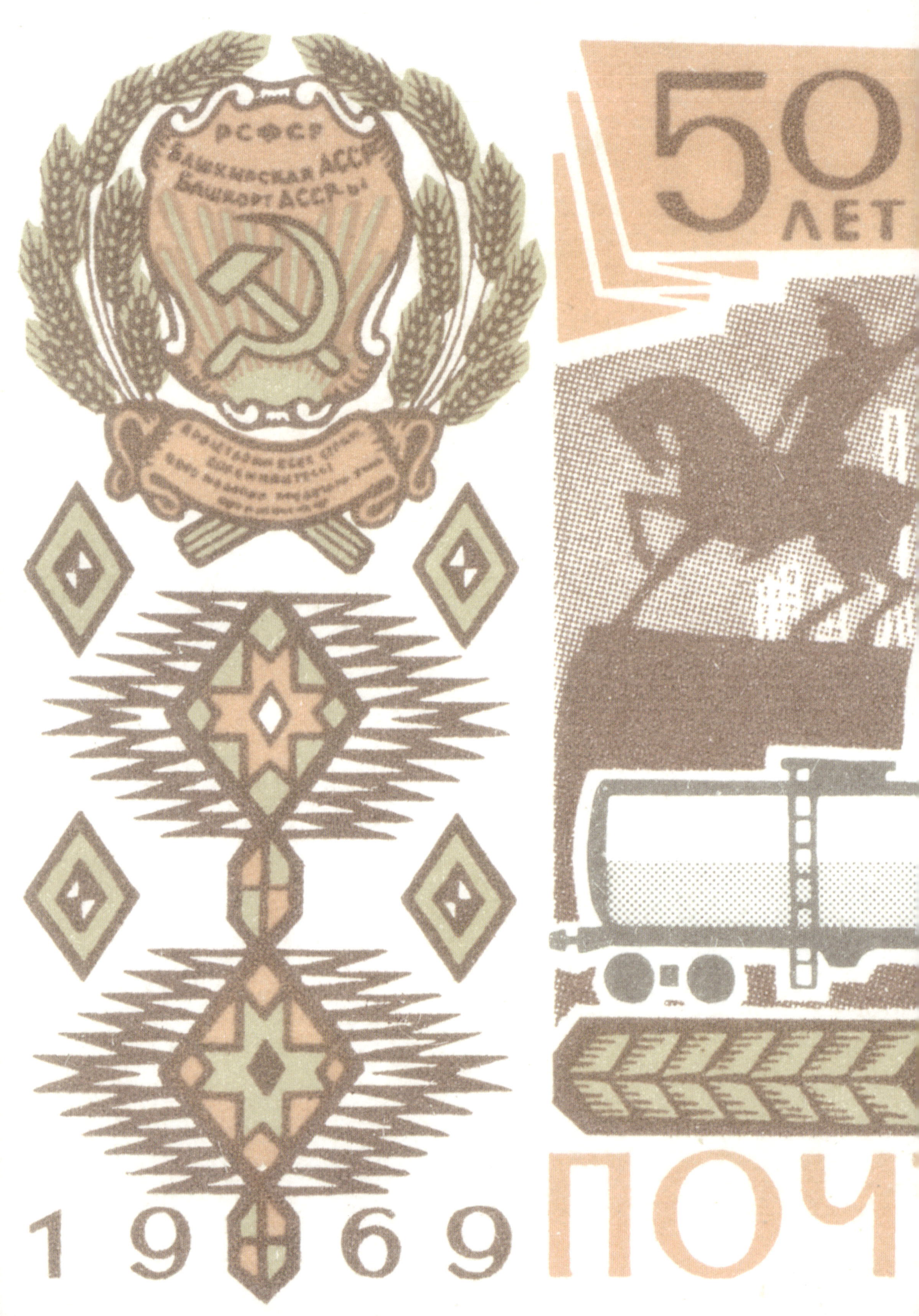
РСФСР
БАШКИРСКАЯ АССР
БАШҠОРТ АССР
50
ЛЕТ
1969
ПОЧ

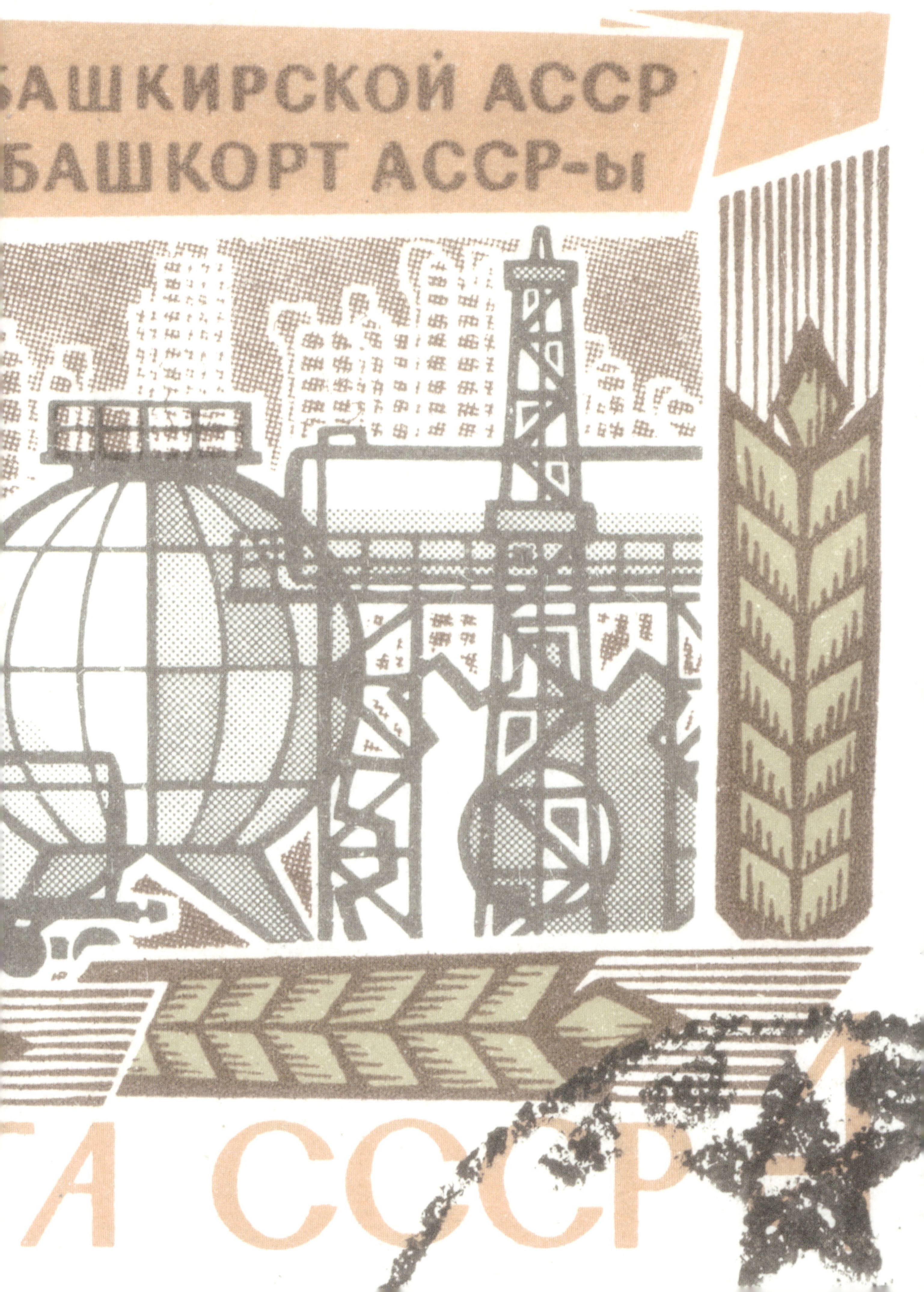

БАШКИРСКОЙ АССР
БАШКОРТ АССР-ы
ТА СССР

IRINA KORINA

At over 2 metres high, Irina Korina's *Capital* (2012), a column-like 'ruin' composed of what looks like refuse material, stands as an ironic monument to contemporary culture. The sculpture is made up of ordinary thin plastic bags filled with discarded, donation clothing, tied up and hung flaccidly from the centre of a banged up corrugated metal pillar. It has been designed with a child-like imagination and simplicity – dumpsite art, made out of a top-heavy consumerism fallen by the wayside.

The work's title seems just as uncomplicated and direct; it's hard to ignore the obvious play it makes between the central Marxist work critiquing capitalism as an economic system and the term for the top element (Ionian, Doric, etc) of a column in classical architecture, here made out of waste. Capitalism, the sculpture seems to be suggesting, is no more than this: the redistribution of excess. Knowing the context in which Korina works, another meaning of 'capital' appears perhaps even more urgent – the general condition of post-Soviet, post-socialist utopian disarray in the city centres of Russia today.

Korina trained as a theatre designer and is known for creating enveloping room installations out of disposable, ordinary materials common to every Russian – a little like Ilya Kabakov's Soviet interiors, but with a heavier dose of whimsy and kitsch. Previously, she's used familiar cheap floral fabric, discarded furniture and magazines to create an unfamiliar materiality verging on the absurd, and to confront us with objects and spaces conjuring memories of a previous time. Behind its comical makeshift appearance, *Capital* stands as a totem to the everyday, leaving us to wonder the meaning of this traditional object reincarnated by Korina.

IK-01

CAPITAL, 2012
Mixed media
220 x 50 x 50 cm

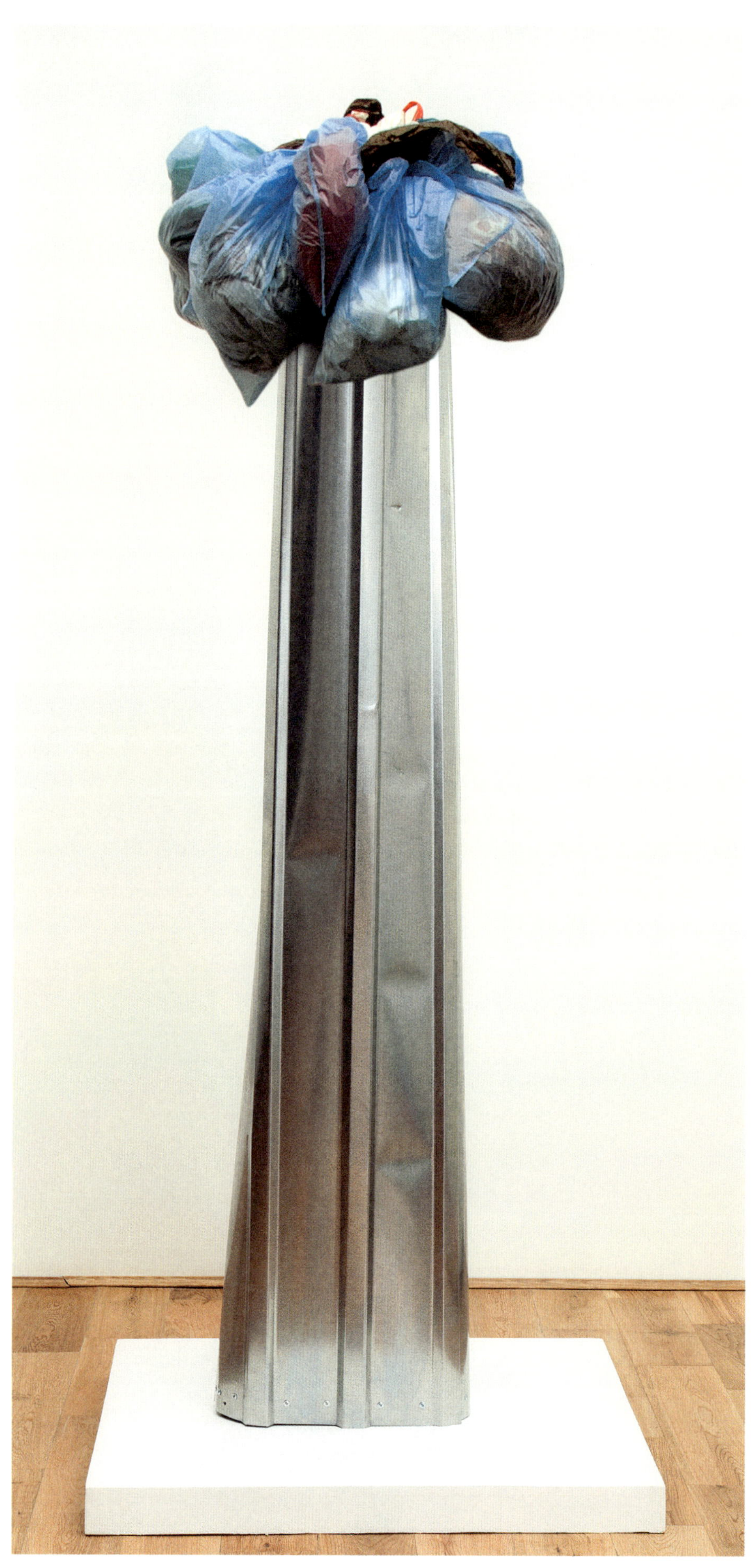

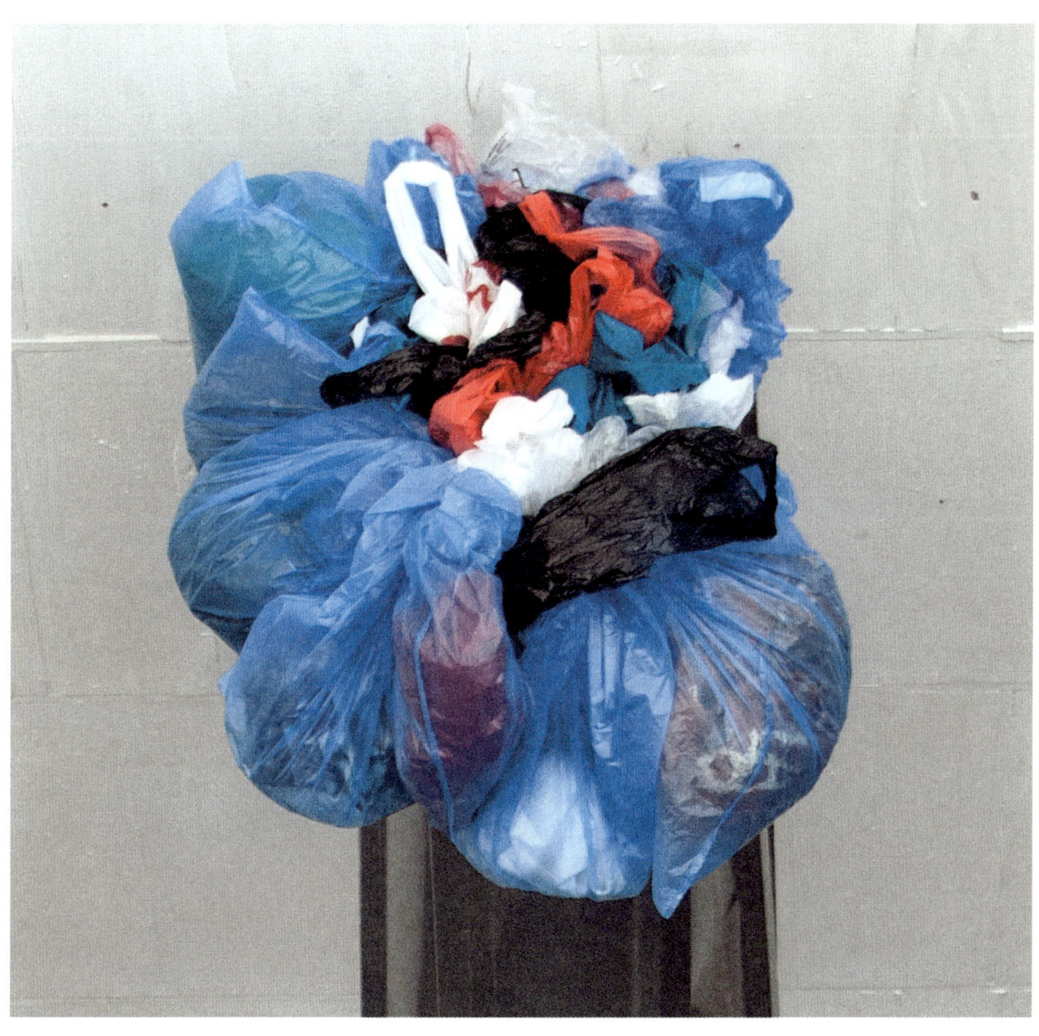

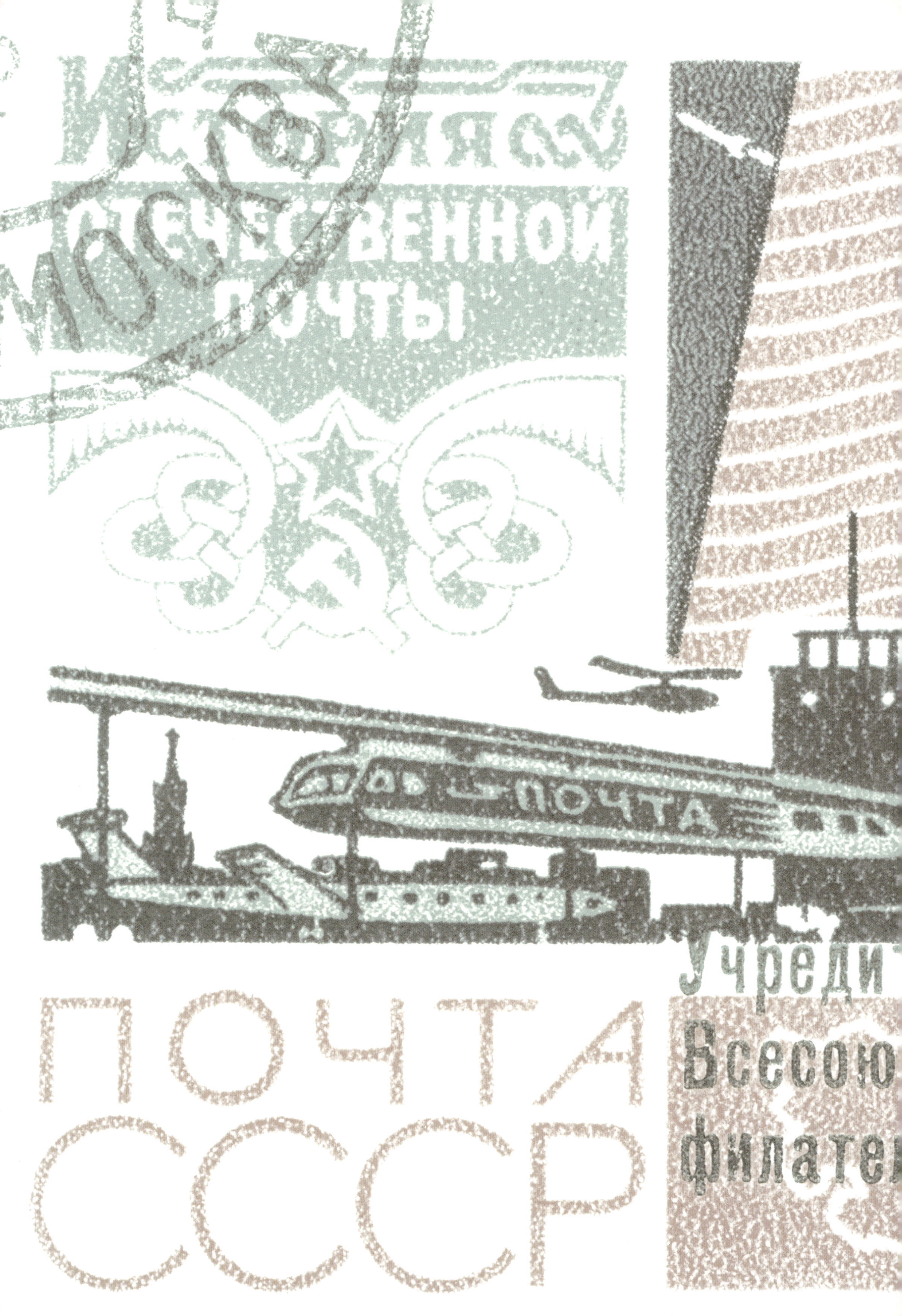
ИСТОРИЯ
ОТЕЧЕСТВЕННОЙ
ПОЧТЫ
ПОЧТА
ПОЧТА
СССР
Учреди
Всесою
филате

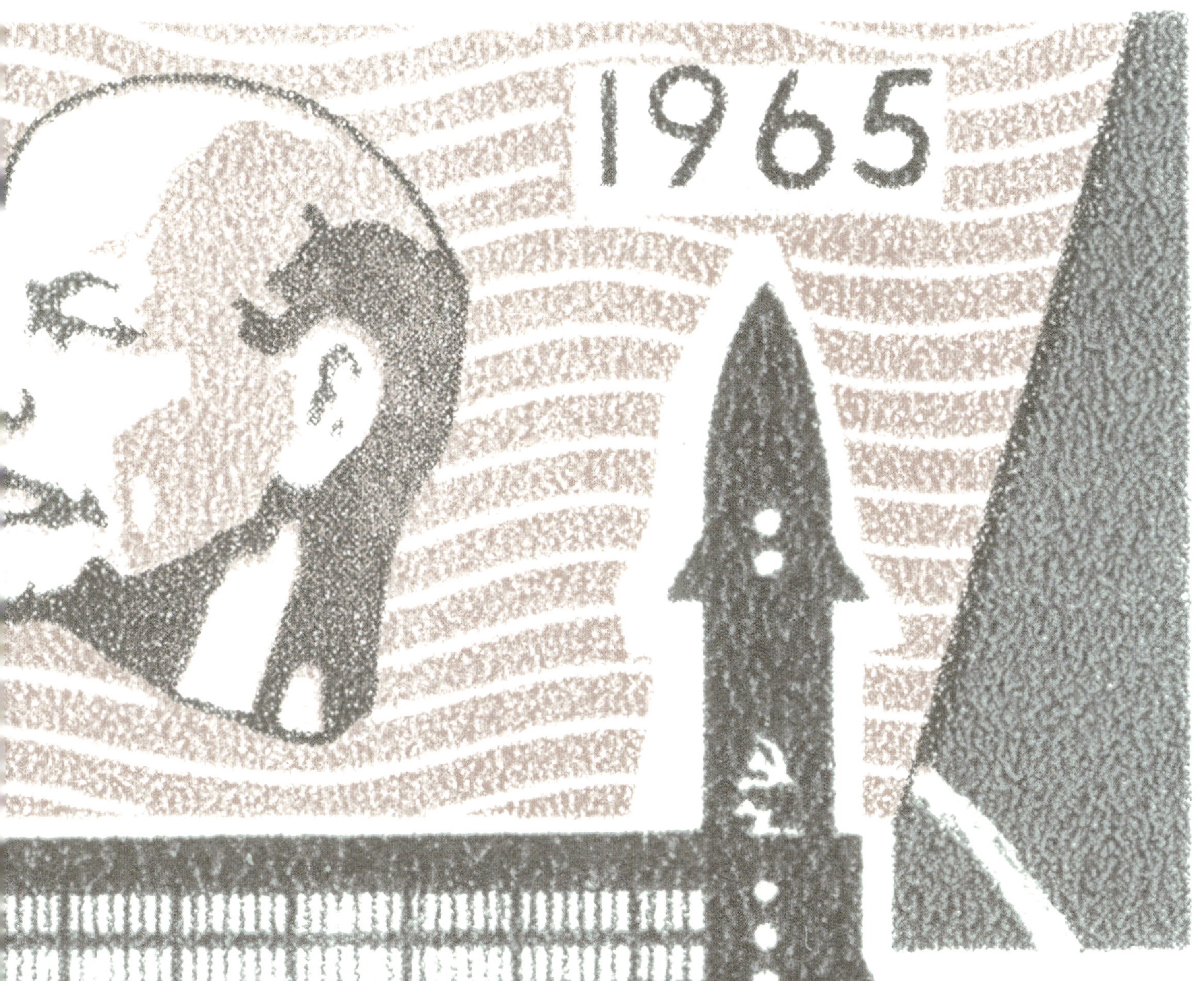

1965
льная конференция
ого общества
стов. 1966
16 коп.

VALERY KOSHLYAKOV

Valery Koshlyakov's large-scale cardboard paintings, collages and installations — sometimes hanging from the ceiling, sometimes made out of sticky tape placed directly onto the gallery walls — irreverently engage with ideas of empire.

Covered in paint drips, his flattened-box panels are blown-up postcard images of state-approved classical and monumental European architecture that have more in common with street art than with photorealistic obedience. They look wet, urgent, quickly rendered, and they show his iconic subjects, from a Soviet stadium to a gothic cathedral, as a madman's fantasy.

The nearly five-metre wide *Grand Opera, Paris* (1995), one of his earlier cardboard works, depicts its subject in a myriad of dizzy unfinished details, washes and vigorous brushstrokes that turn the solid structure into a half-idealized, half-non-existing precarious castle in the air. We see the building from below, in traditional composition, but the uneven surface on which it is painted makes it fragmented, unhinged, as if it were breaking away from its support.

The work's grand subject and pompous gestural painting accentuates the kitsch factor — this could be a slightly psychotic version of the common hack-painted tourist souvenir. Similarly with *High-rise on Raushskaya Embankment* (2006), painted with tempera on cardboard, which is evocative of an avant-garde architectural masterpiece, yet the painting's visibly flimsy support, in contrast with the monumentality of its subject, also somehow chimes in with the irony of a failed utopia.

Koshlyakov's re-reading of symbols of empire is all-encompassing, taking imagery from ancient ruins and sculpture to modern government buildings, but the monumental scale of his works also suggests an additional, particularly charged reference — that of Stalin-era murals and political myth-building.

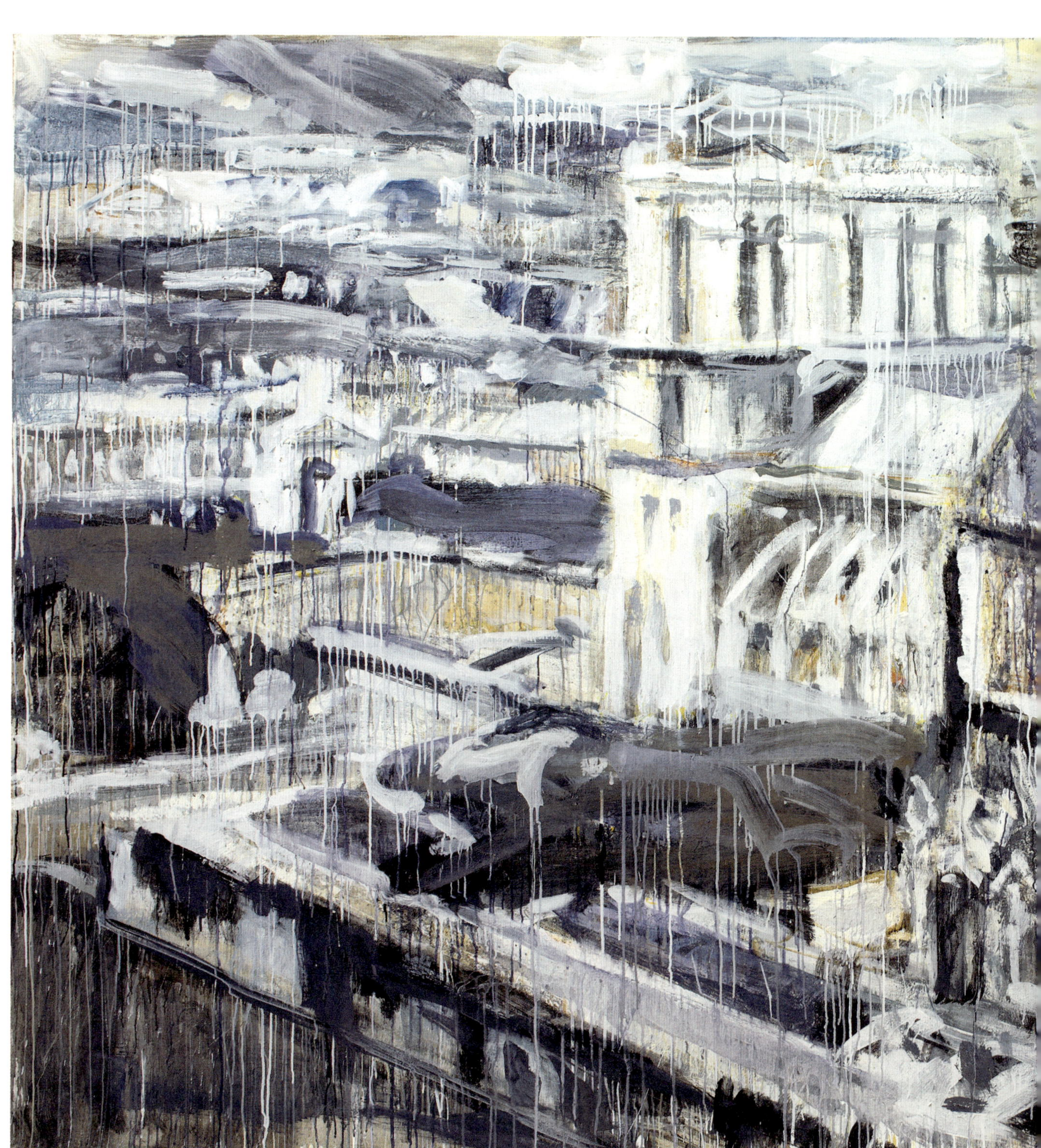

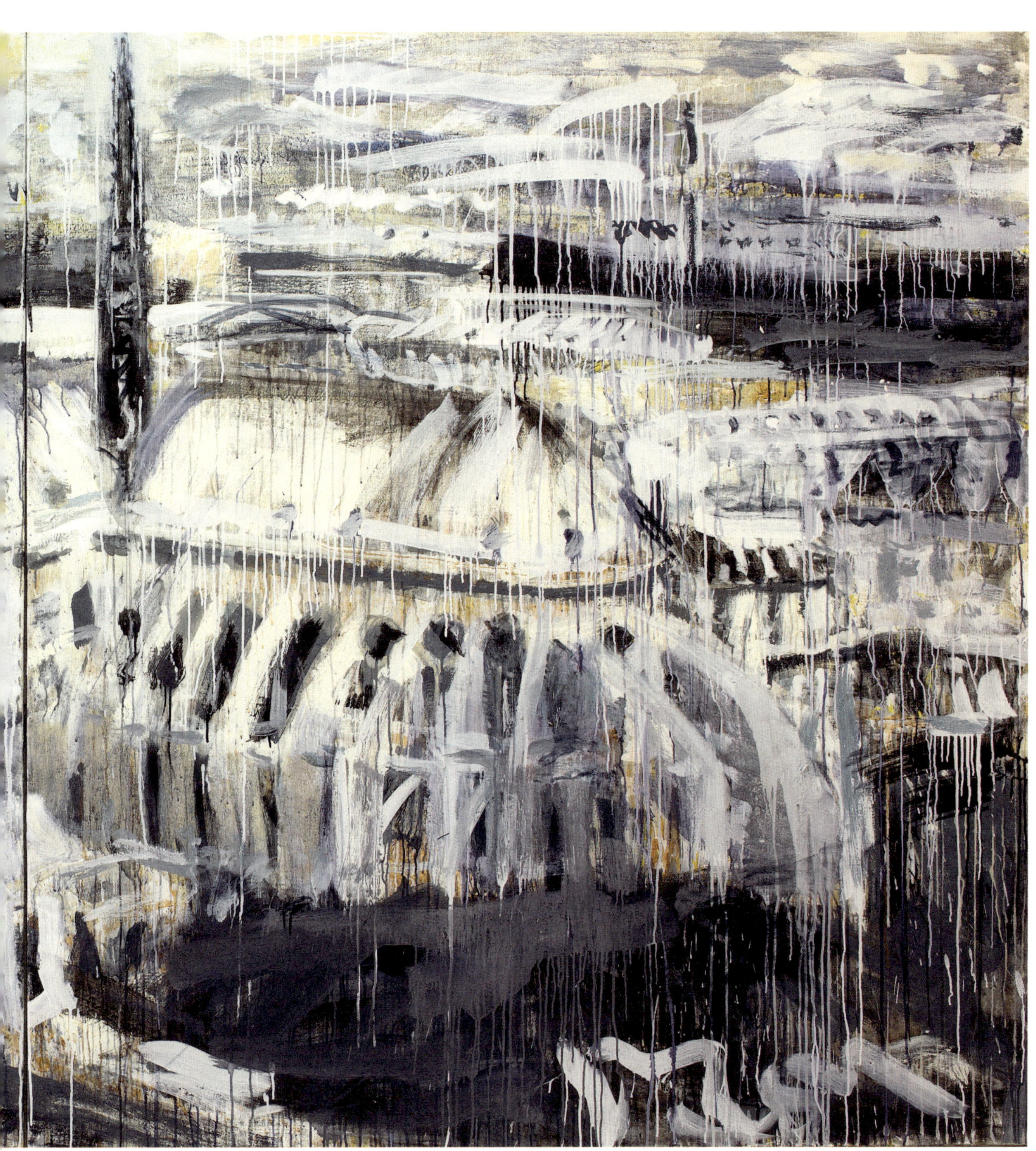

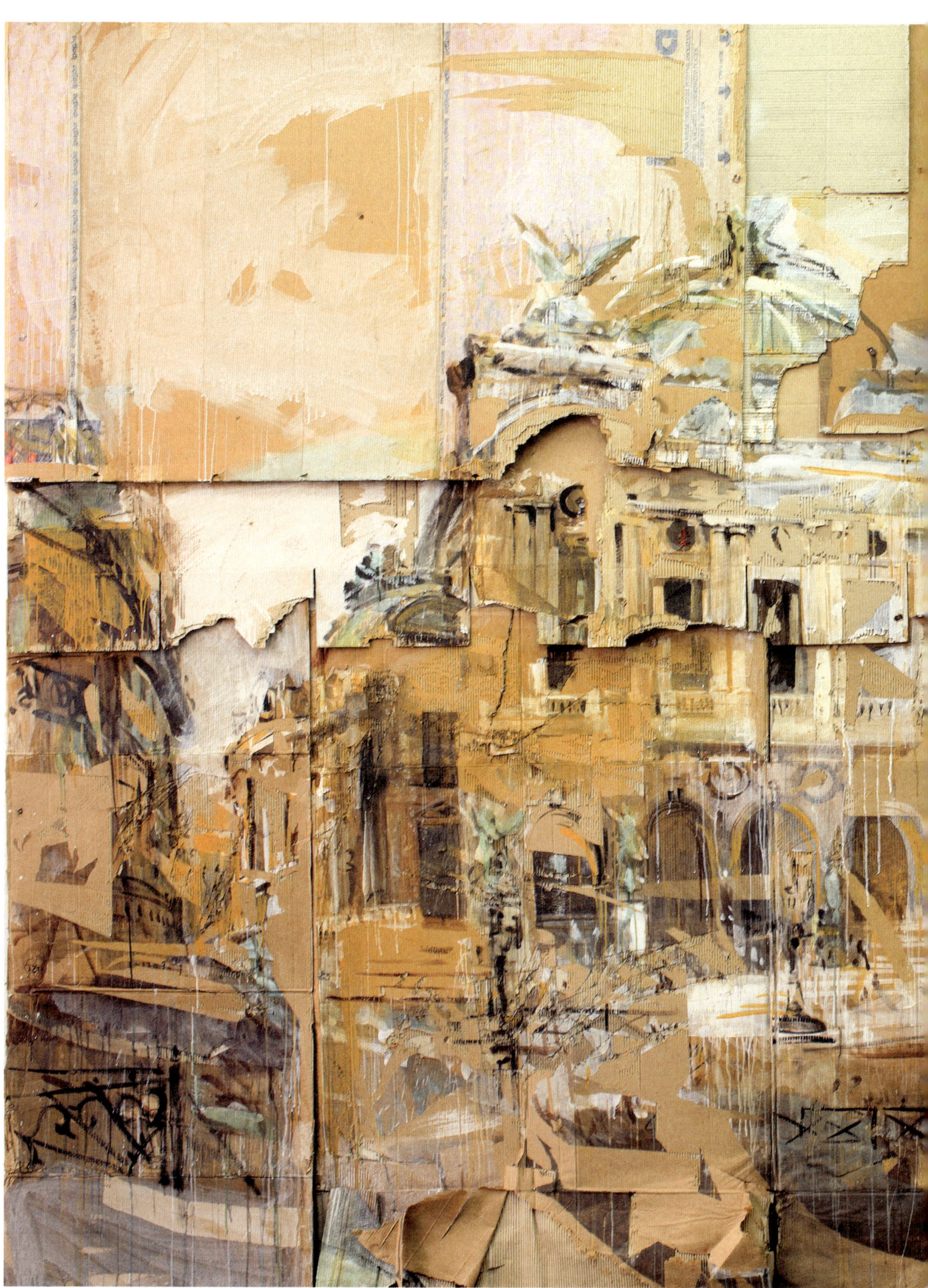

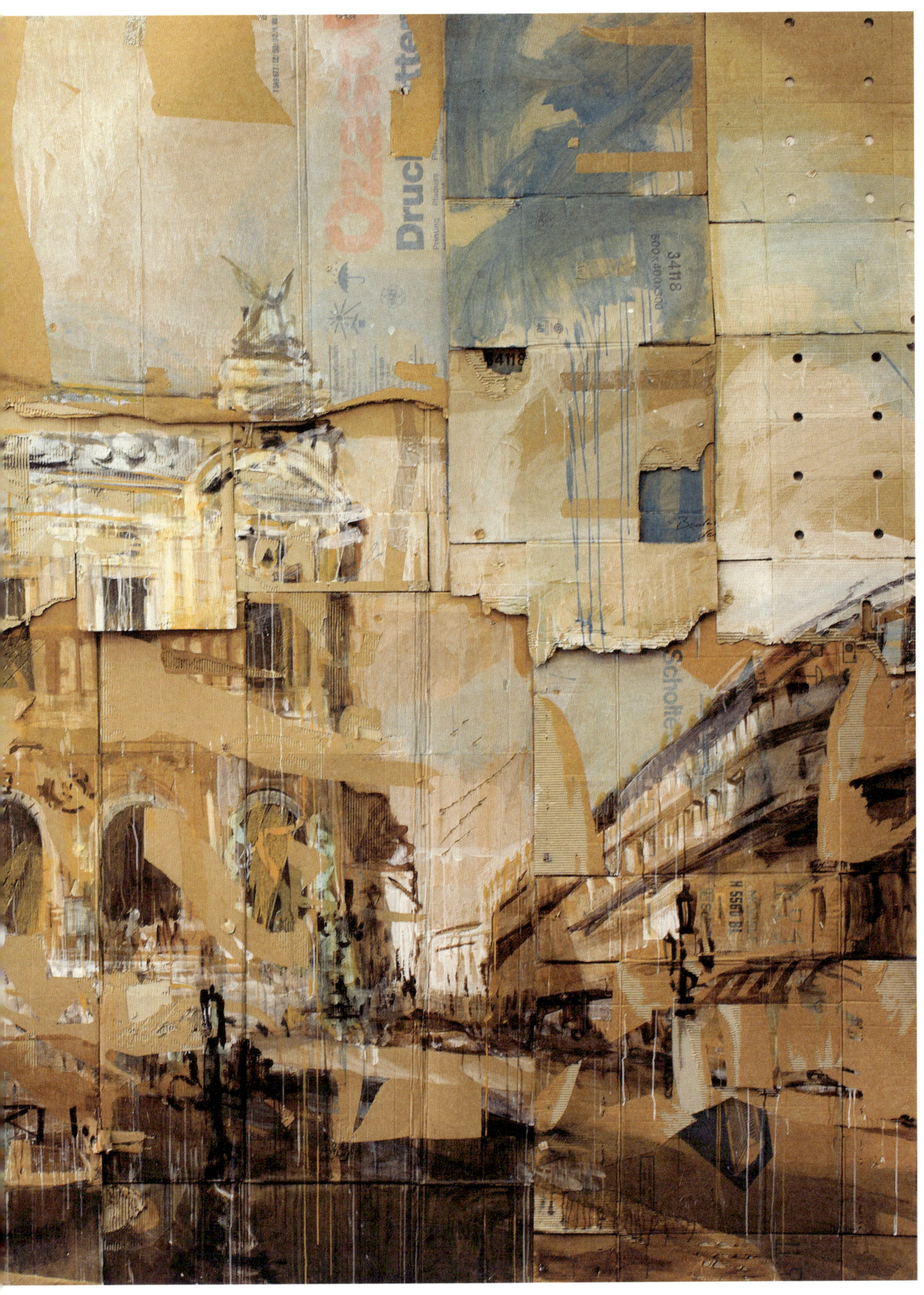

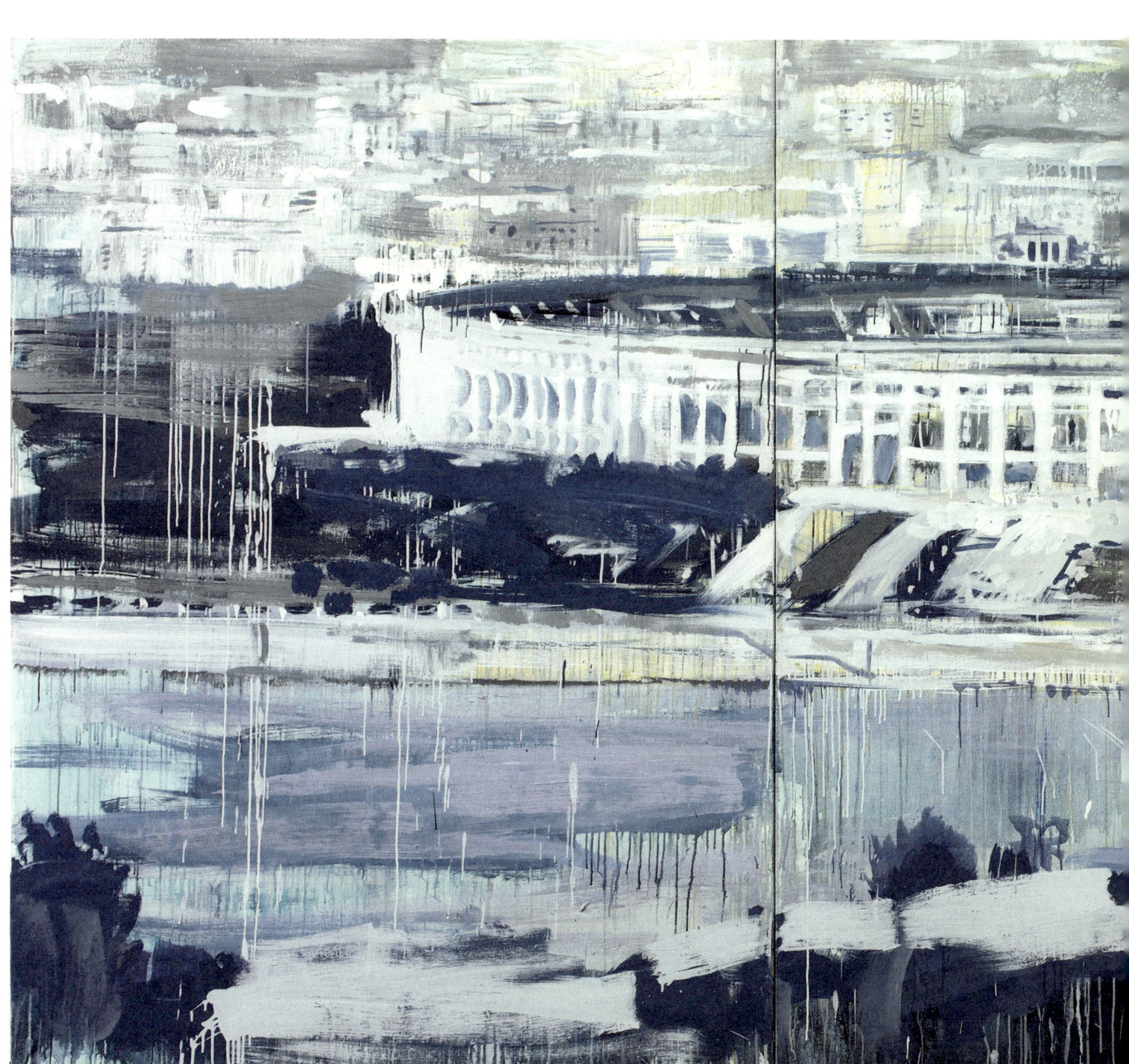

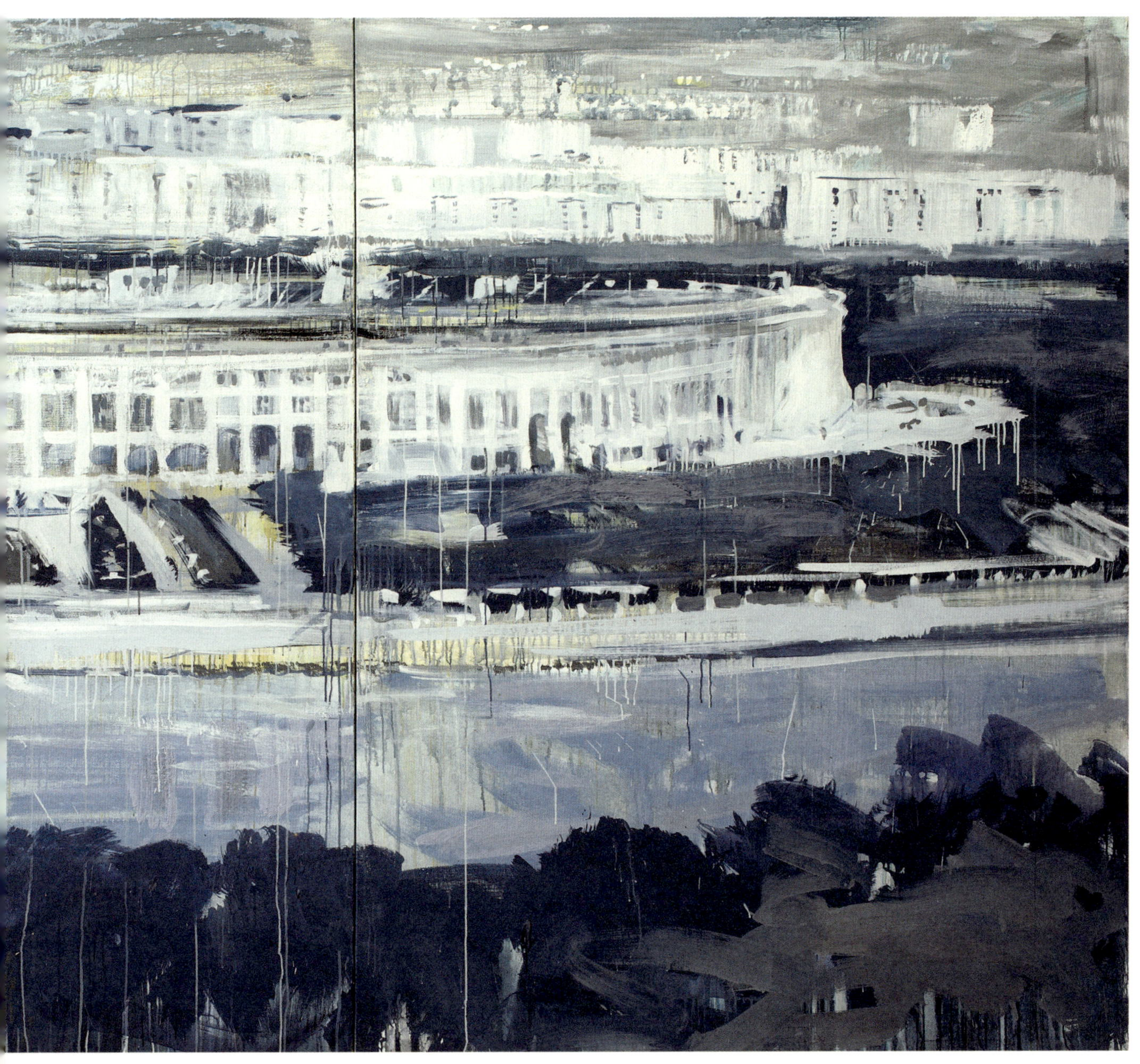

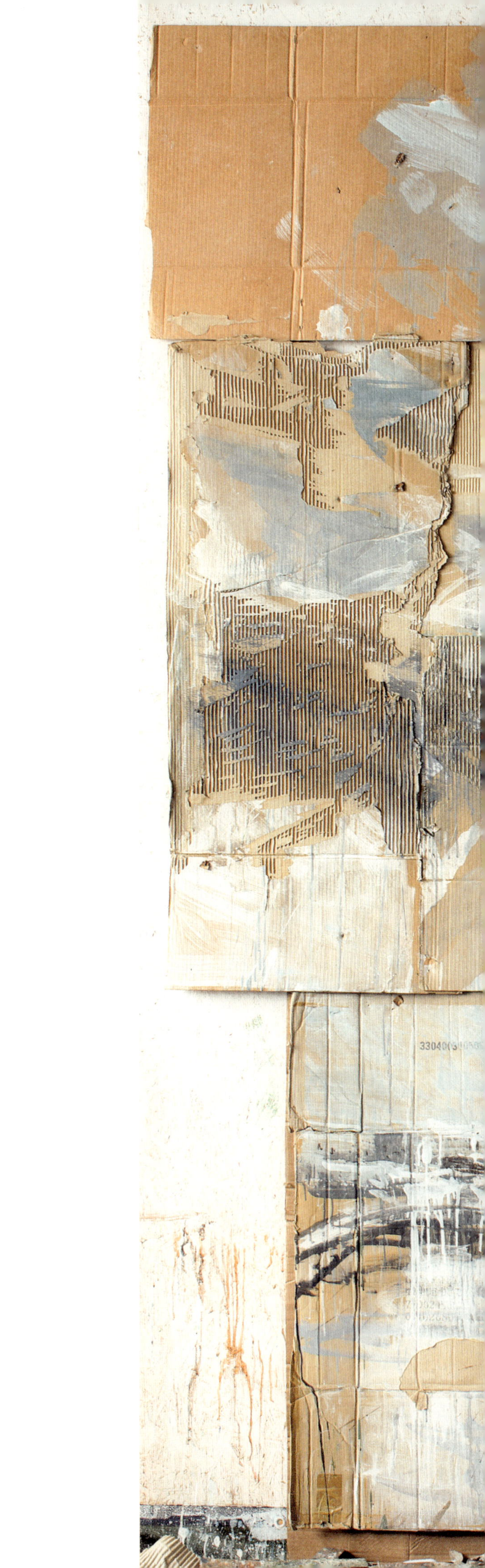

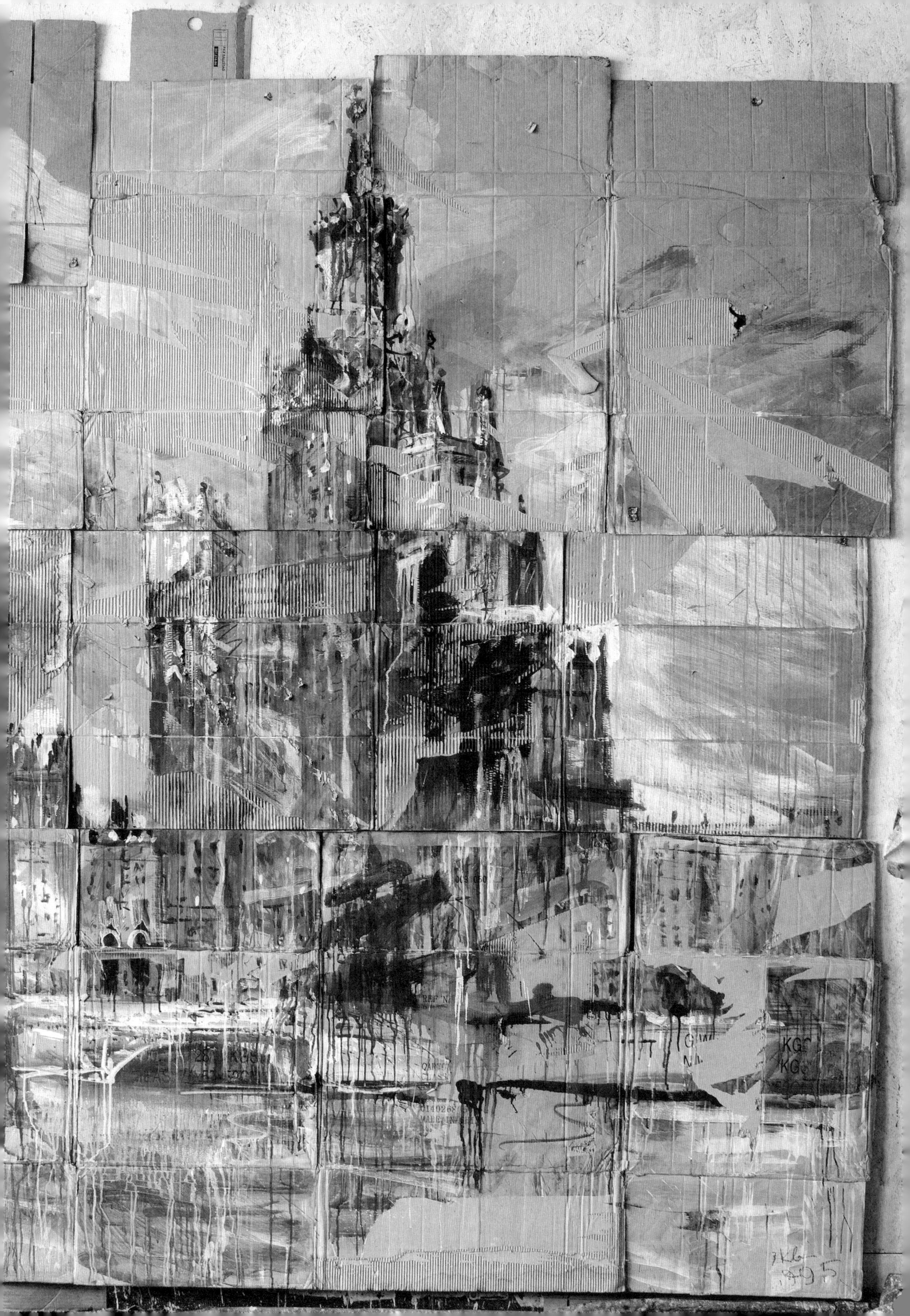

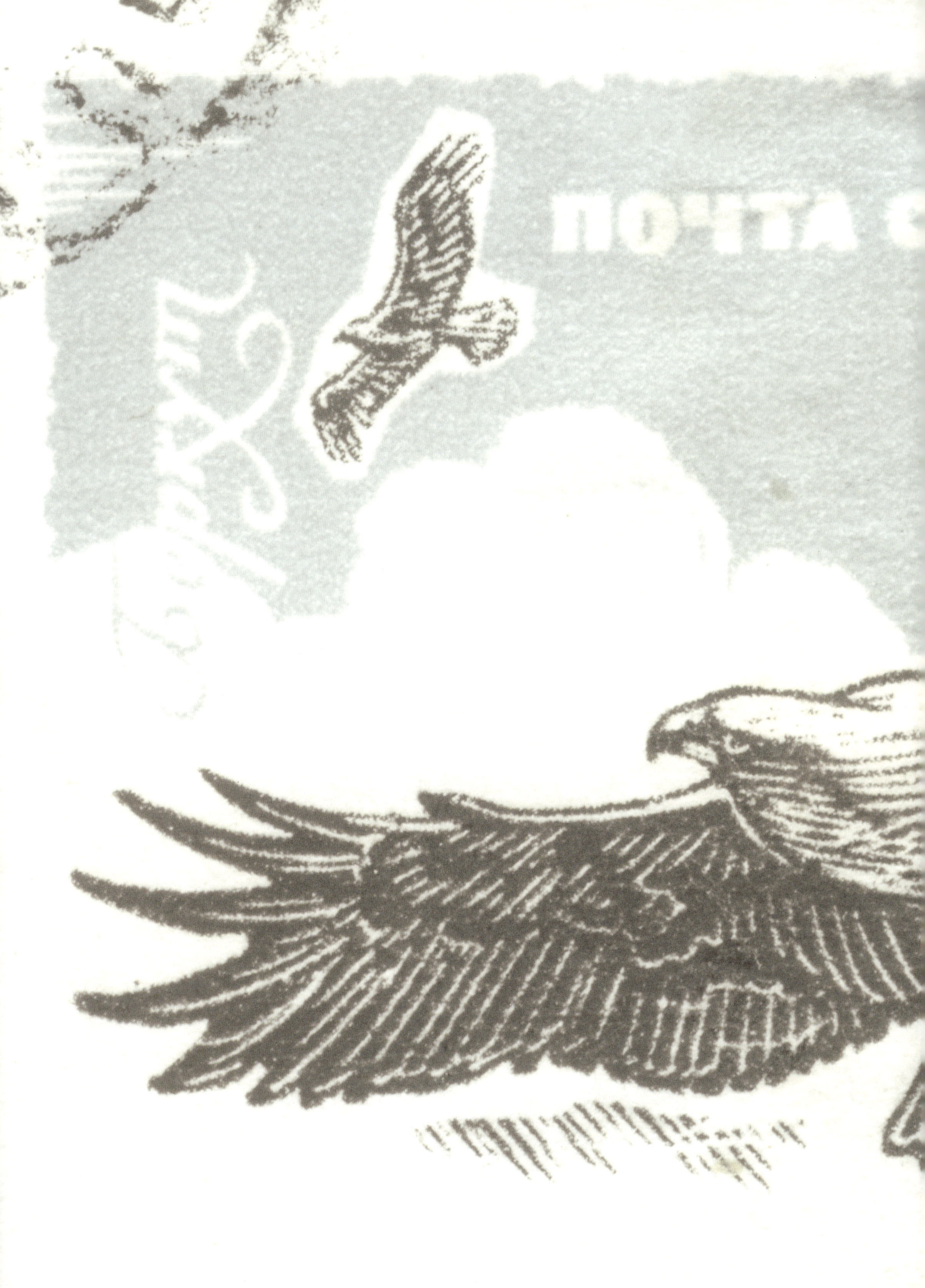

ПОЧТА С

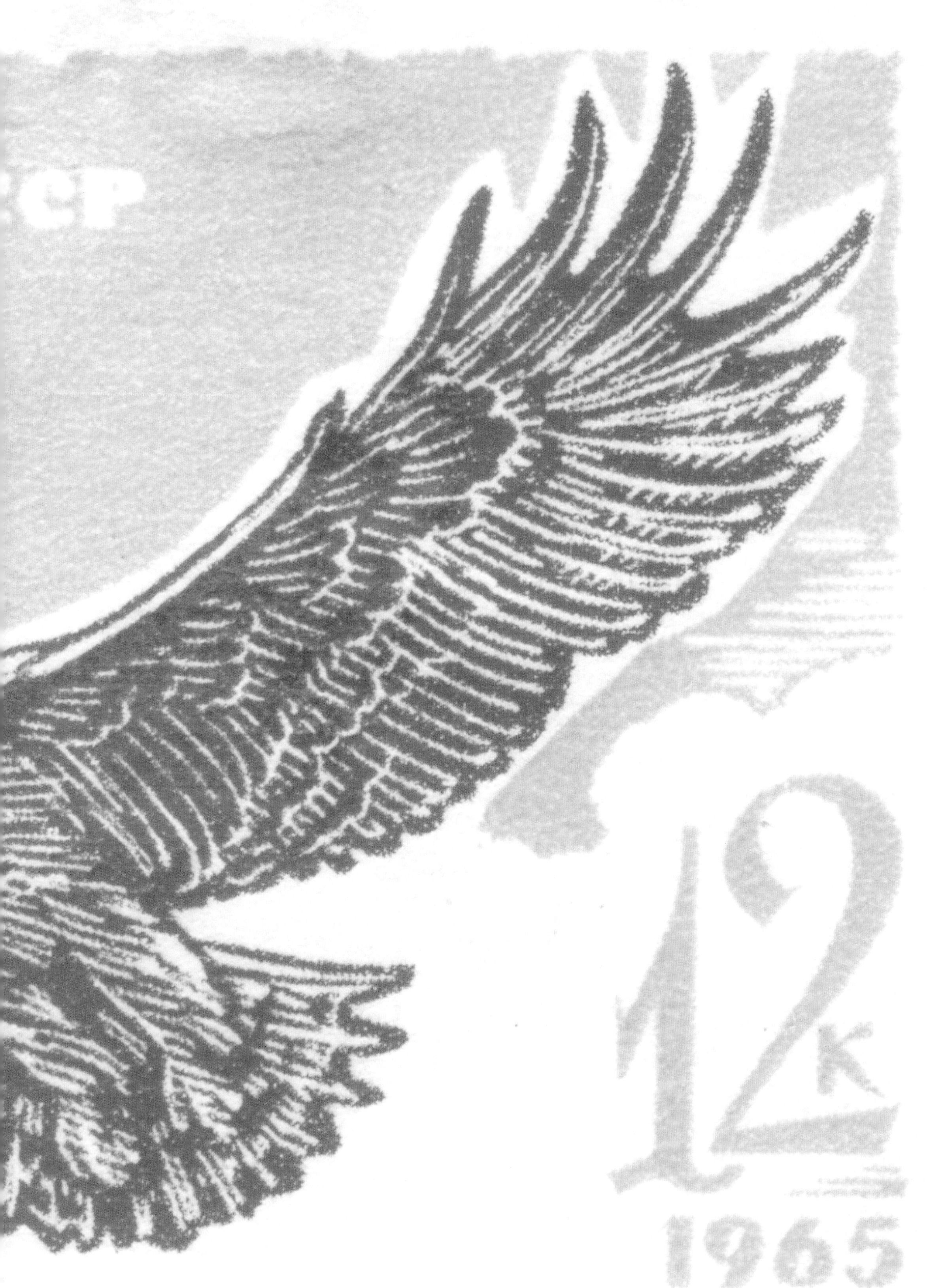
ССР
12 к
1965

DARIA KROTOVA

Daria Krotova's works use purposefully fragile media, such as thin sheets of paper or soft clay, to explore the delicate, material, 'living' nature of art. She makes objects, drawings and installations that become worn down during the very process of their making, and that invite their audience's erosive touch. Her work's symbolic on-going damage questions the notion of art, and of the art establishment, as permanent.

Krotova's work focuses on the representation of real, living shapes – heads, faces and hearts – isolated from their usual physical contexts. Her visual language raises our consciousness of the representation of life, even of imaginary creatures, within the art historical tradition. Her installations are sometimes composed of thin, papier-mache-like sculptures; other times of porcelain, another material that could be easily shattered. For some projects she has created sites with 'archeological' objects – not pottery shards but bones and teeth and horns made out of ceramics as a way of underscoring the fragility and fetishisation of historical remains.

Heart, Organ Of Love (Sometimes My Heart Turns Into A Chicken), (2011) is a series of layered and pinned together watercolours depicting human hearts, rendered particularly tangible and evanescent by the depth of texture and colour of Krotova's wet on wet, torn crepe paper pasting. "I like working with materials, which are perishable, which often break and fade during the process of work," Krotova explains, "even before it's finished, like ceramics, or paper, because for me they convey the 'living' quality to the object to be made in the best way." But she does not forego the possibility of working with more solid materials, say marble. "Fragile and perishable can be written in any heavy block."

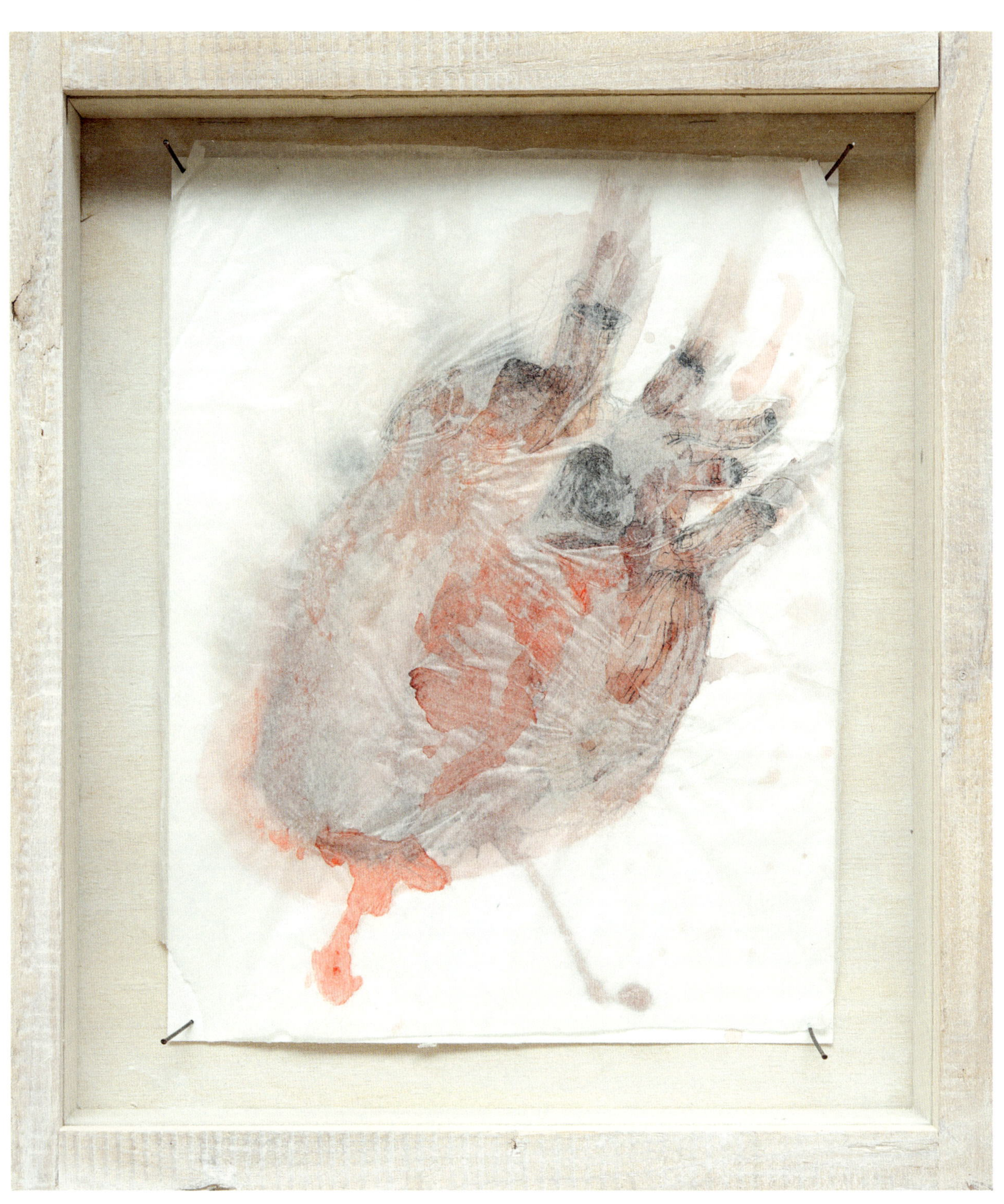

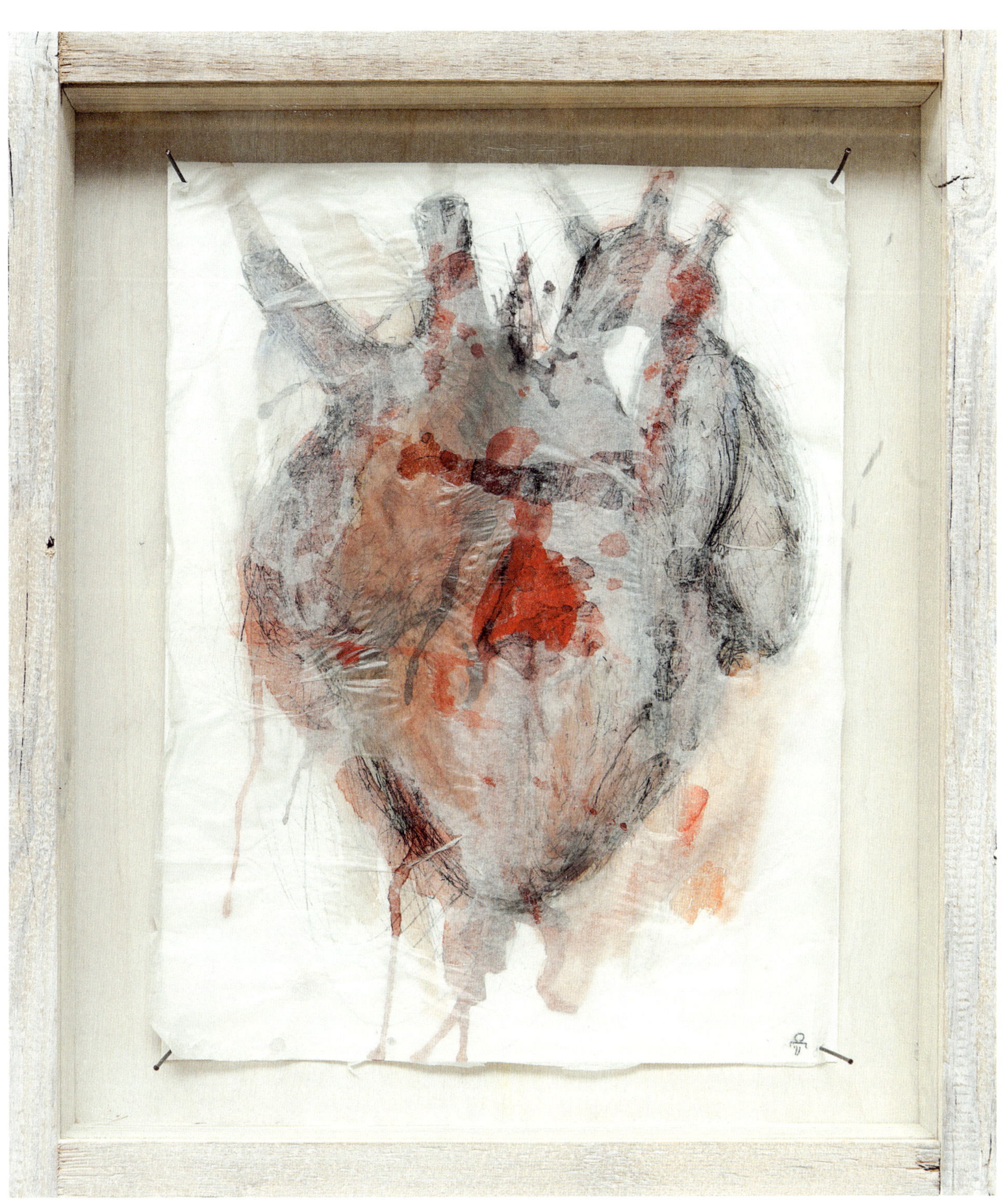

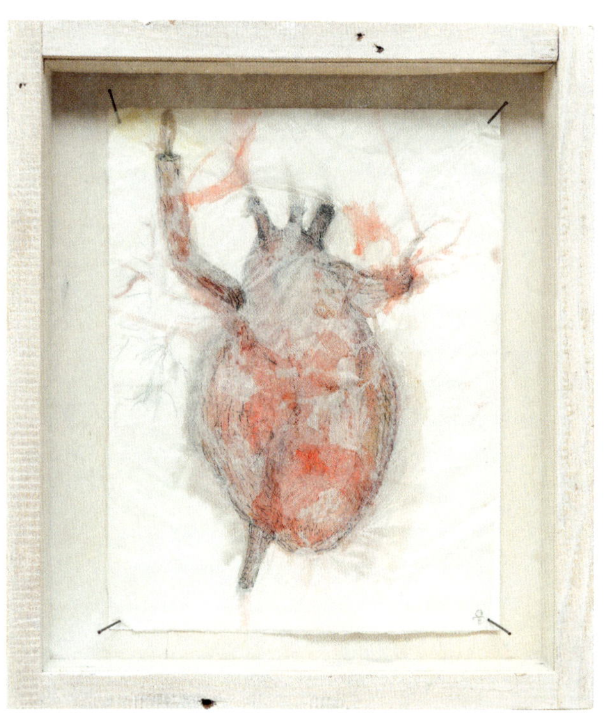
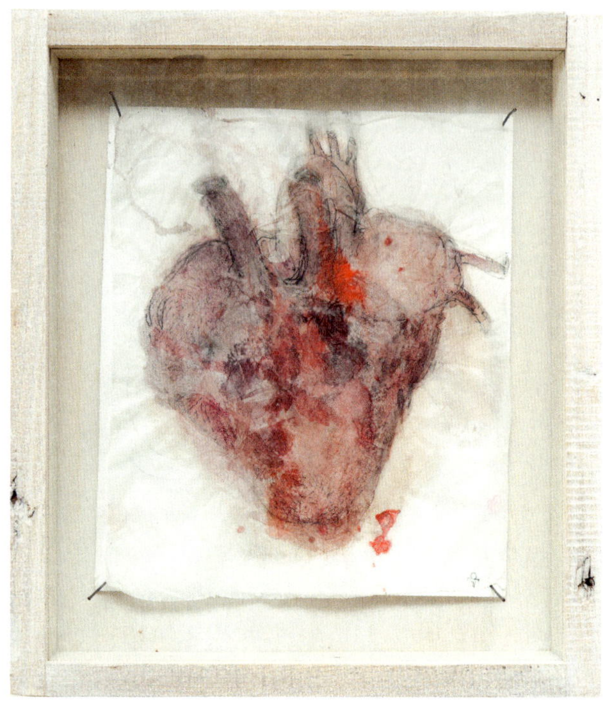
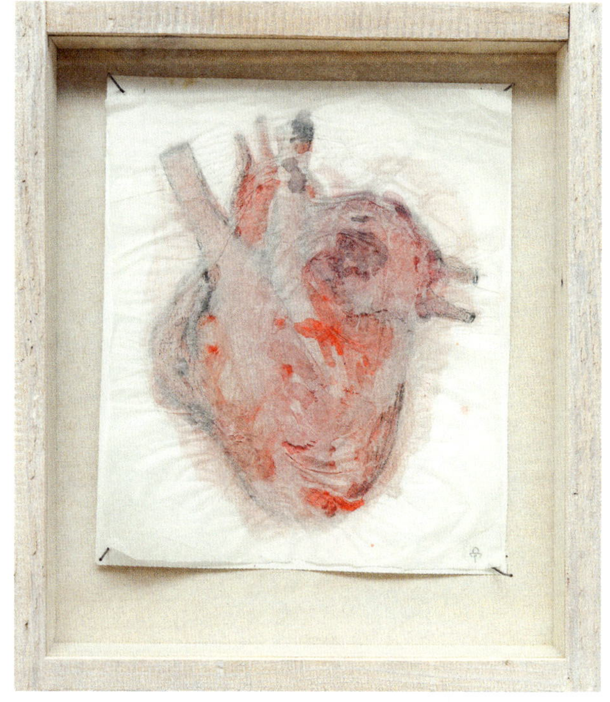
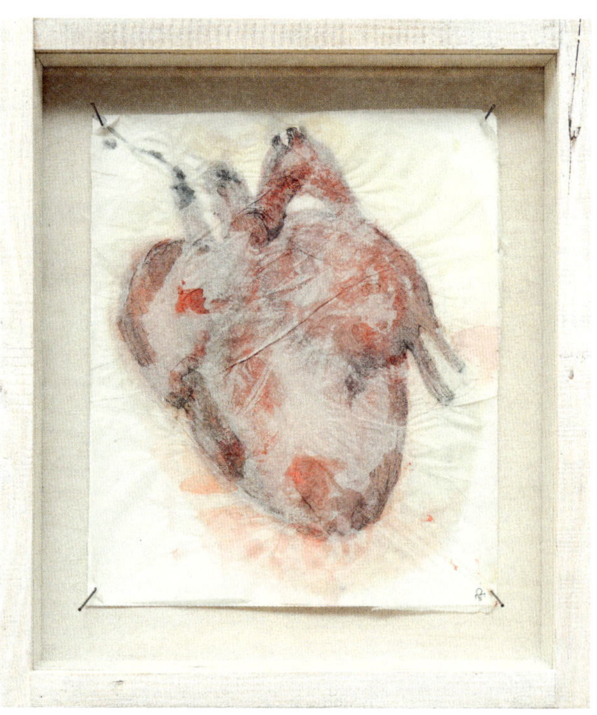

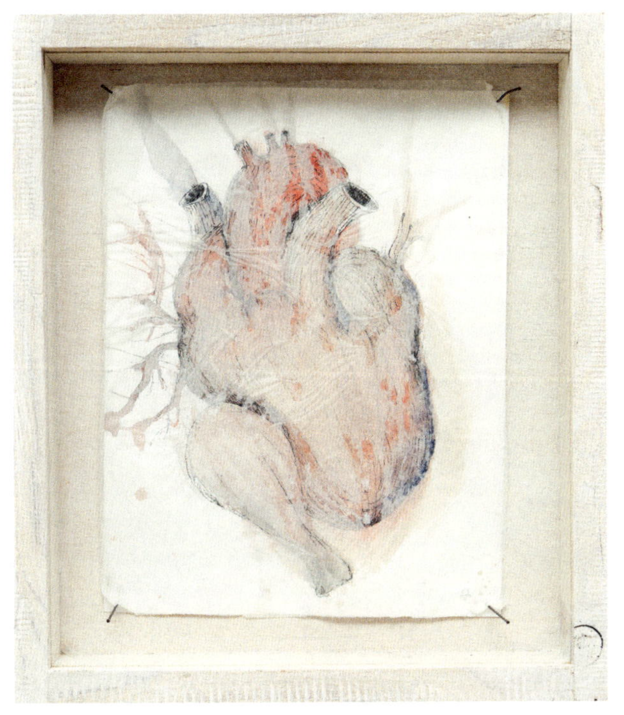
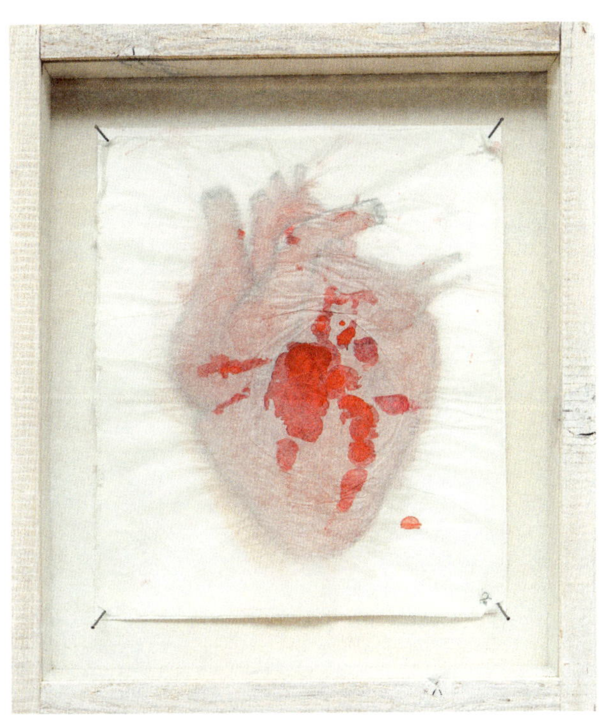
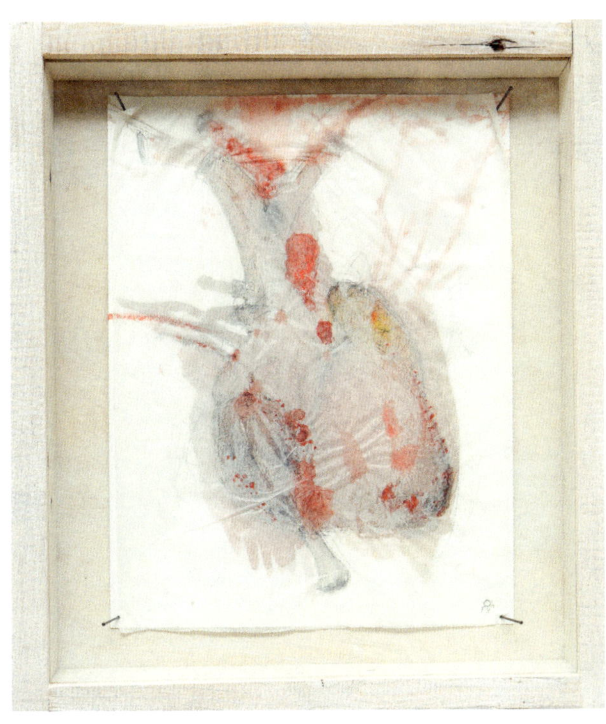

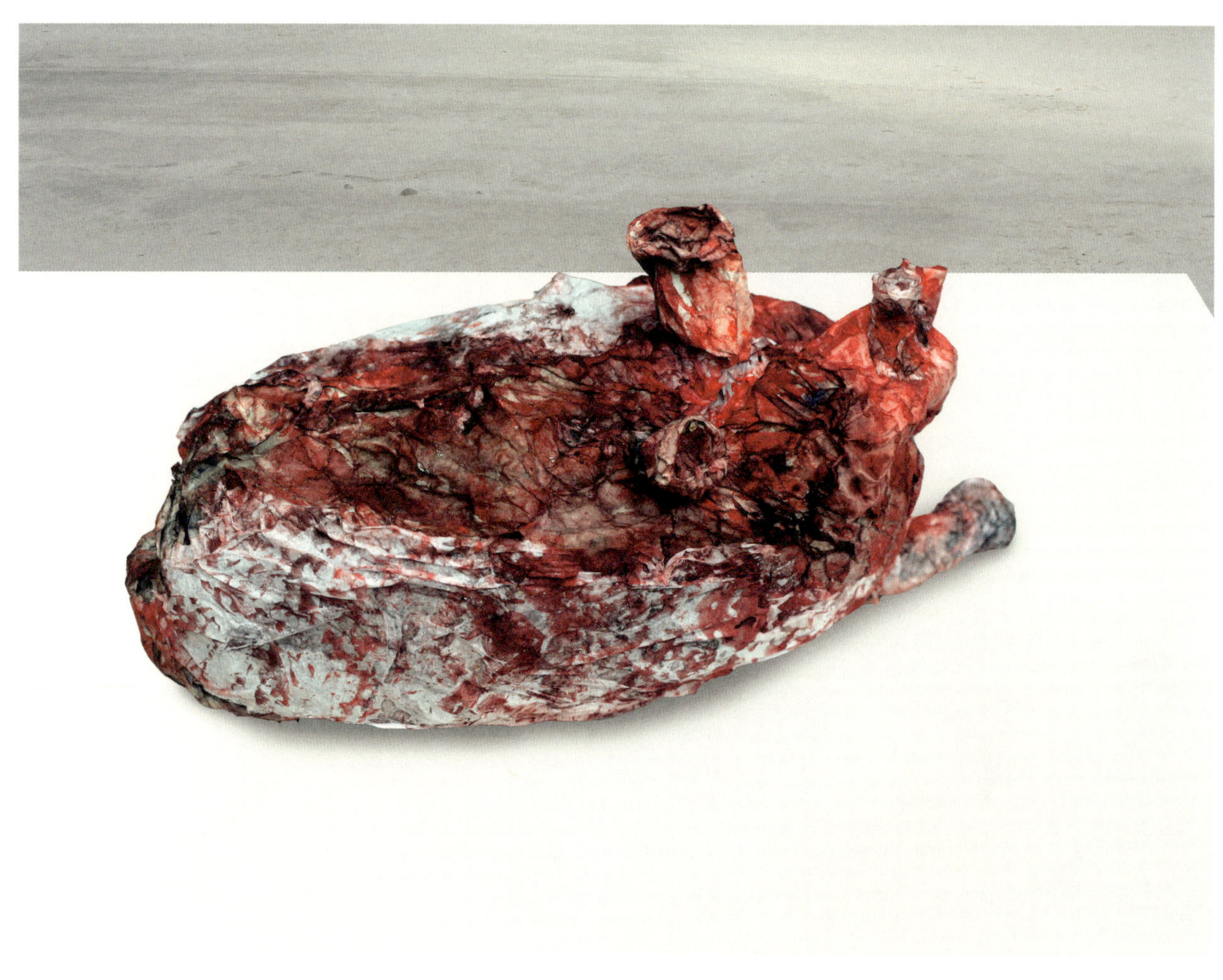

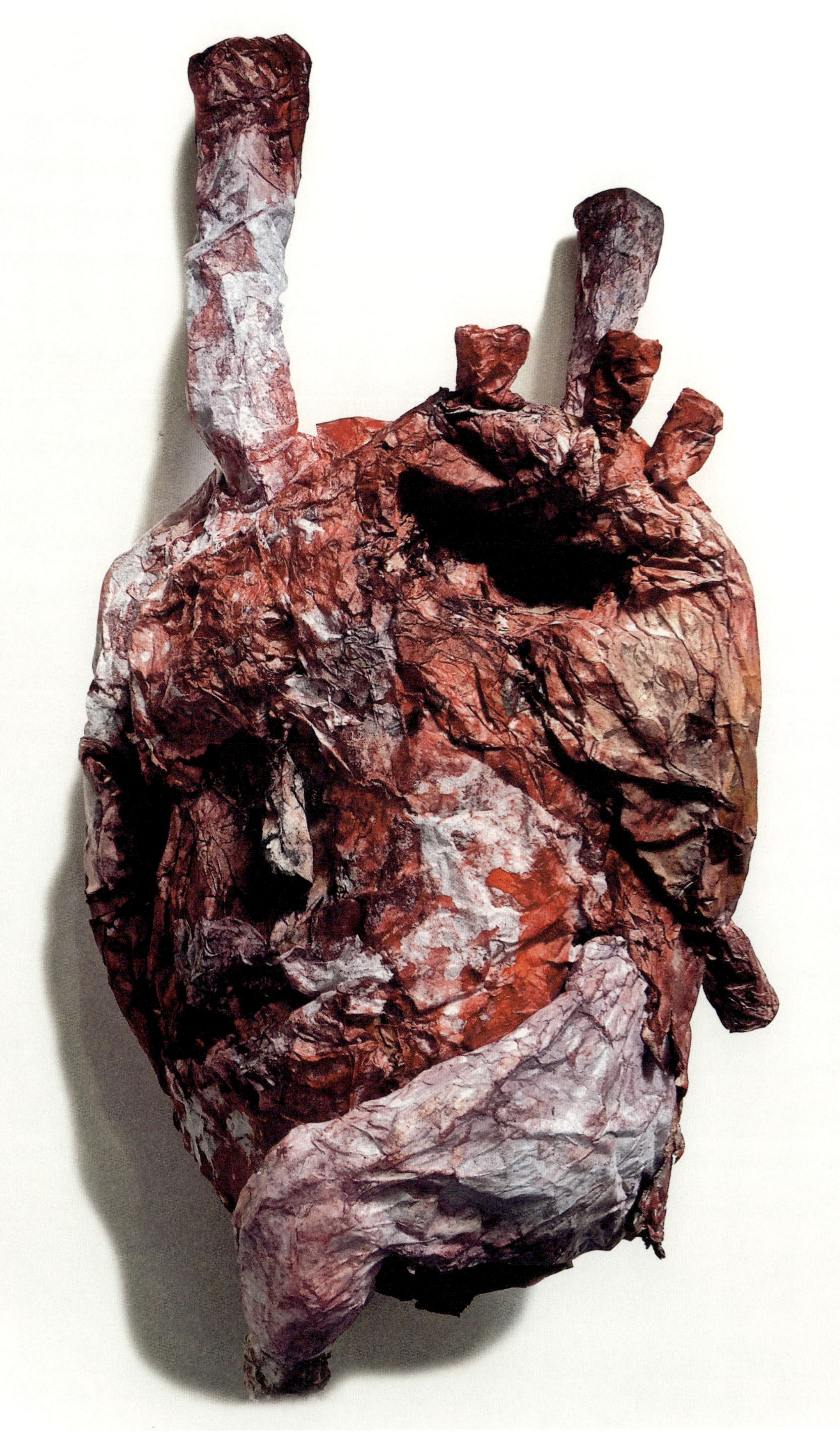

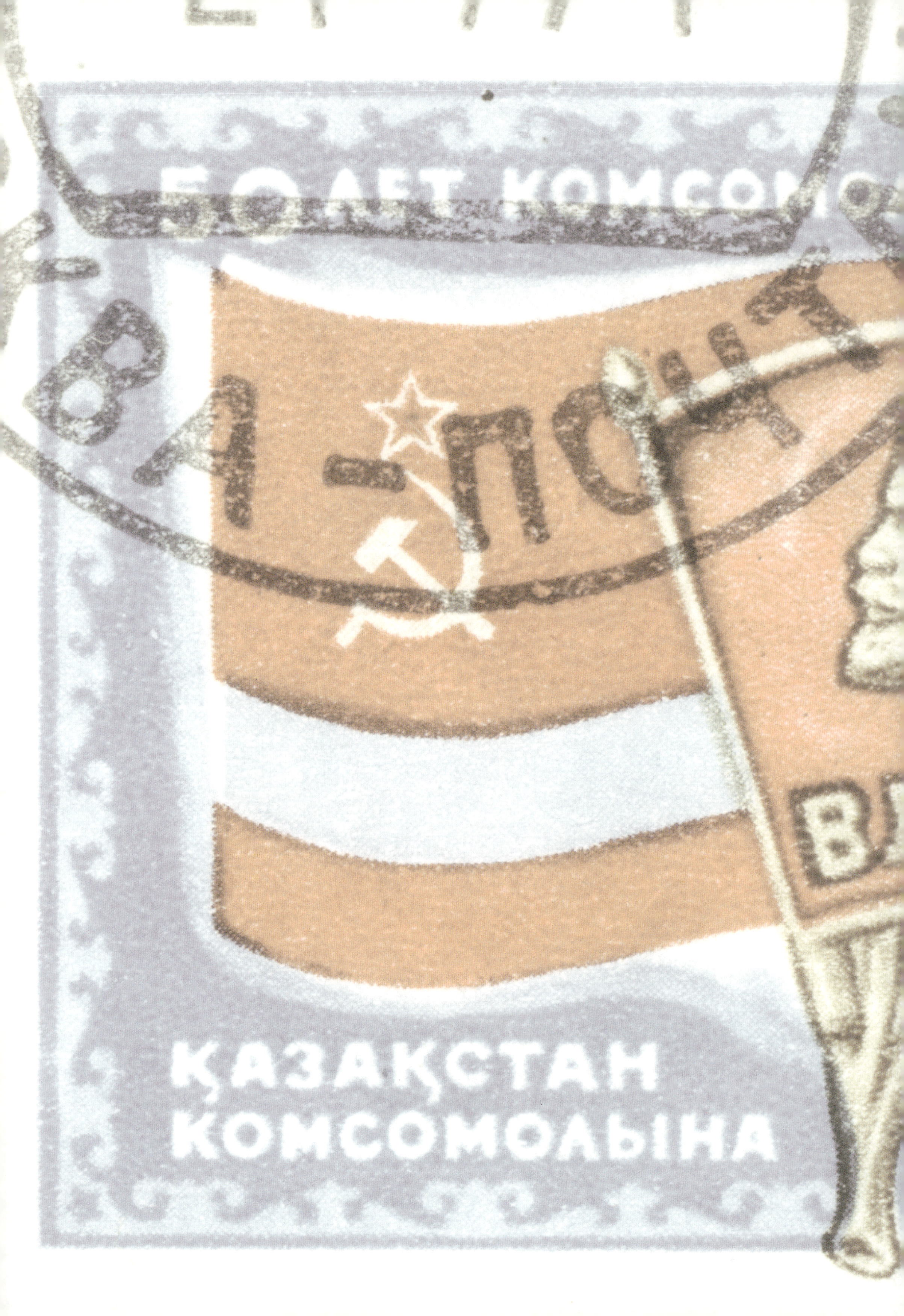

50 ЛЕТ КОМСОМО

ҚАЗАҚСТАН
КОМСОМОЛЫНА

КАЗАХСТАНА

ЛКСМ

50 ЖЫЛ

1971

ПОЧТА СССР

4

BORIS MIKHAILOV

Boris Mikhailov, probably the most influential photographer working in Russia today, has spent decades documenting the social condition of individuals living in the Soviet Union and the aftermath of its collapse. His work, both conceptual and documentary in nature, is guided by personal impression. His projects create a composite, alternative portrait of the political status quo in post-communist society drawn out of individual situations and faces.

Case History (1997–98) encompasses 413 photographs of people taken between 1997–98 in his hometown of Kharkov, in the Ukraine, ten years after the dismantlement of the Soviet system. Fifteen years on, it is still a startling chronicle of the extremes of life on the streets for suddenly destitute members of society – the abandoned working class, young and old, chronically poor, and newly homeless individuals who fell through the cracks of a system now without a net, failed by the promises of Perestroika and capitalism. A carnival of desperate characters, whether under the influence, lost or larking about, his Goya-like players put a face to the anonymous despair of a public ideology gone bankrupt.

The artist explains he "might equally call [the project] the 'clinical file of a disease'… A big city, such as Kharkov, offered me a great deal of raw material. And I did not miss it, I did not ignore it." But this is decidedly not a photojournalistic project; Mikhailov controversially paid and fed his subjects to pose for him. Yet these images don't claim to be objective. Perhaps because of this personal involvement, his graphic portrayal of bleakness stands as one of the most frank documents of the human condition in times of desperation.

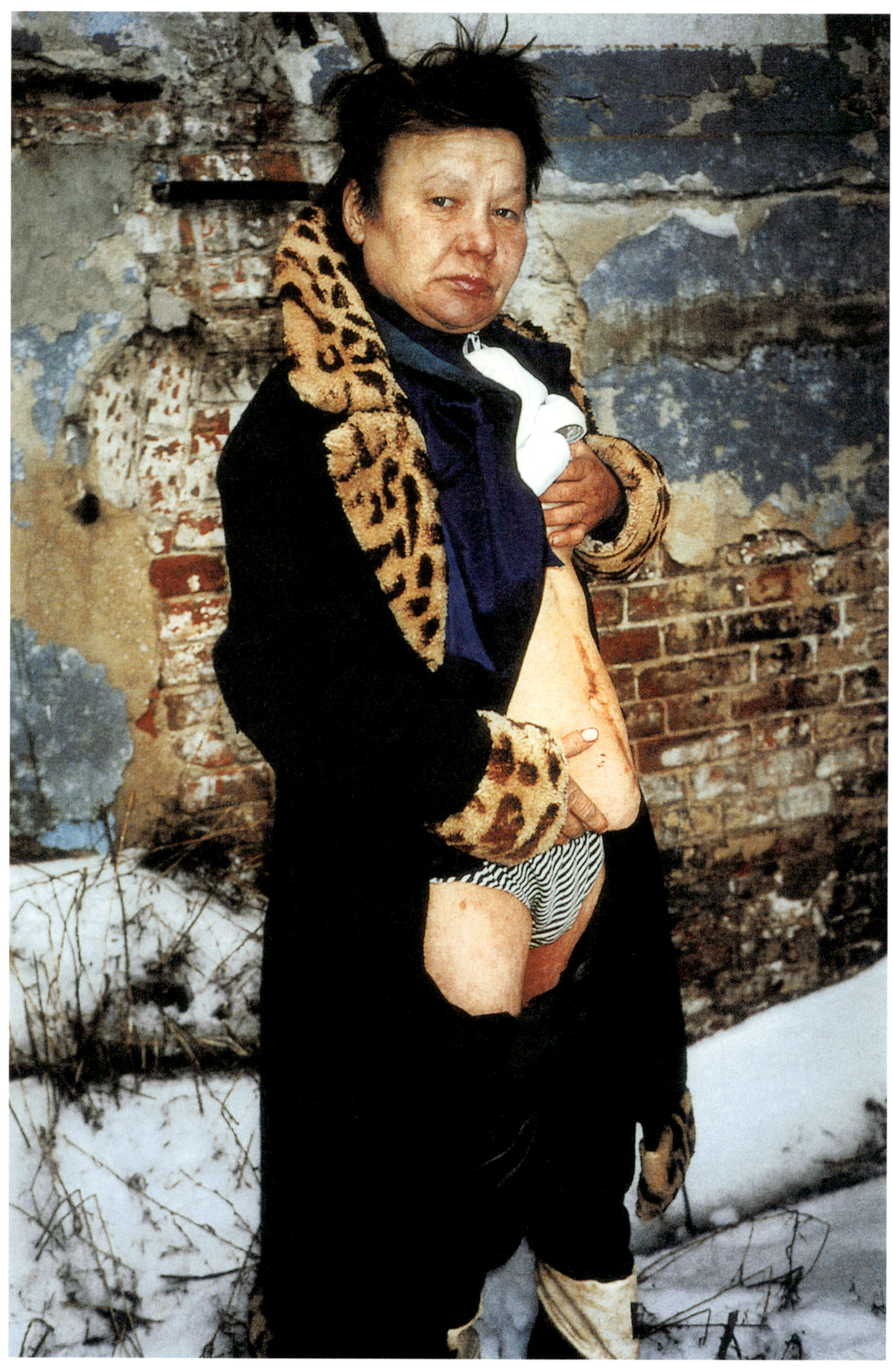

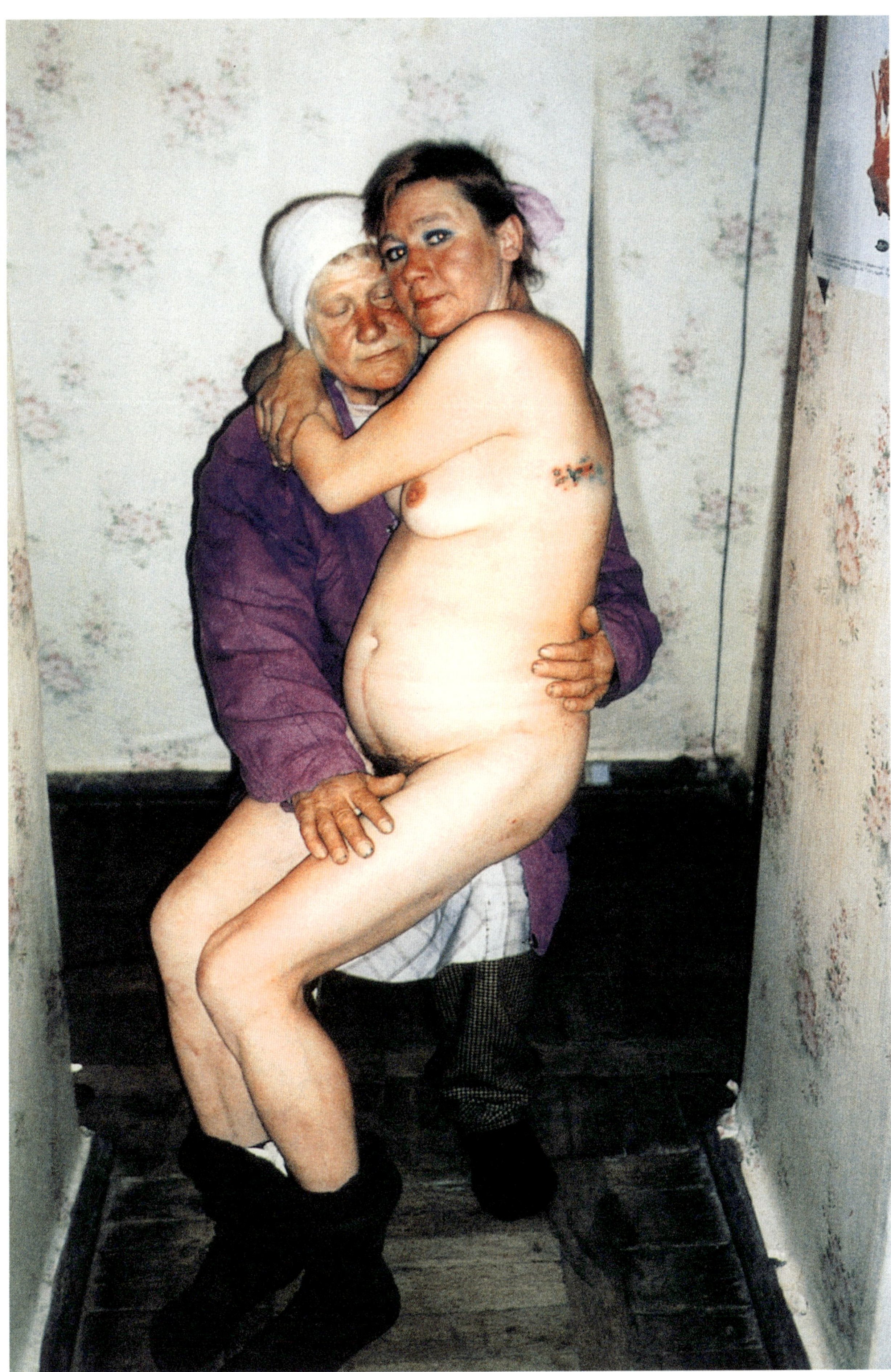

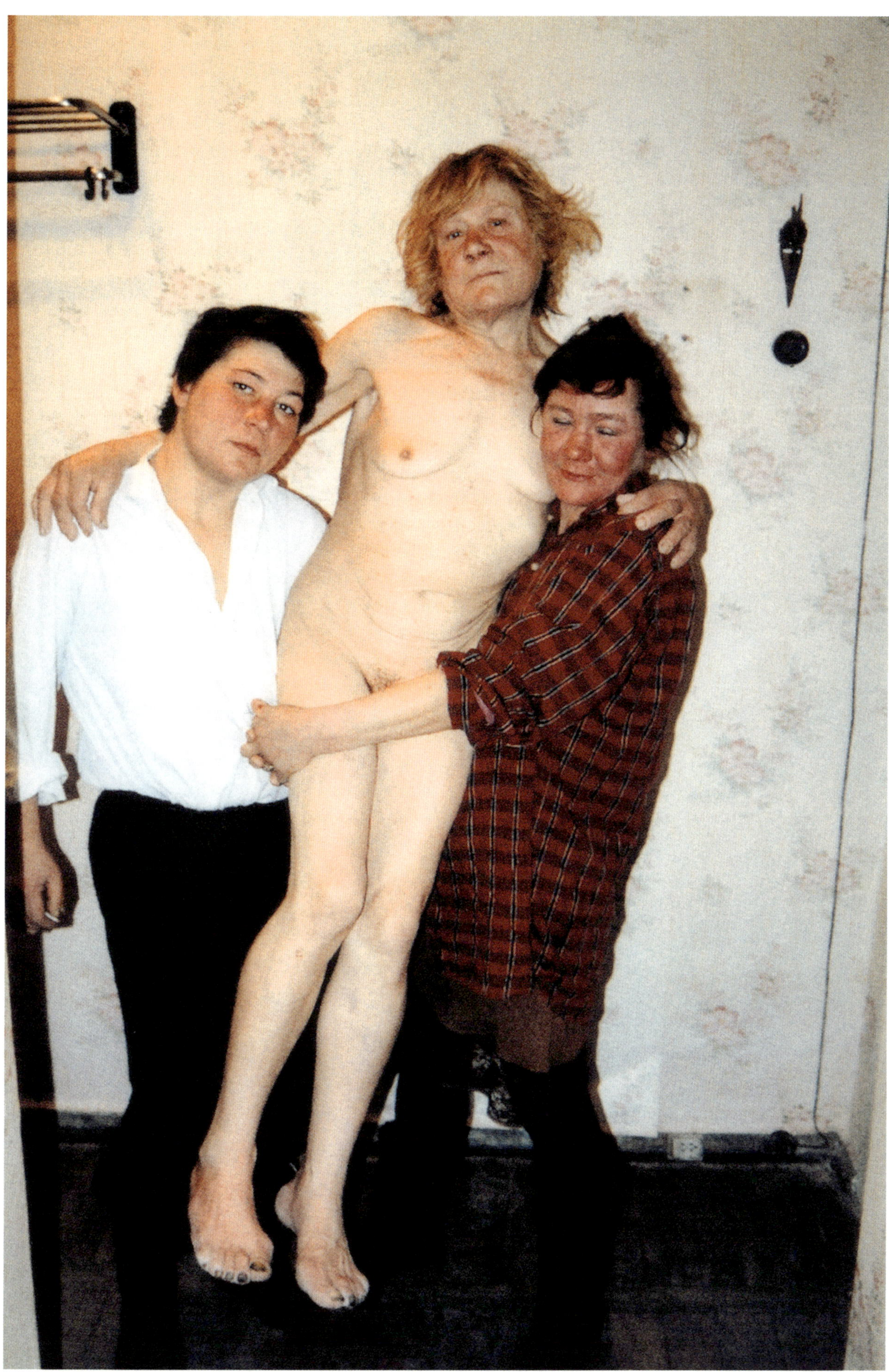

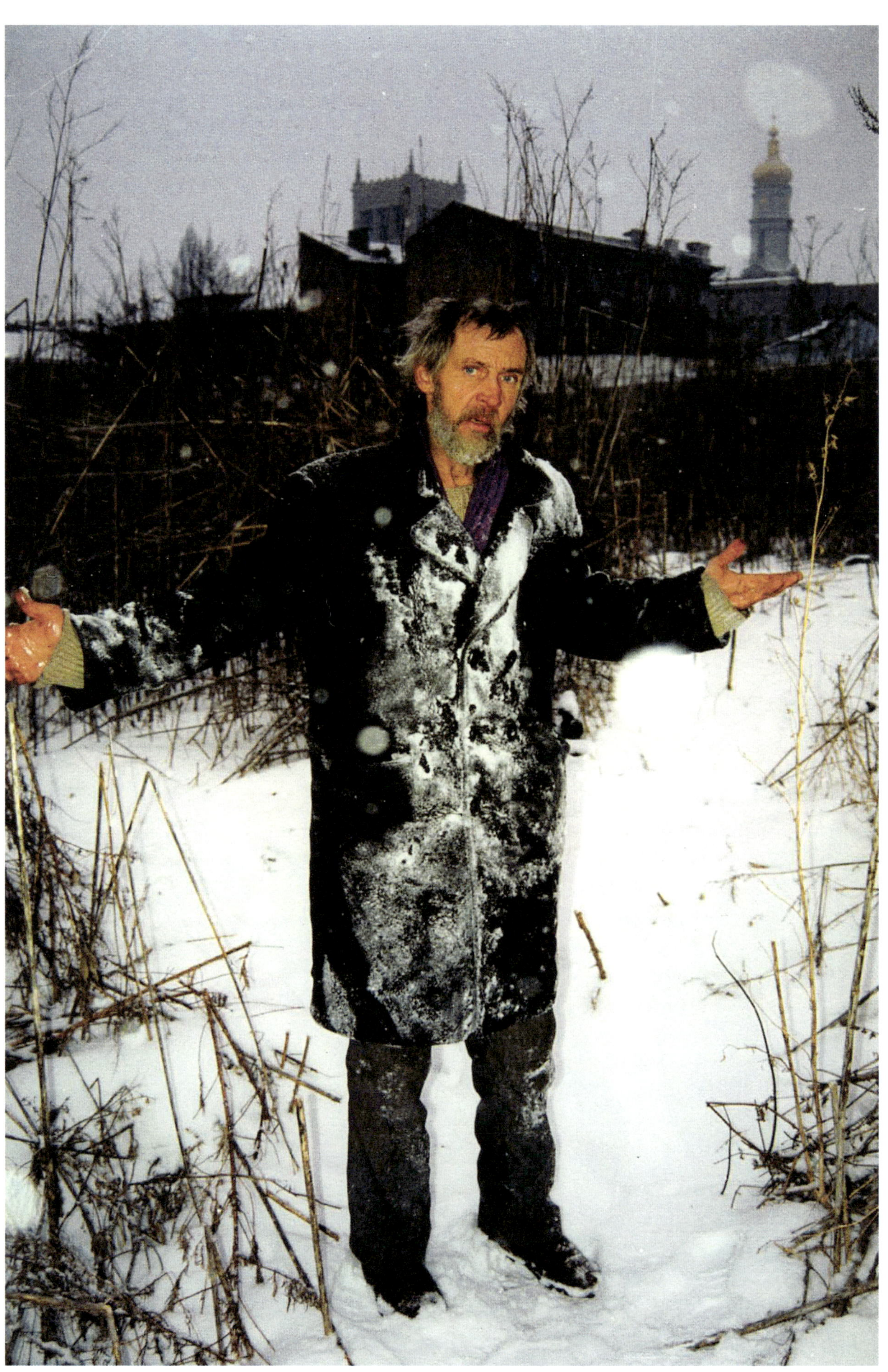

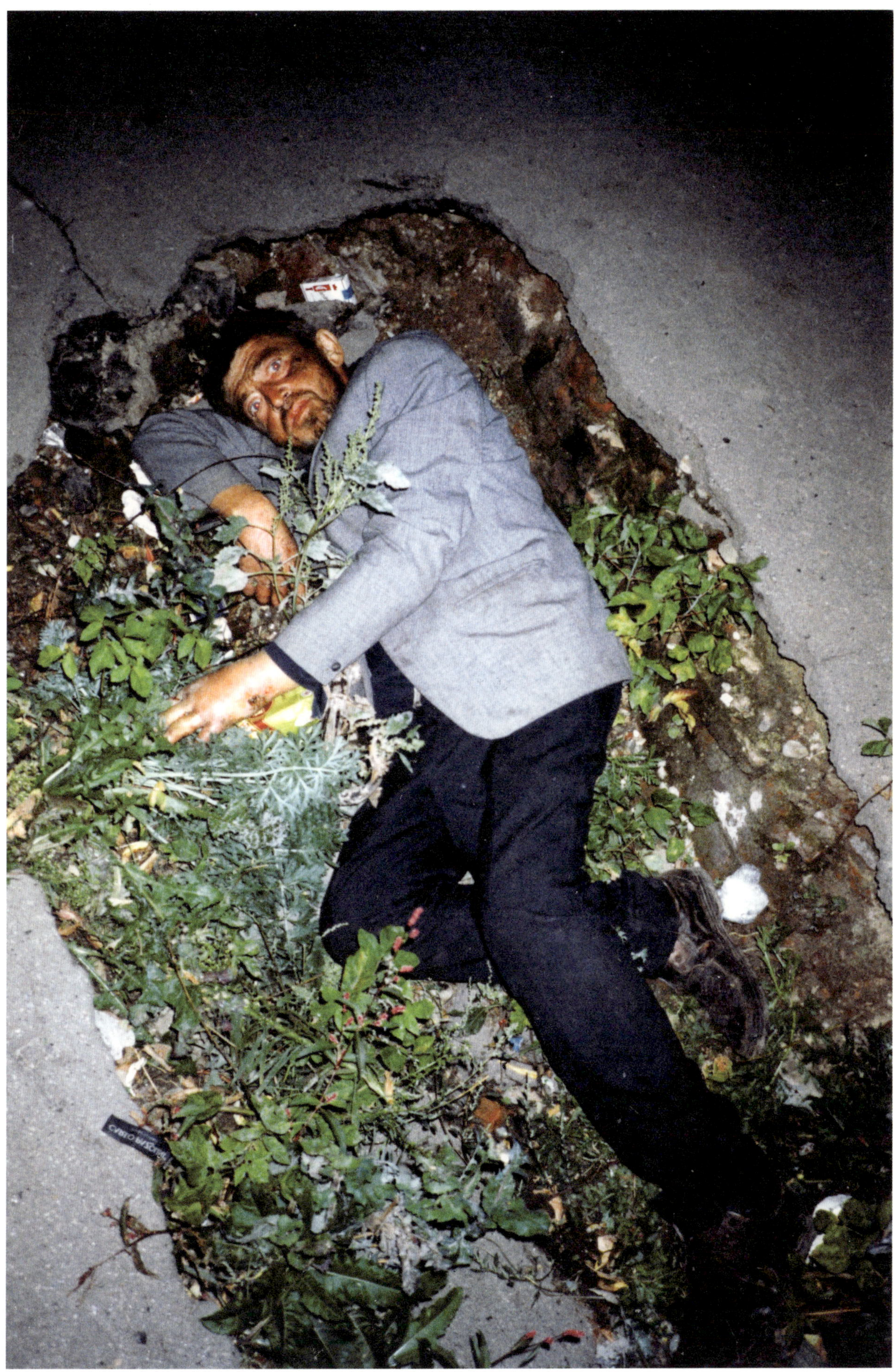

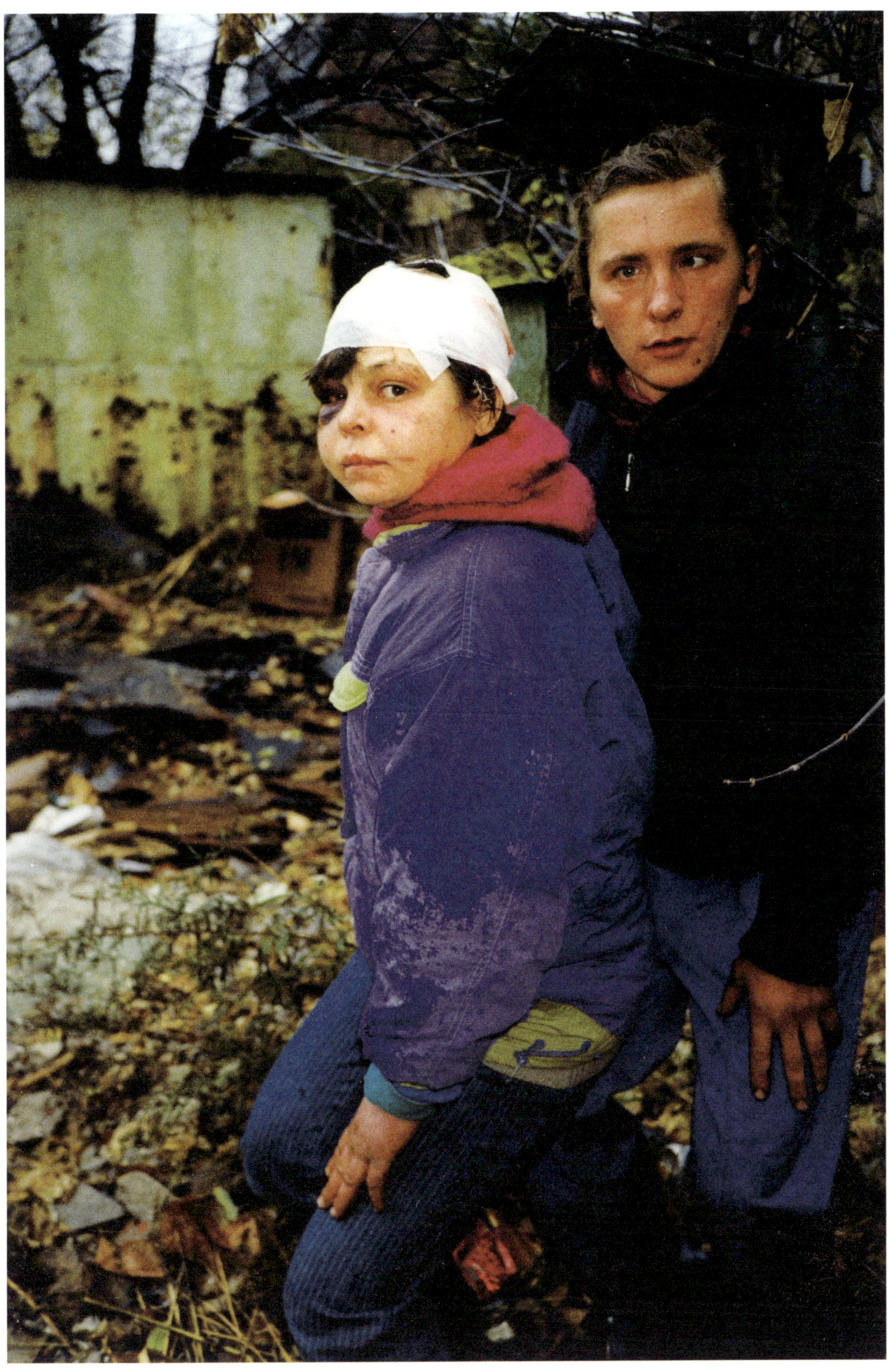

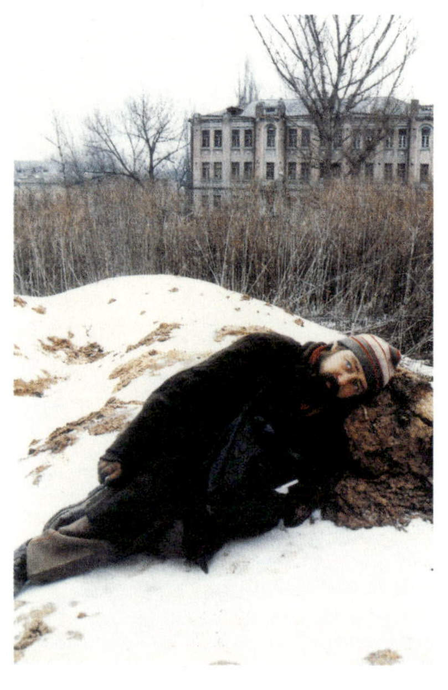 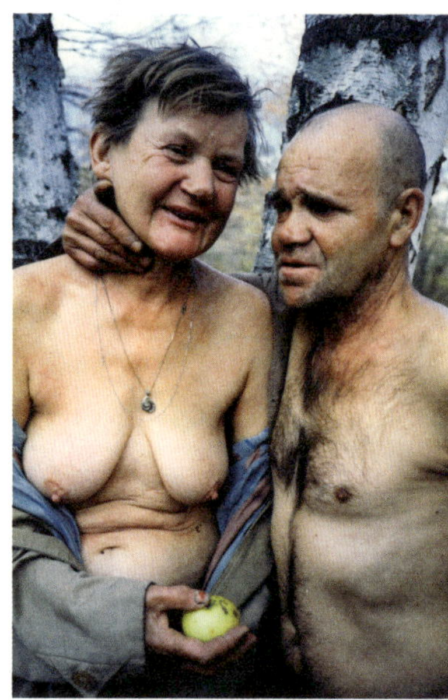 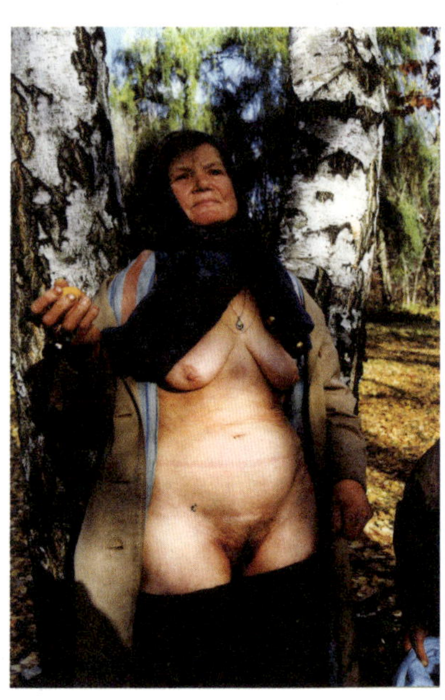

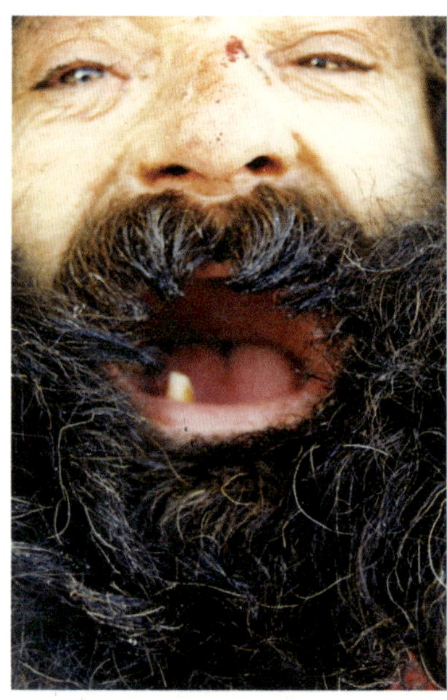 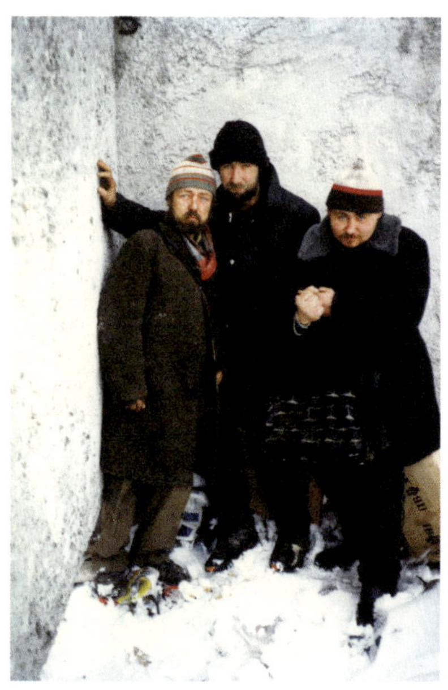 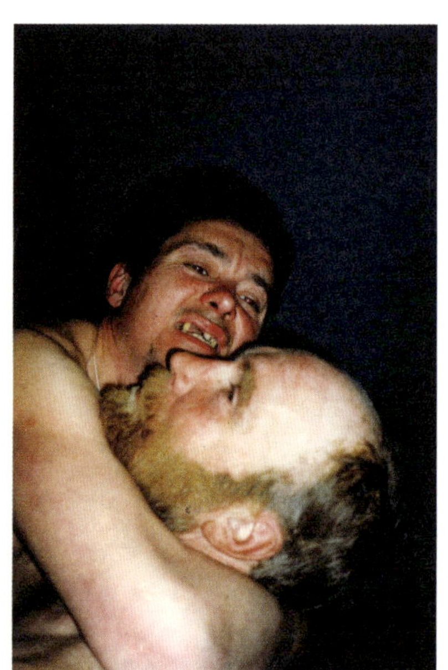

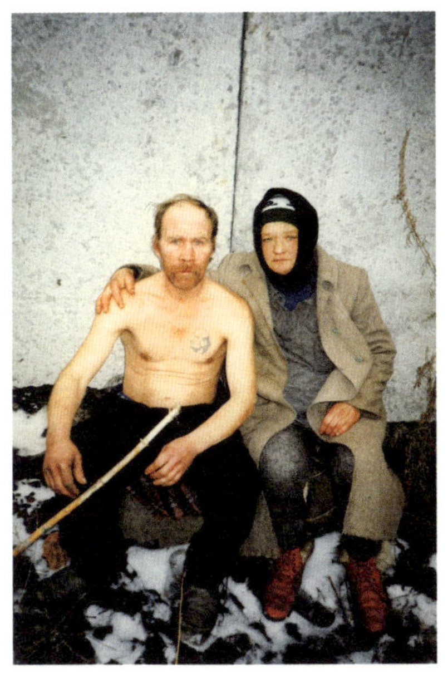
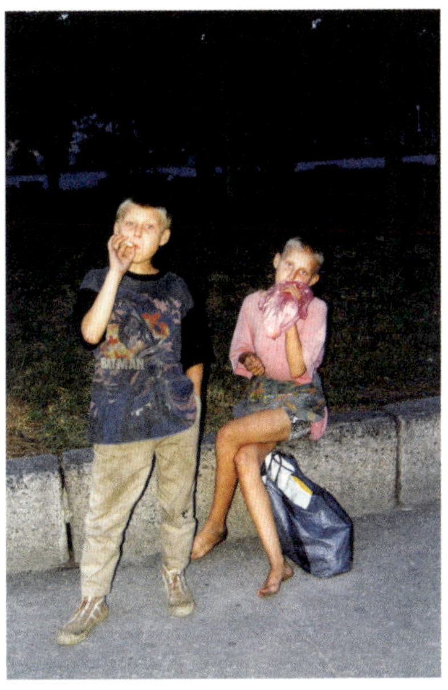
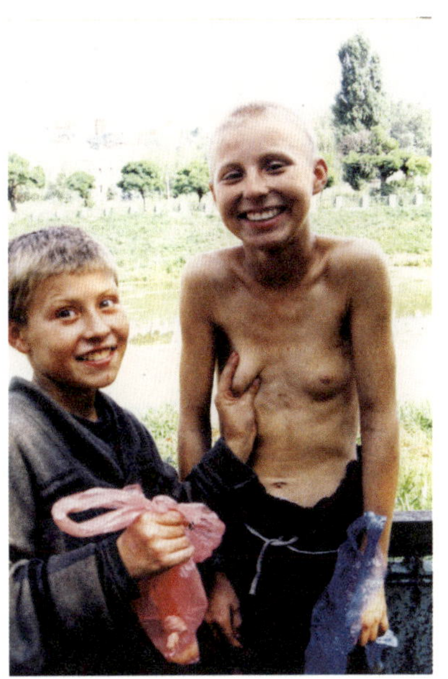
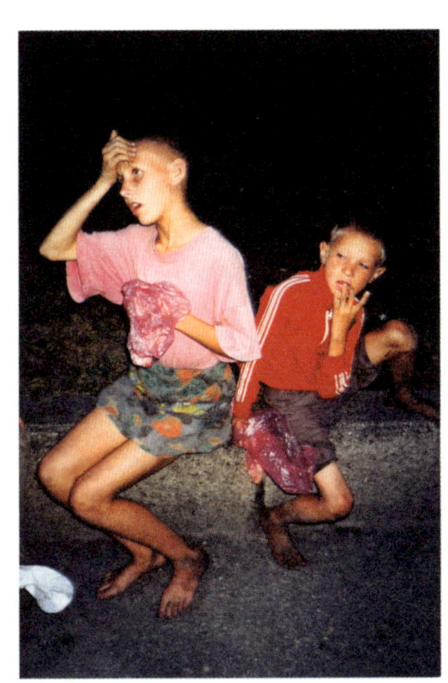
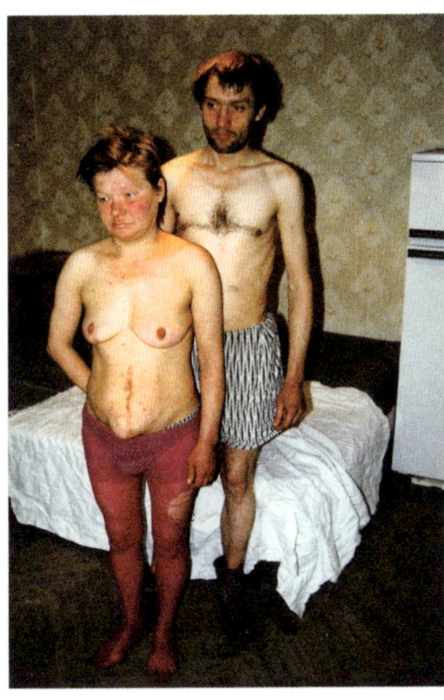
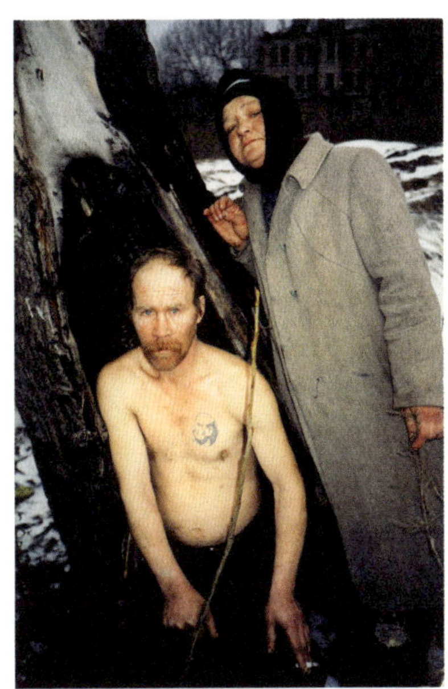

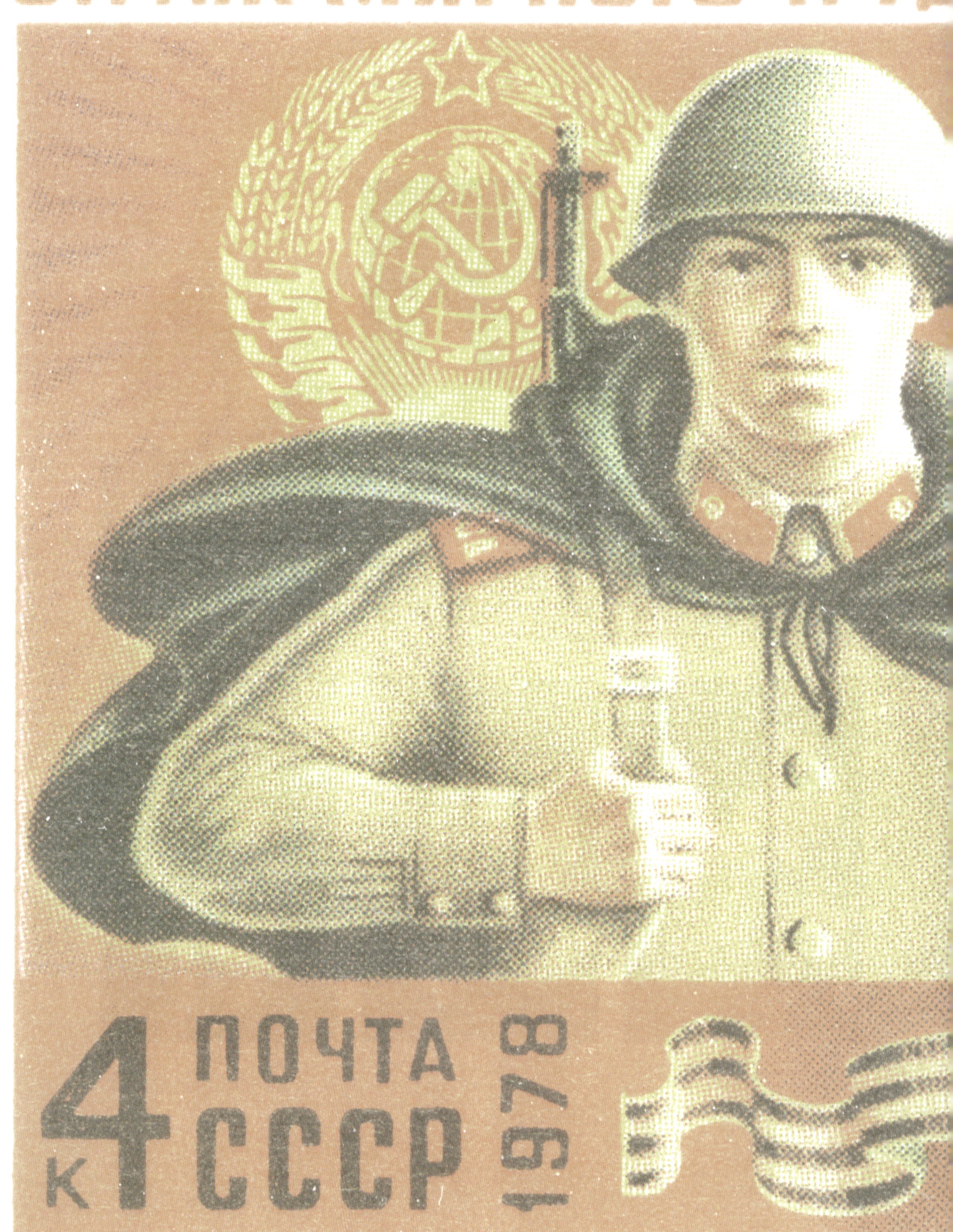
СТРАЖ МИРНОГО ТРУД
ПОЧТА
СССР
1978
4
к

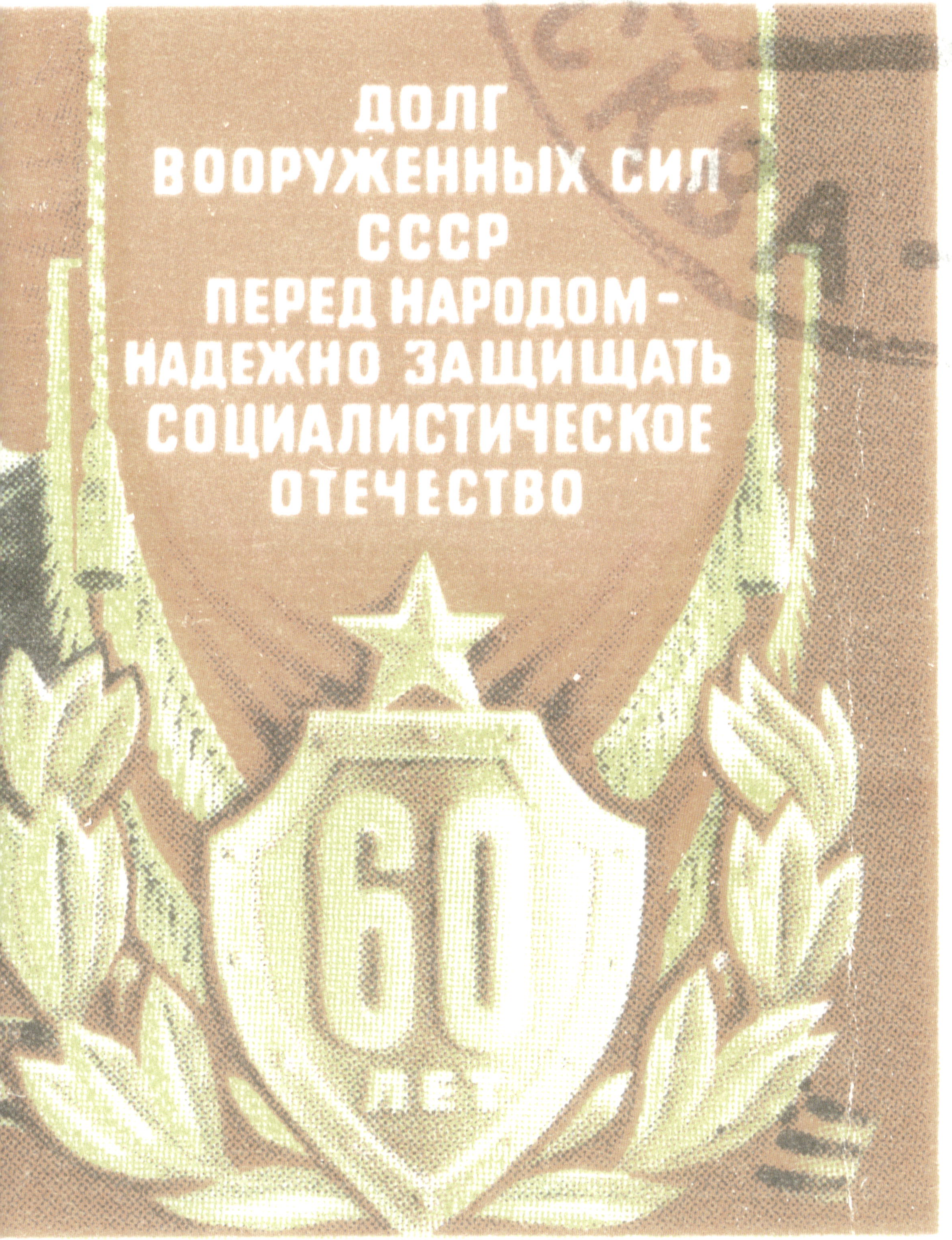
ДОЛГ
ВООРУЖЕННЫХ СИЛ
СССР
ПЕРЕД НАРОДОМ -
НАДЕЖНО ЗАЩИЩАТЬ
СОЦИАЛИСТИЧЕСКОЕ
ОТЕЧЕСТВО
60
ЛЕТ

NIKA NEELOVA

Nika Neelova makes sculptural installations out of reclaimed architectural features and burnt timber. Disassociated from their original use and re-composed in her new arrangements, these old beams, casts and worn ropes exude their own original energy as well as their heritage. They have become something other than what they were, while retaining a feeling of oneiric repetition – claiming a life of their own and a new purpose, but still clawing onto a past one.

Principles of Surrender (2010) is constructed out of six burnt wood posts which, with its slight cantilevers, support beams and mortise and tenon joints, resembles age-old vernacular architecture. Tied to the platform created by these posts are huge bell clappers which the artist has cast in wax infused with ash, creating an enormous congregation of bell pulls.

But there is no bell to ring, because this structure is not a bell tower. Yet both of these images, and what they can connote, hover around as poetic associations within the same space. Similarly, *Scaffolds Today, Monuments Tomorrow* (2011) distressingly reads both like a seaside pier and a platform used to hang people.

Neelova's works stand as odd, transparent altars to their elements' origins, made up of elements that have survived despite being charred. They open up the distorted manner in which the past is read by the present, and what she refers to as "the historical memory that is embedded in materials."

SCAFFOLDS TODAY, MONUMENTS TOMORROW, 2011   PRINCIPLES OF SURRENDER, 2010
Burnt and waxed wood, paper and ink   Burnt timber, bell clappers cast in wax infused with ash, rope
200 x 150 x 400 cm   250 x 150 x 300 cm

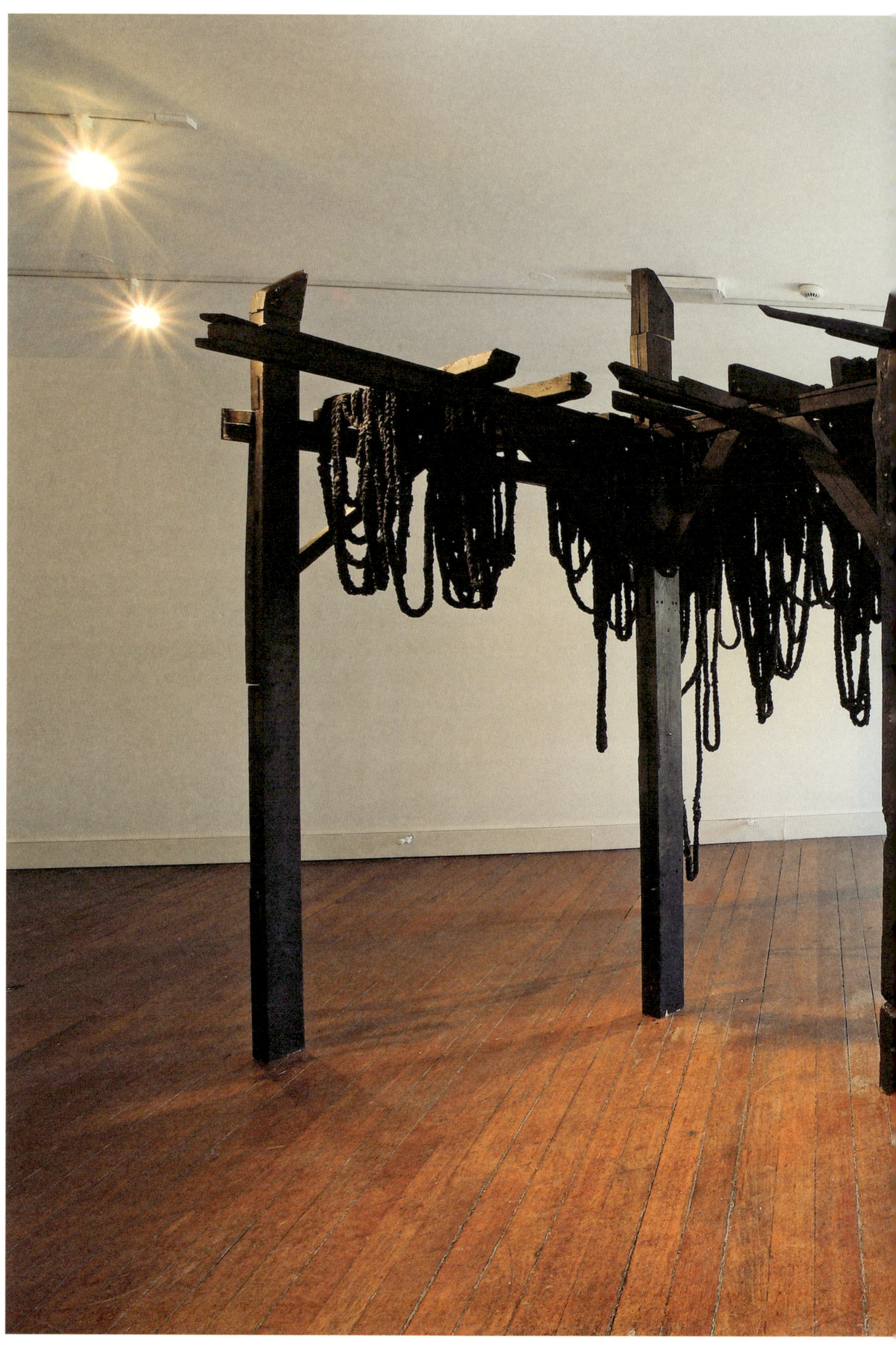

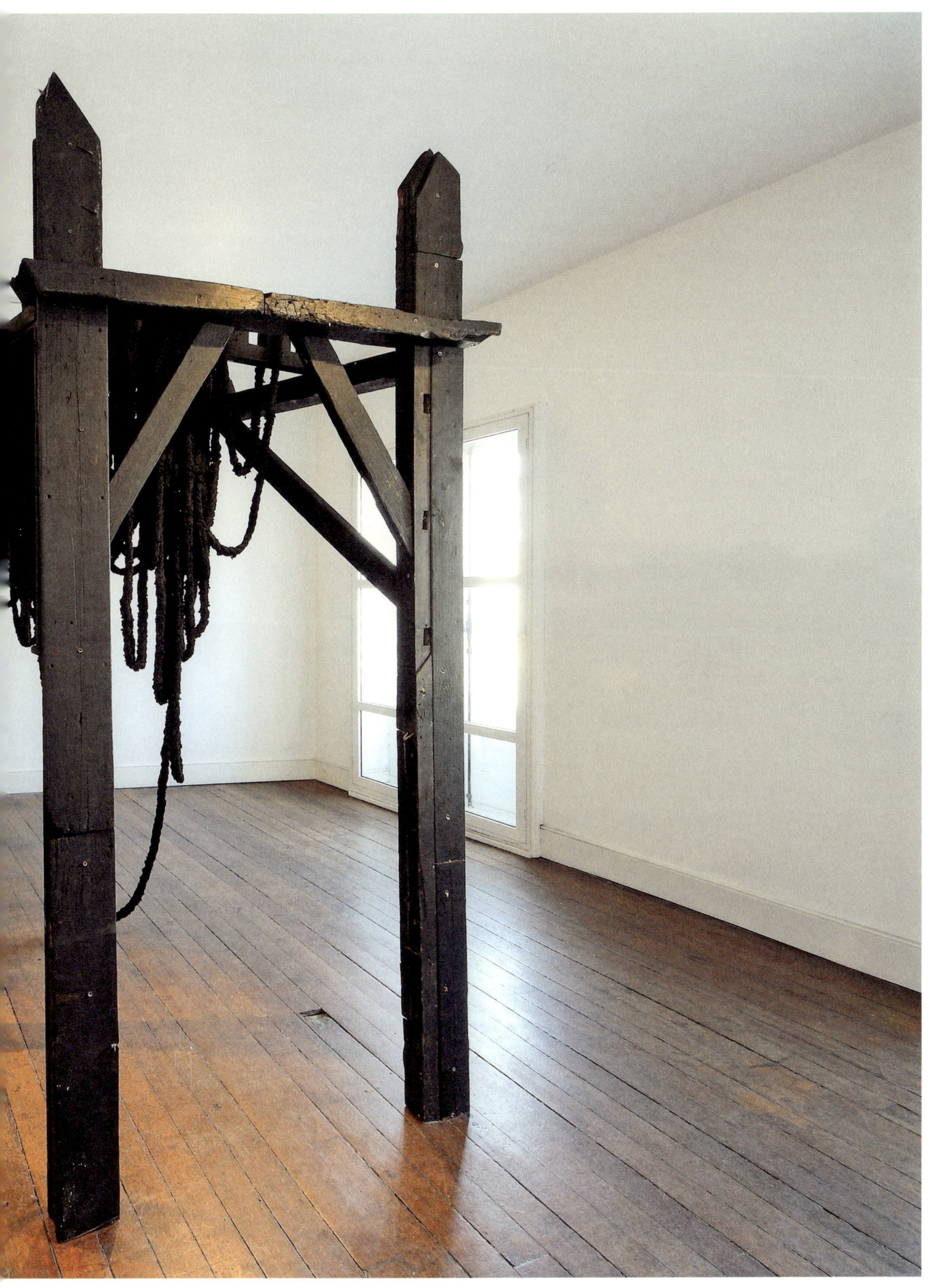

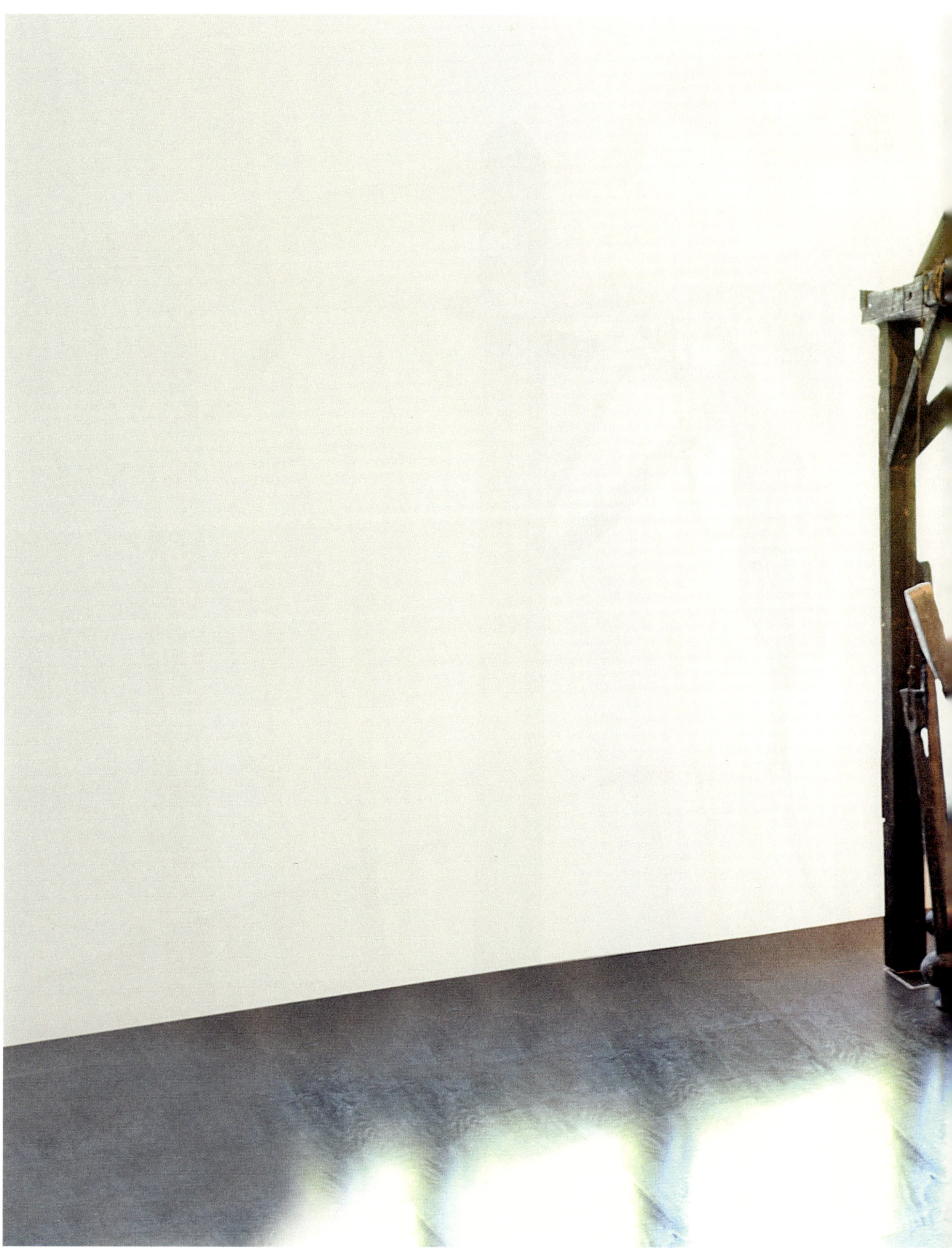

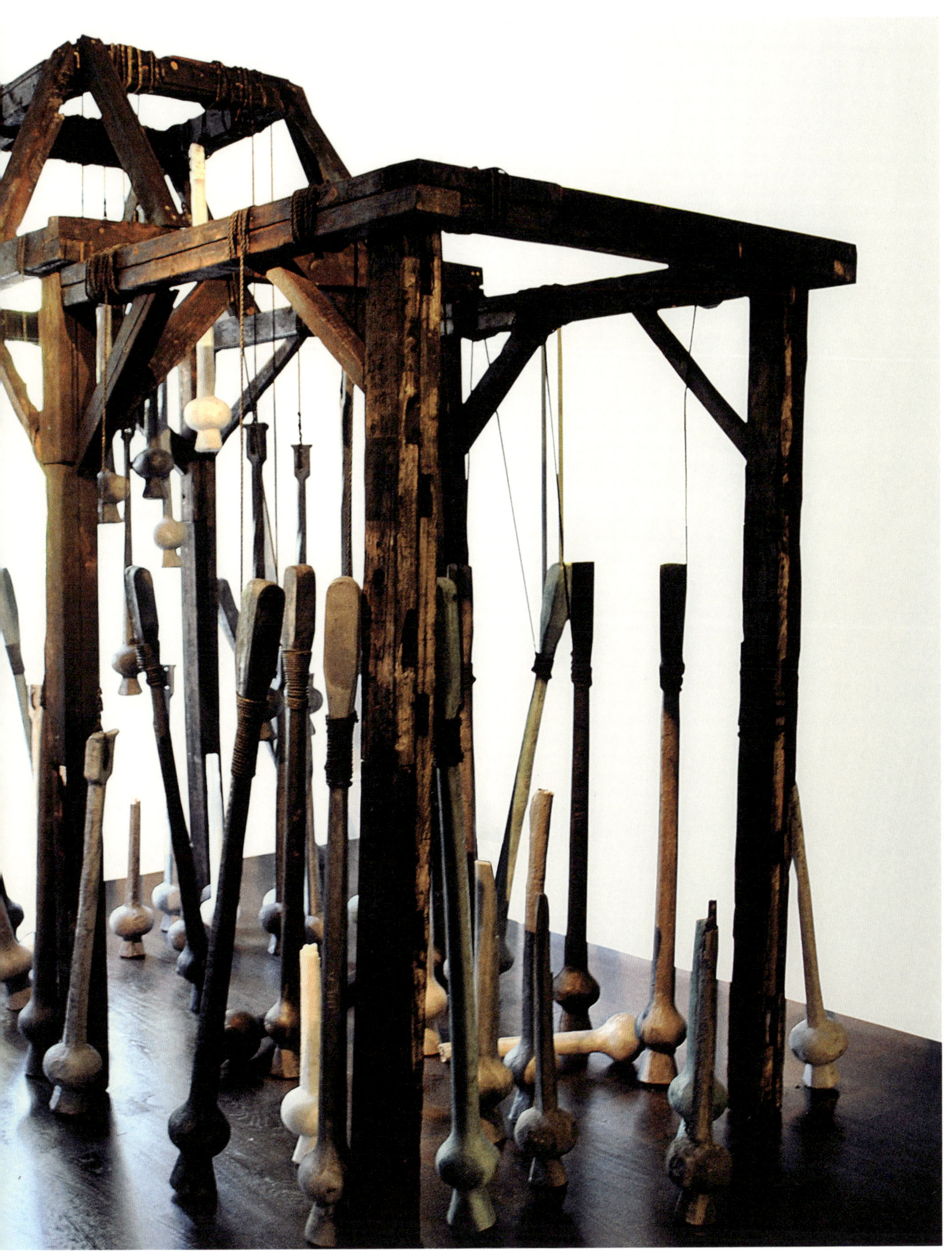

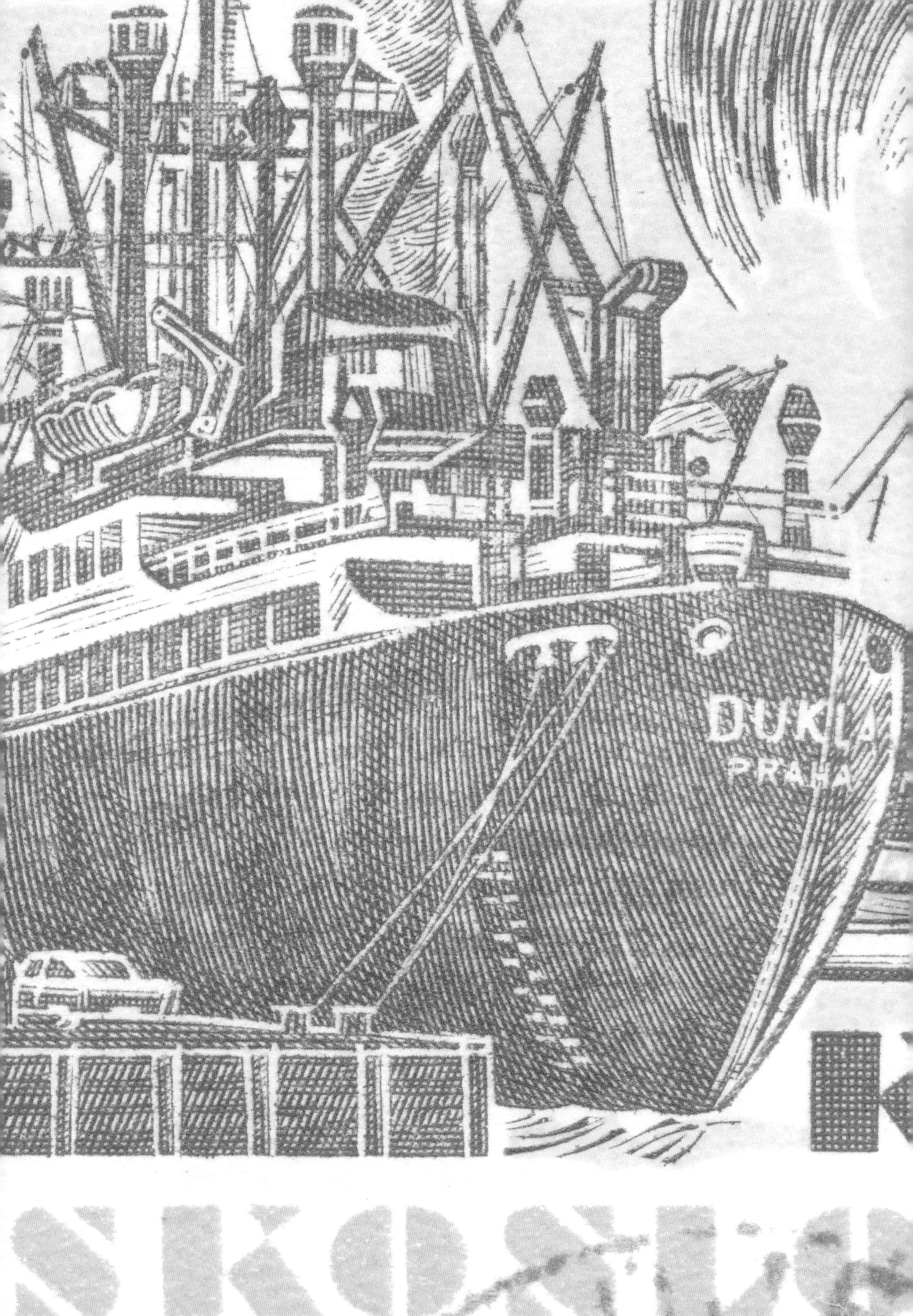

DUKLA
PRAHA

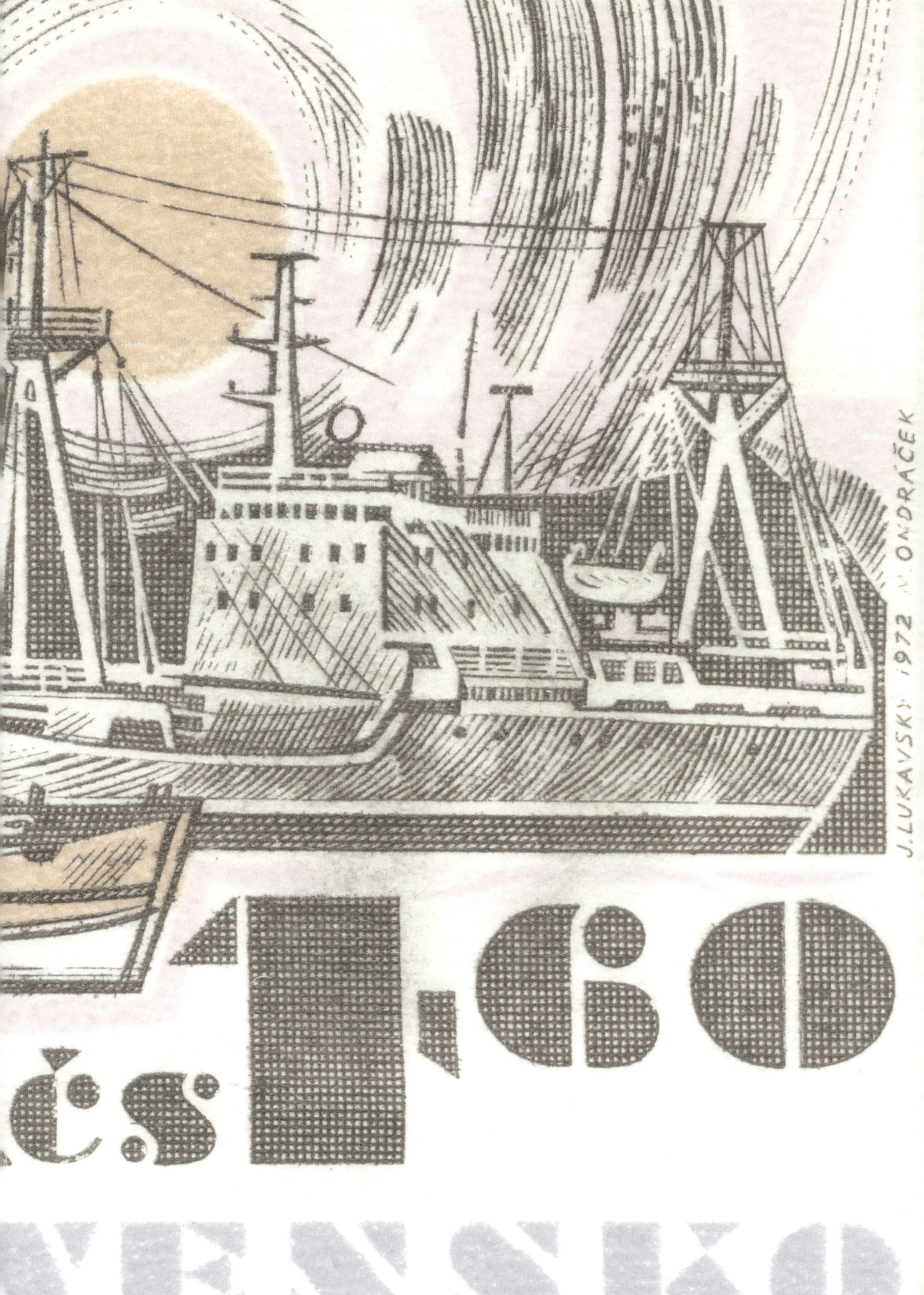
J. LUKAVSKÝ 1972 M. ONDRÁČEK
Č.S.
1,60
VENSKO

VIKENTI NILIN

The stars of Vikenti Nilin's 'Neighbours' series (1993 - present) probably come from all walks of life but they have one thing in common: they are staring into their own abyss, conveniently found in the familiar surroundings of the commonplace Soviet tower block. Yet they don't seem in the least bit worried. Deadpan doesn't begin to sum up the mood hanging around Nilin's black and white portraits. The expressions on his subjects, as they perch on the edge of windowsills and balconies, are phlegmatic, unimpressed, relaxed and almost bored.

Vikenti Nilin's photographs and installations are glacially sardonic, direct and to the point, but their oblique meaning can end up provoking nervous laughter. His images suggest a state of incarnate passivity, suspension and permanent transition, perhaps morosely alluding to the state of politics in his home country.

The 'Neighbours' series, taciturnly described by the artist as "the current state of practice, started in 1993", are cryptic yet self-explanatory. We don't really need to ask why these people are sitting so comfortably on the edge of their windowsills and balconies; possible reasons for falling can be intuited, but the suspension is Nilin's magic trick.

Pidjak Dla Khodby Na Rukakh (2006) is made up of a transparent mannequin wearing a modified tweed jacket with upside down pockets bulging with cables and other things, wearing a smiley face badge on it, and a hook with nothing hanging on it. The set-up is unclear, but it seems that this object too is immune to the physical laws of the universe. Asked to discuss both of these works, Nilin opts for an a propos epigram taken from a Talking Heads song: "...Somewhere in South Carolina/gravity don't mean a thing..."

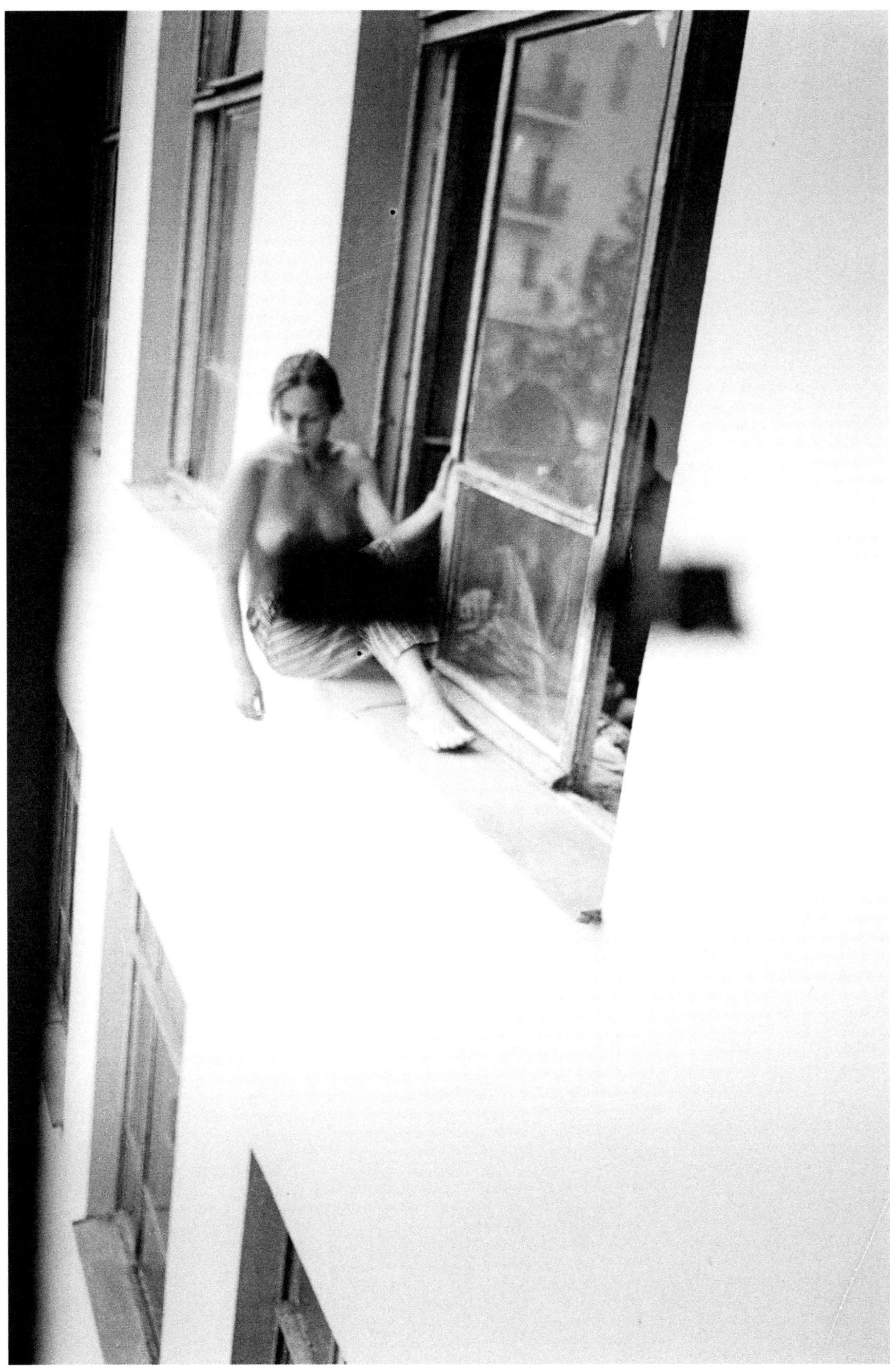

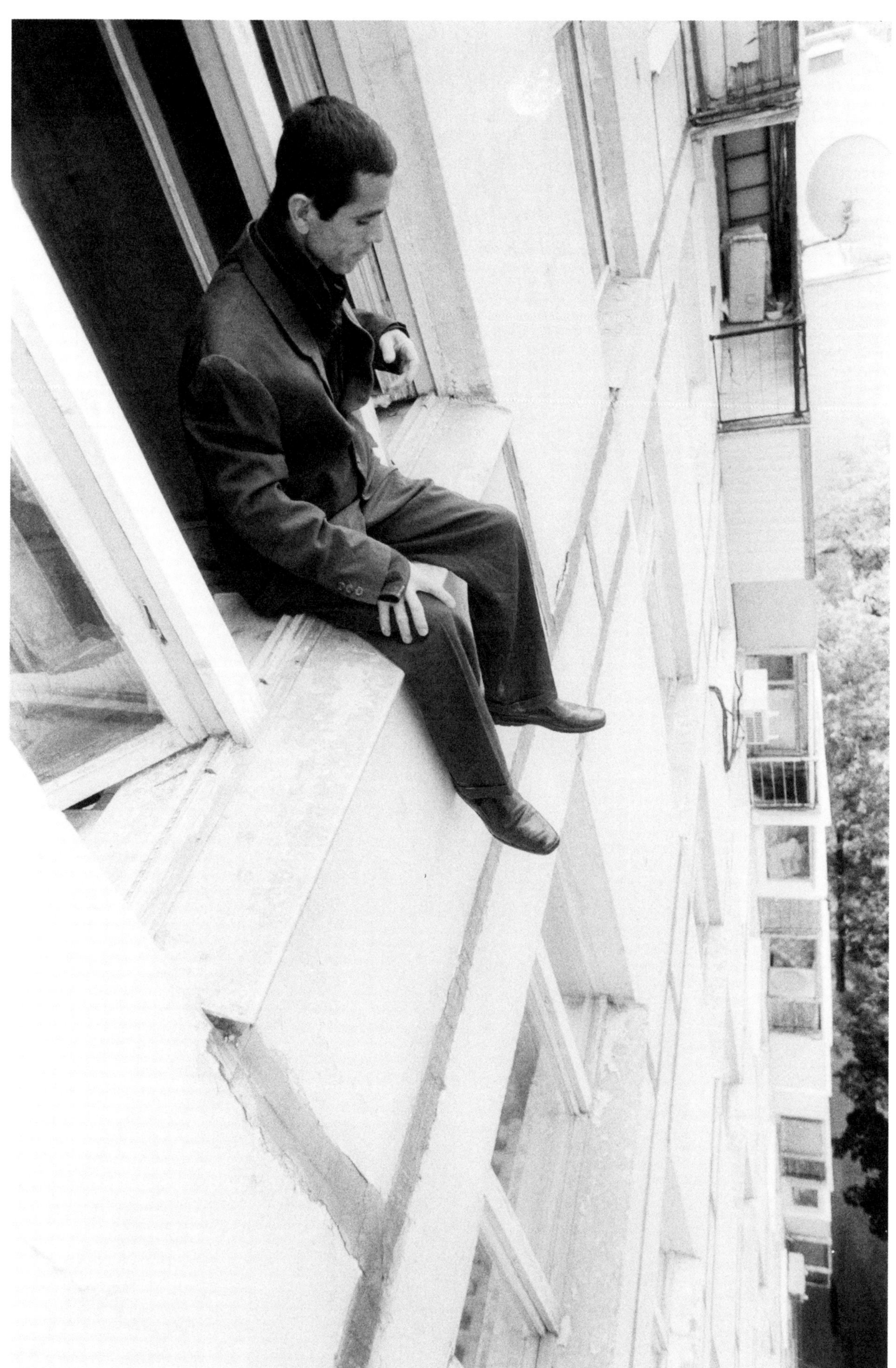

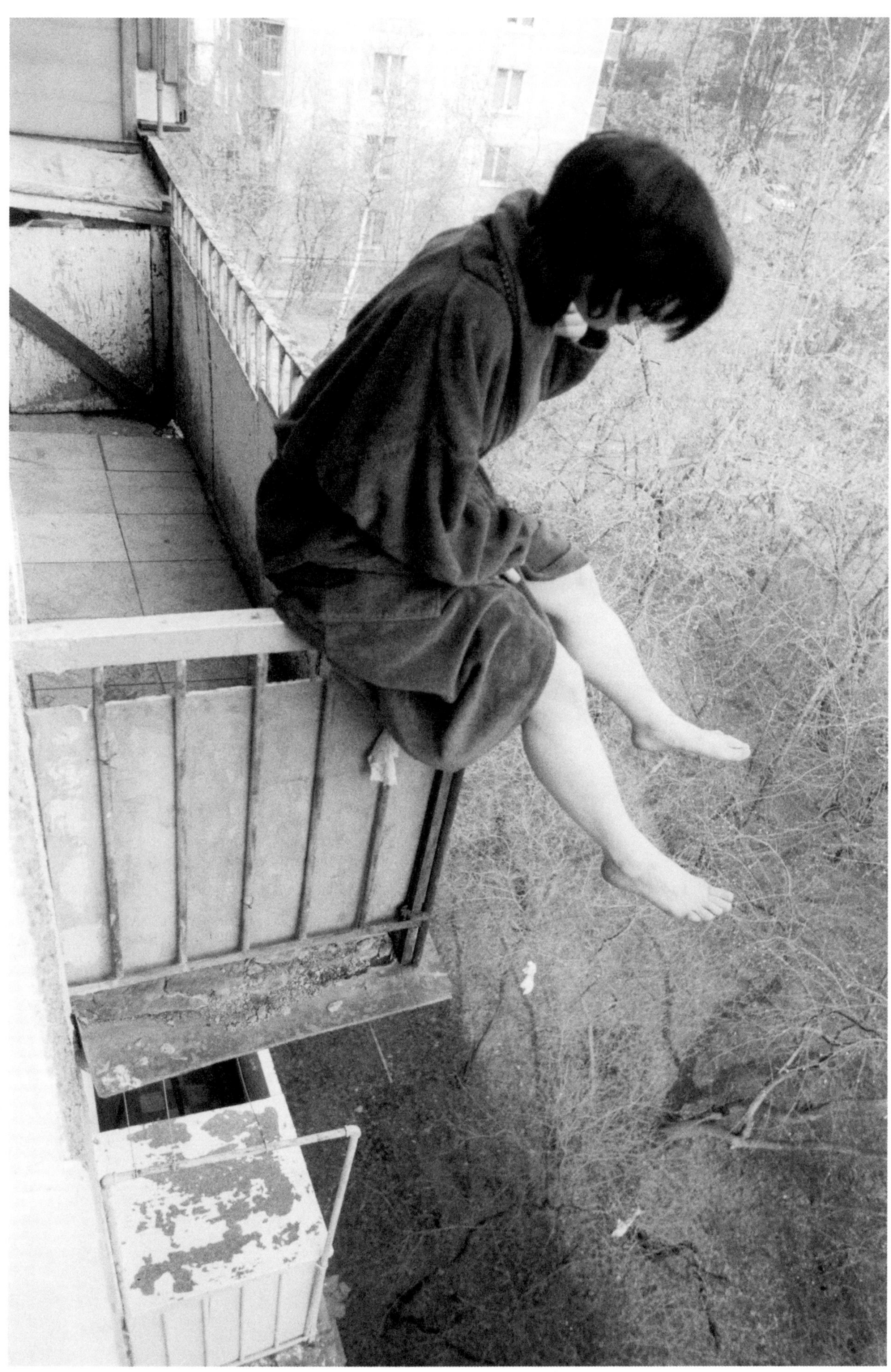

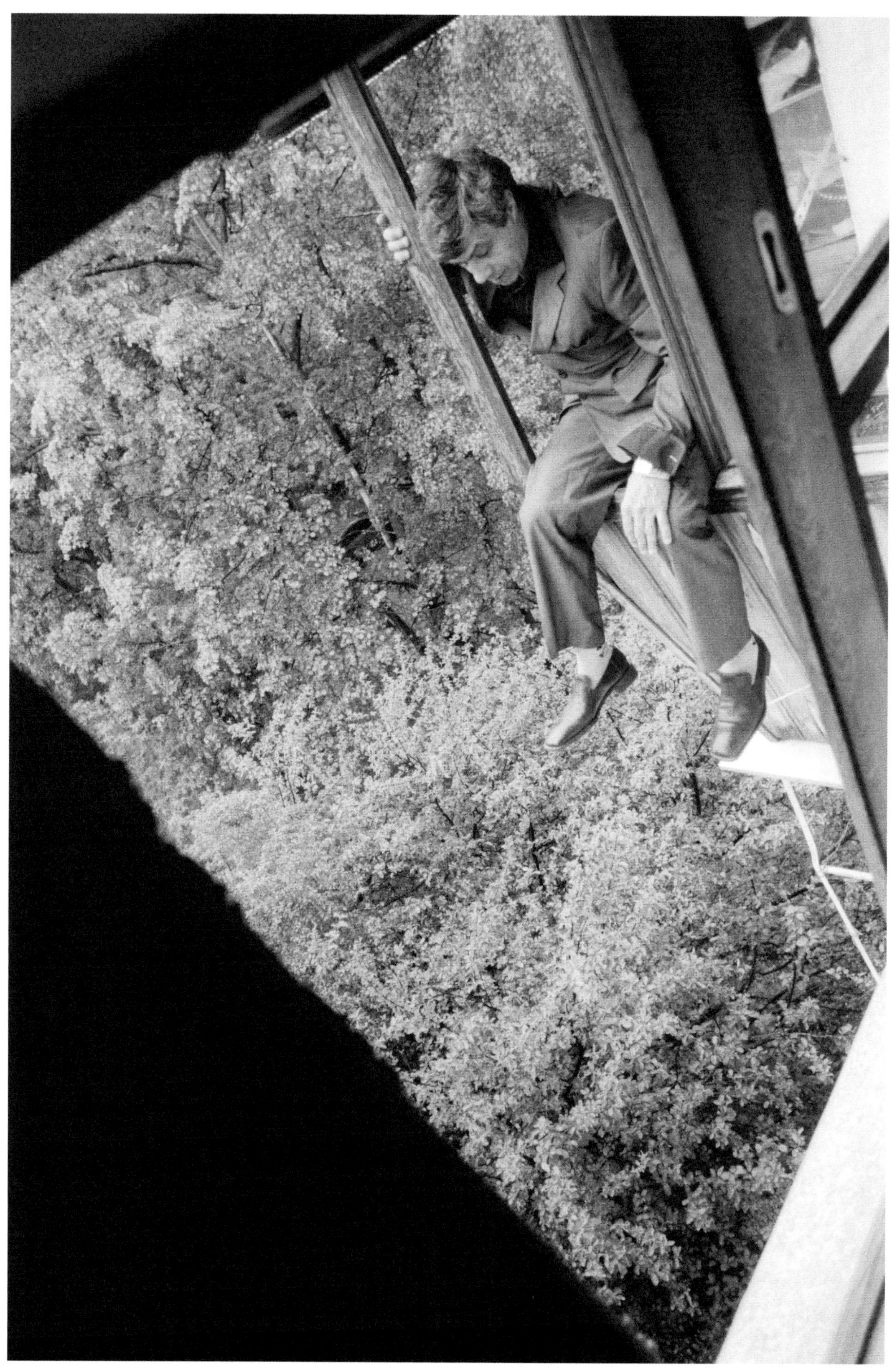

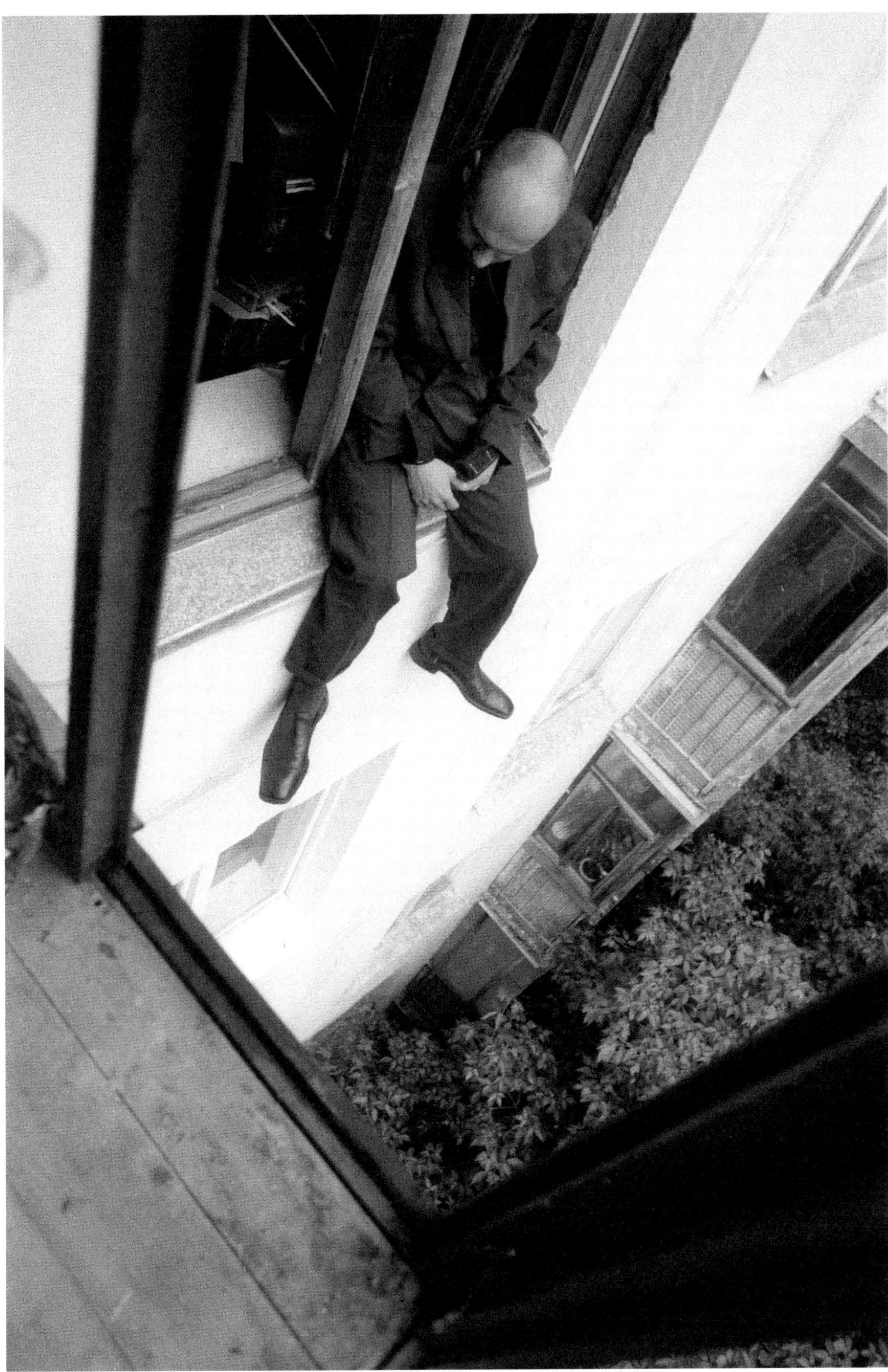

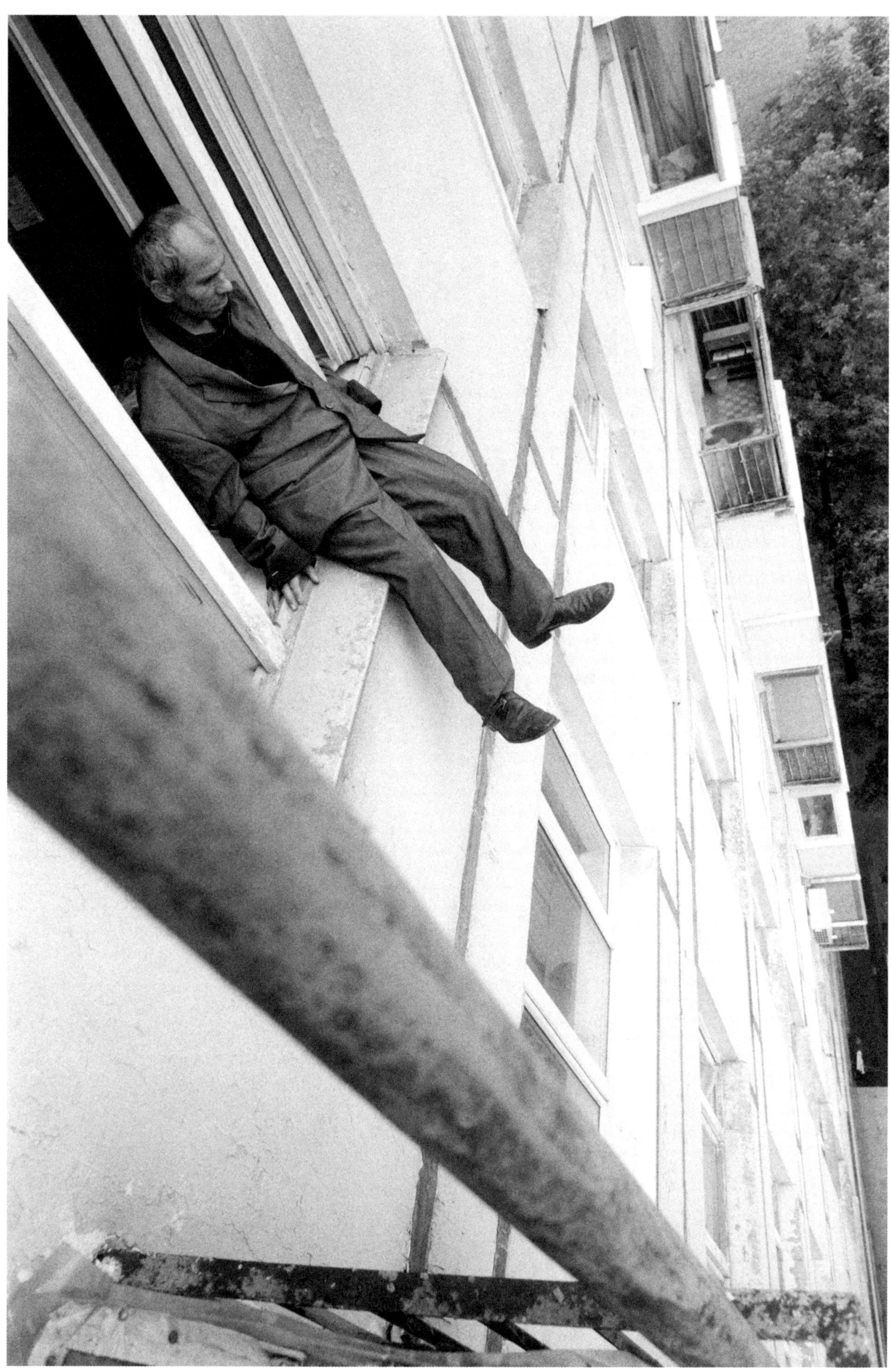

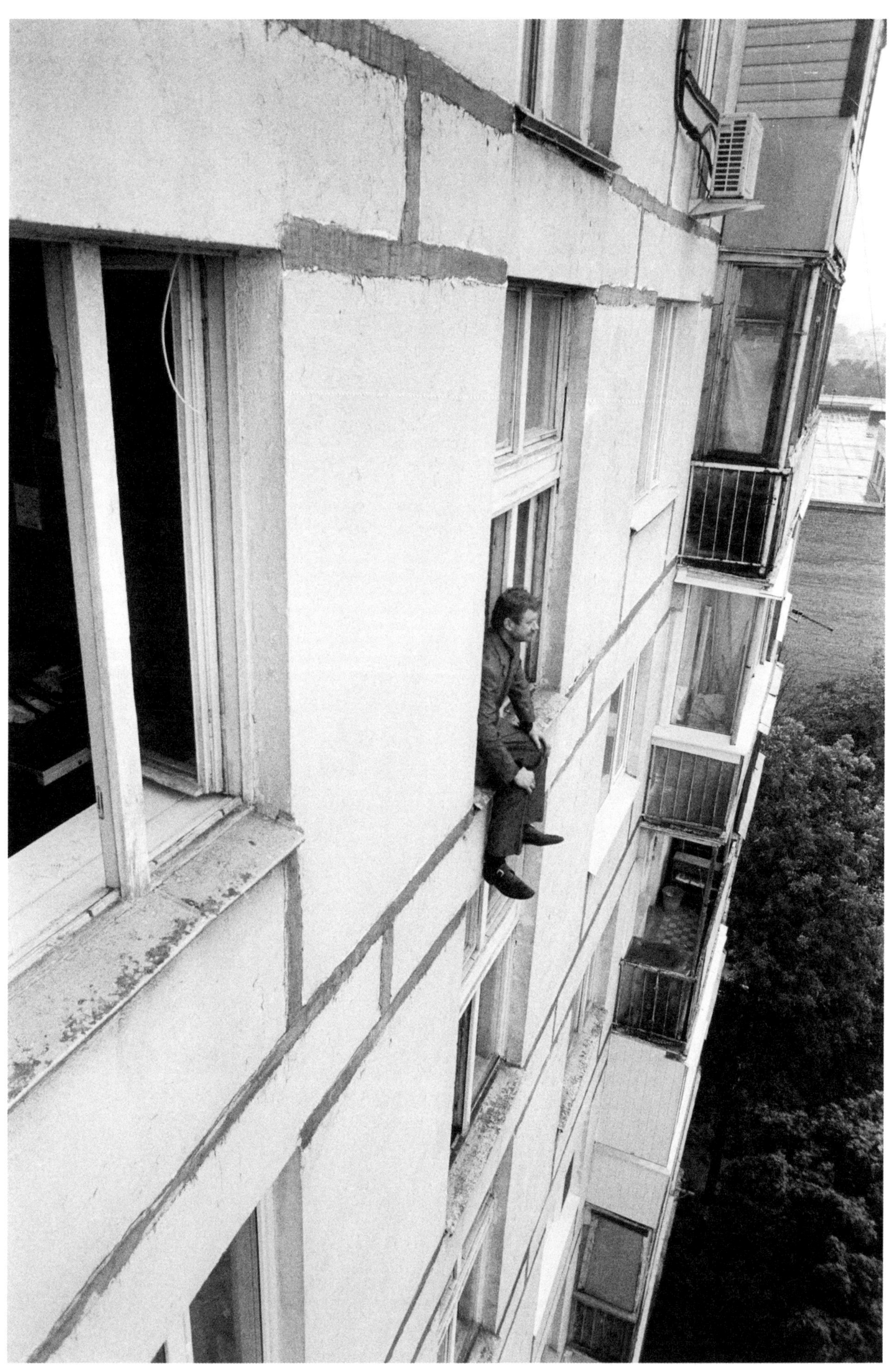

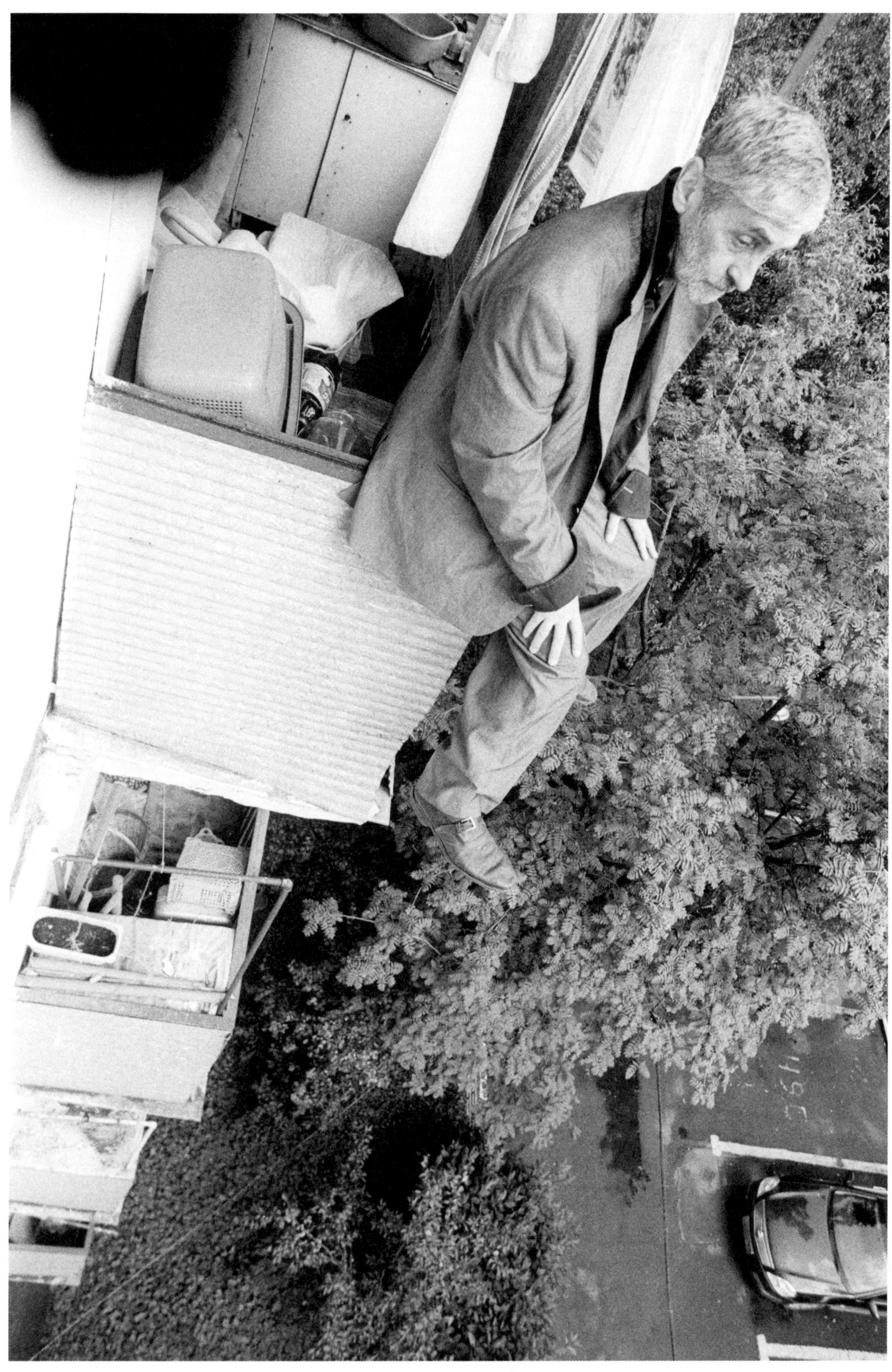

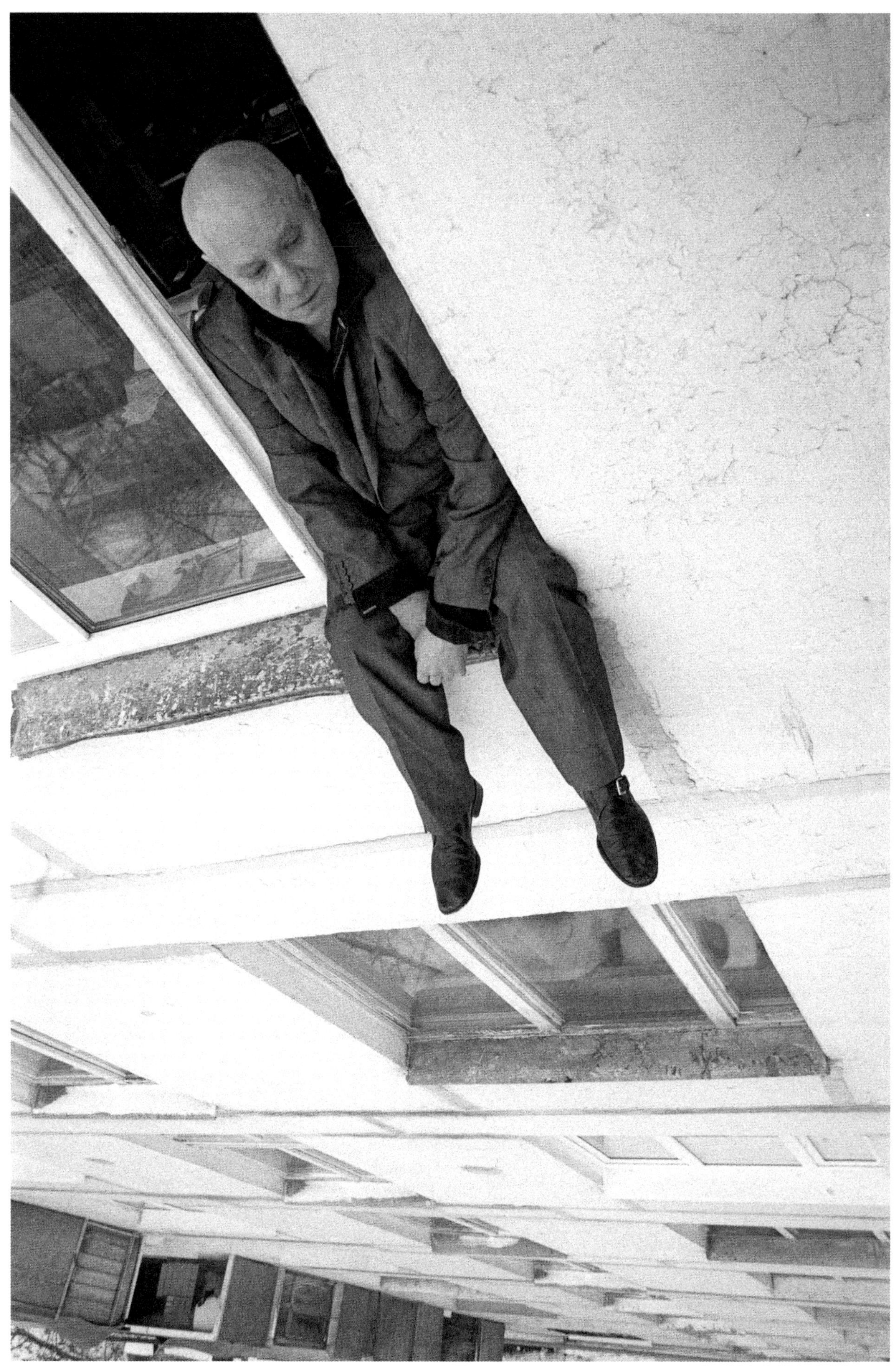

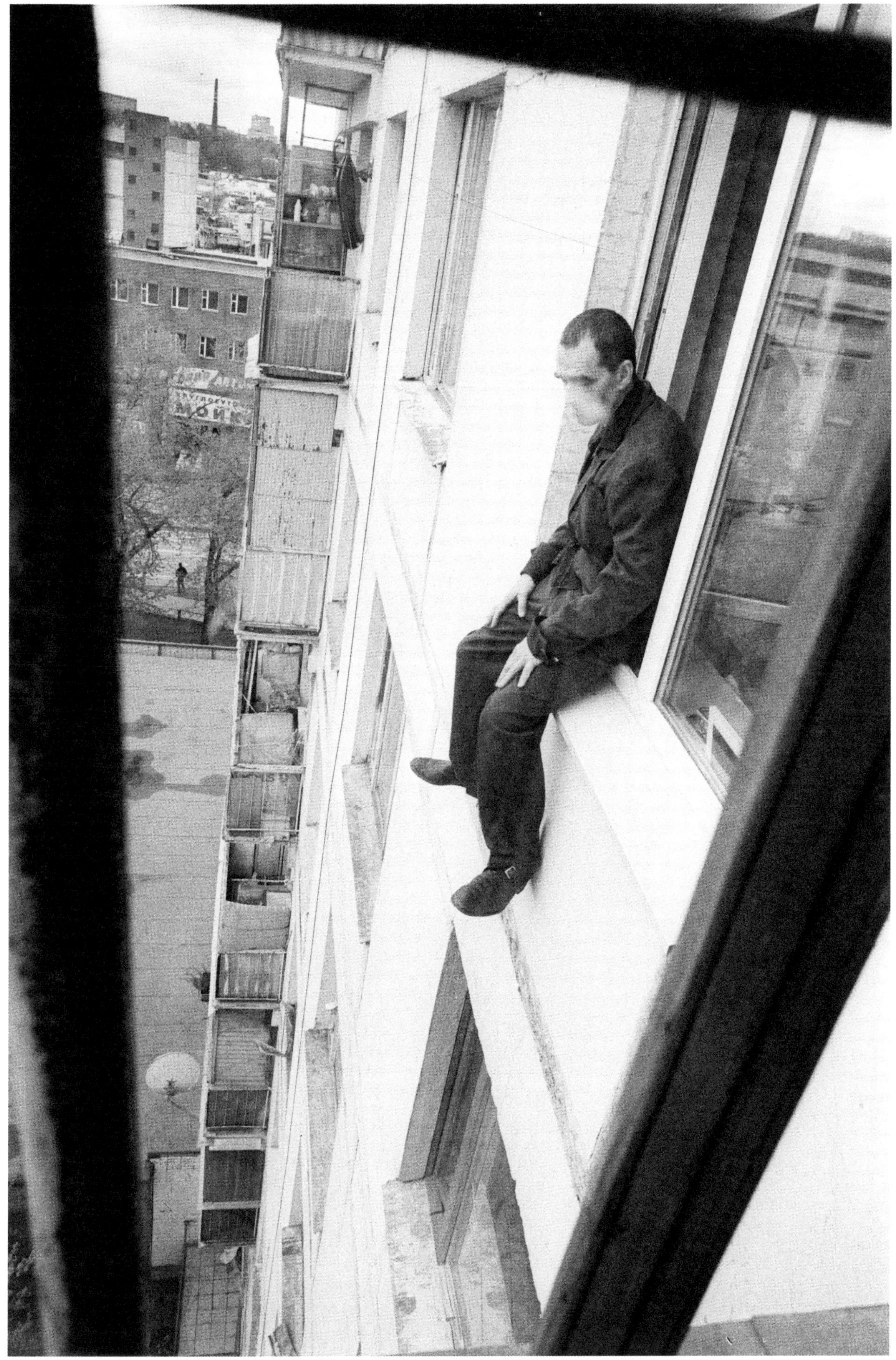

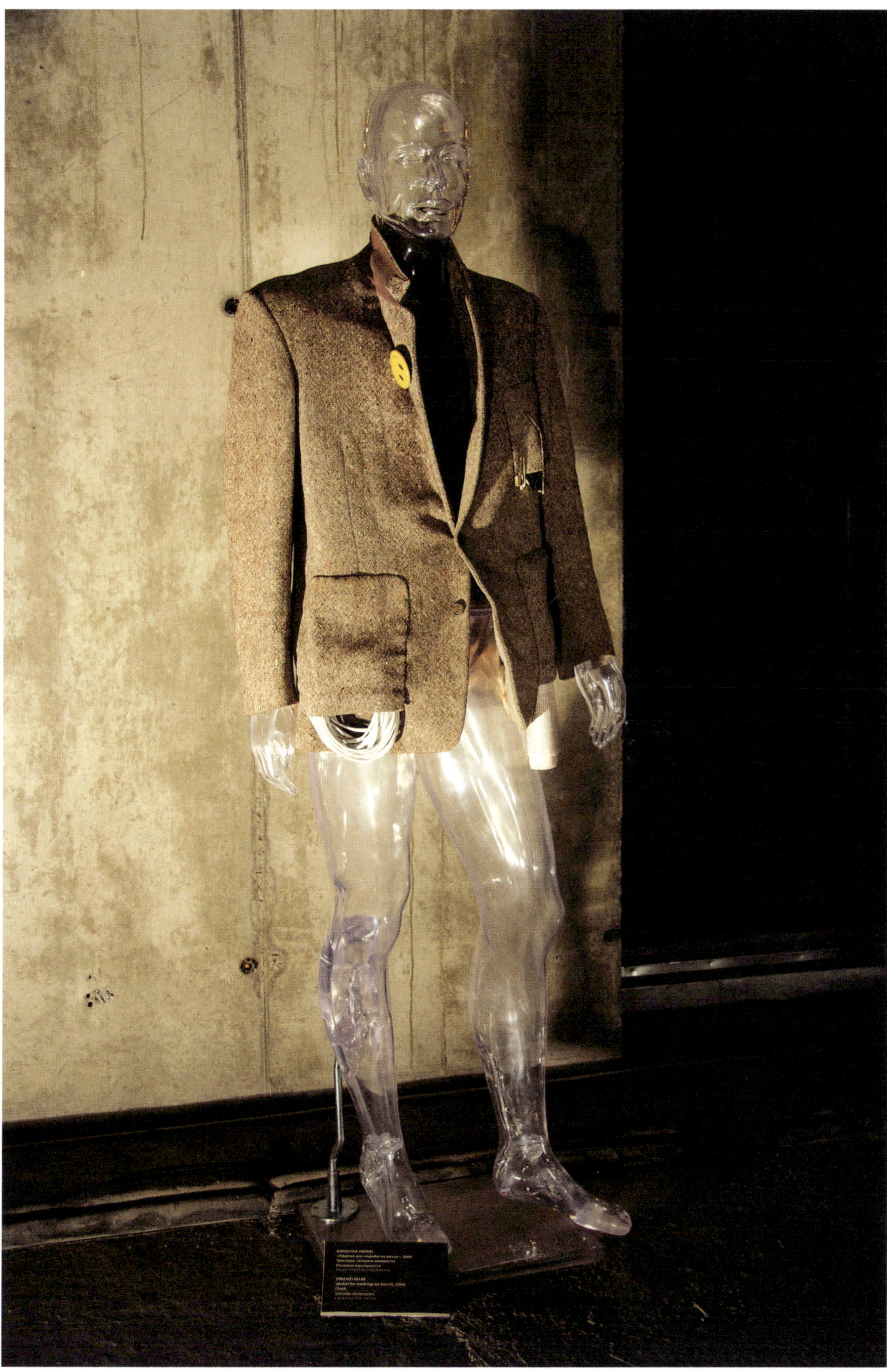

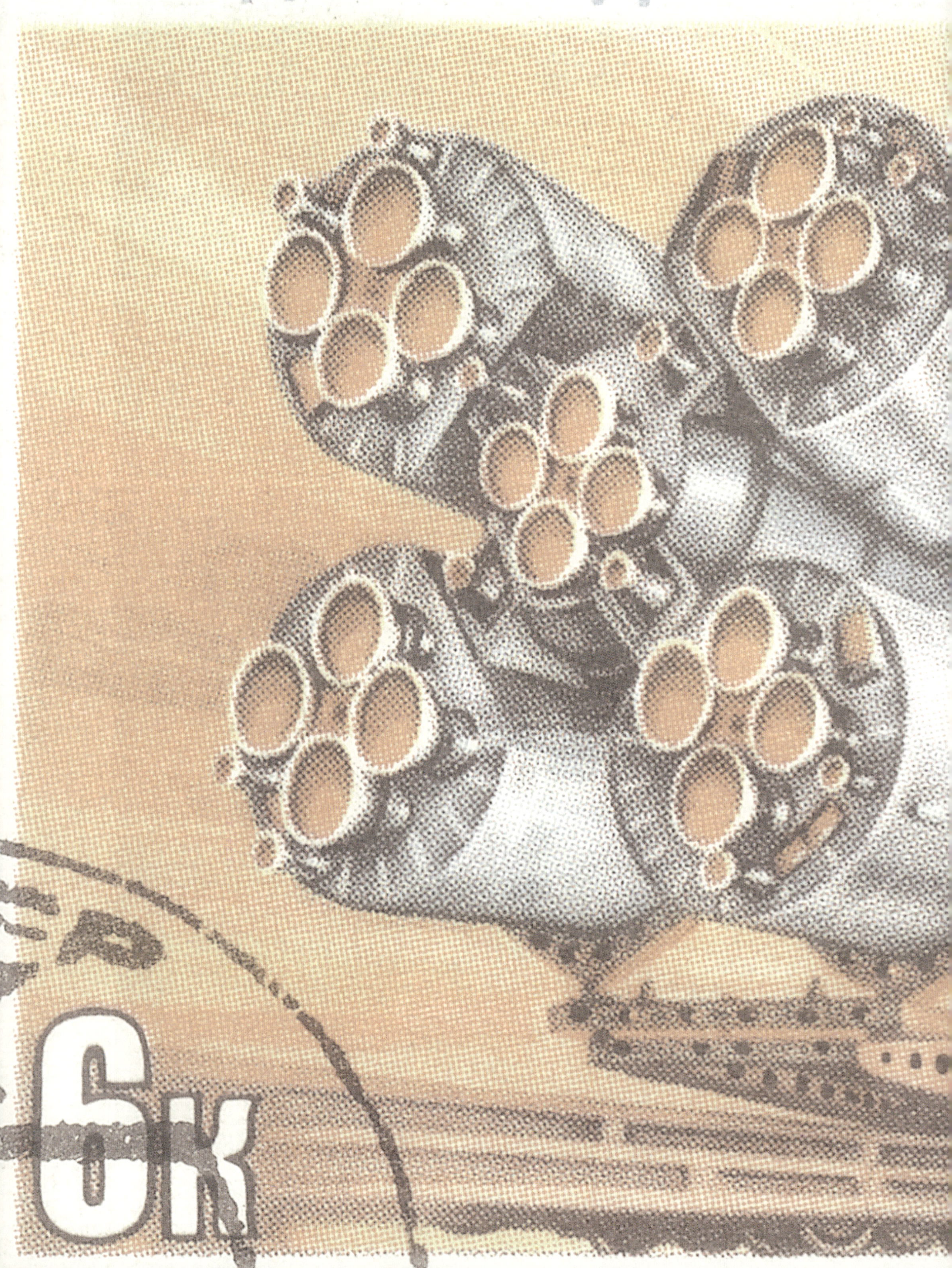
МЕЖДУНАРОДНЫЕ ПО
6к

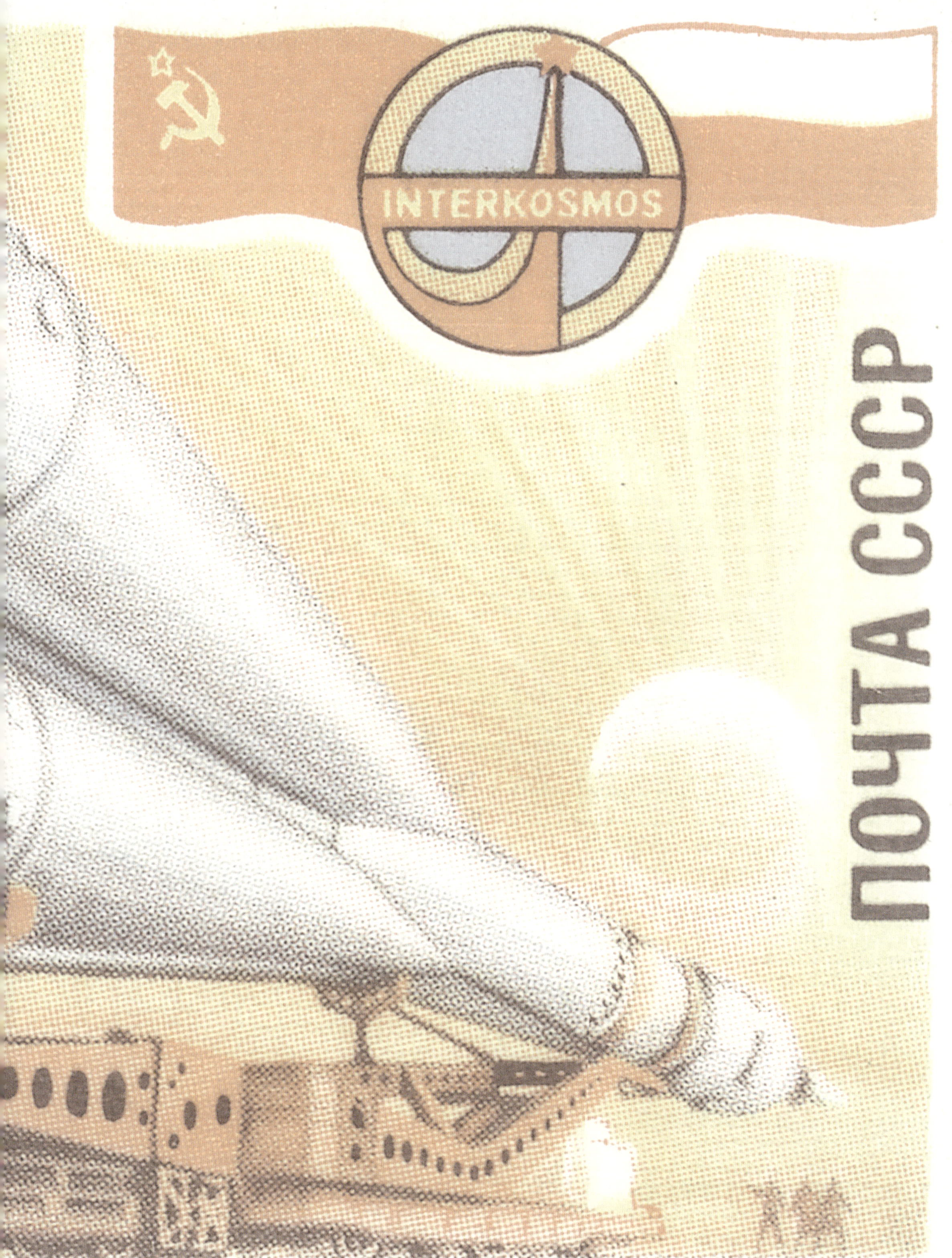
ЛЕТЫ В КОСМОС · 1978
INTERKOSMOS
ПОЧТА СССР

GOSHA OSTRETSOV

Gosha Ostretsov's multimedia practice is informed by a variety of subjects, such as early avant-garde art movements and cutting-edge contemporary fashion, but above all, by a fascination with comics and their strange contextualisation within post-Soviet culture.

Working in the Paris fashion world in the 1980s and '90s, Ostretsov became more and more involved with costume-art and performance. His interest in comic-strip and superhero culture led him to make grotesque latex masks, which have since then played a central role in his exploration through 'action figures' of the representation of power.

Comics have not been assimilated into Russian art in the same way as they were by Pop artists in the West. In fact, they are still considered somewhat alien and certainly not the medium with which to convey anything serious. Ostretsov has knowingly subverted this received idea by co-opting the resistance to comics and pop culture in works such as *Sex in the City* (2008), using them as a colourful, mass culture form "[to polemicize] with the profound, rather heavy-handed conceptualist approach".

His *Criminal Government* (2008) cells hold realistic figures in bloodied business suits, some with limbs missing and all with slightly terrifying abstract-shaped heads. Crude graffiti and symbols of interrogation and torture (bare light bulbs, cut-off hands) abound. In this fantasy comic-book world, government officials, usually acceptable 'baddies', are dehumanized and punished, or pushed to suicide, like prisoners of war. The bluntness of cartoon language is used to invert real-life situations and unveil such horrors.

The comparatively sober *Wounded Deer* (2012), with its mask-like head and arrow turned into antlers, is playfully reminiscent of decapitated communist-era statues, of pieces found and nominally re-arranged into a junkyard-style re-formation of history.

CRIMINAL GOVERNMENT, 2008
Mixed media
Overall size: 250 x 900 x 245 cm

SEX IN THE CITY, 2008
Mixed media
Dimensions variable

WOUNDED DEER, 2012
Lime wood, painted pine, iron
Deer: 150 x 60 x 94 cm
Plinth: 15 x 150 x 150 cm

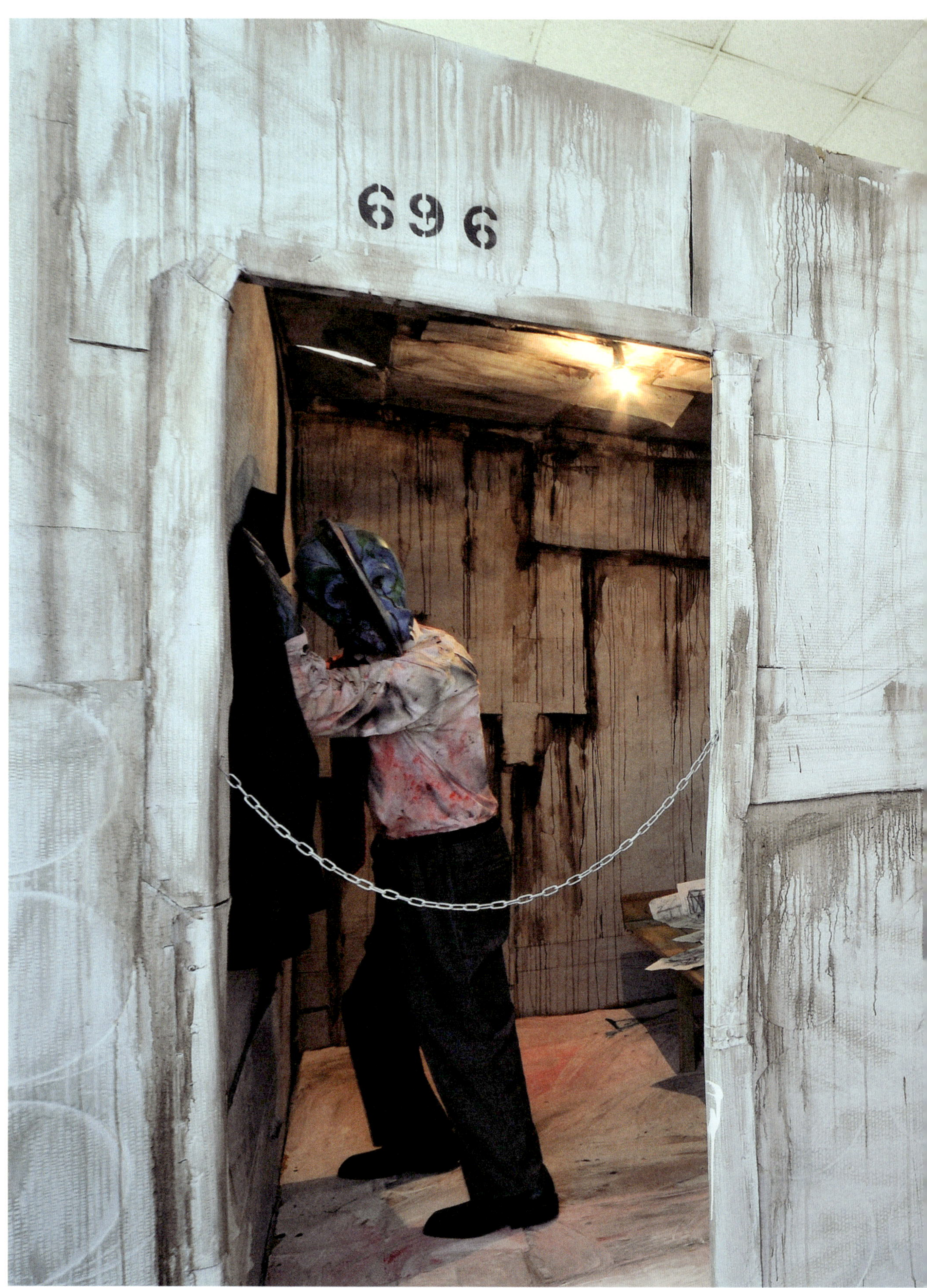
696

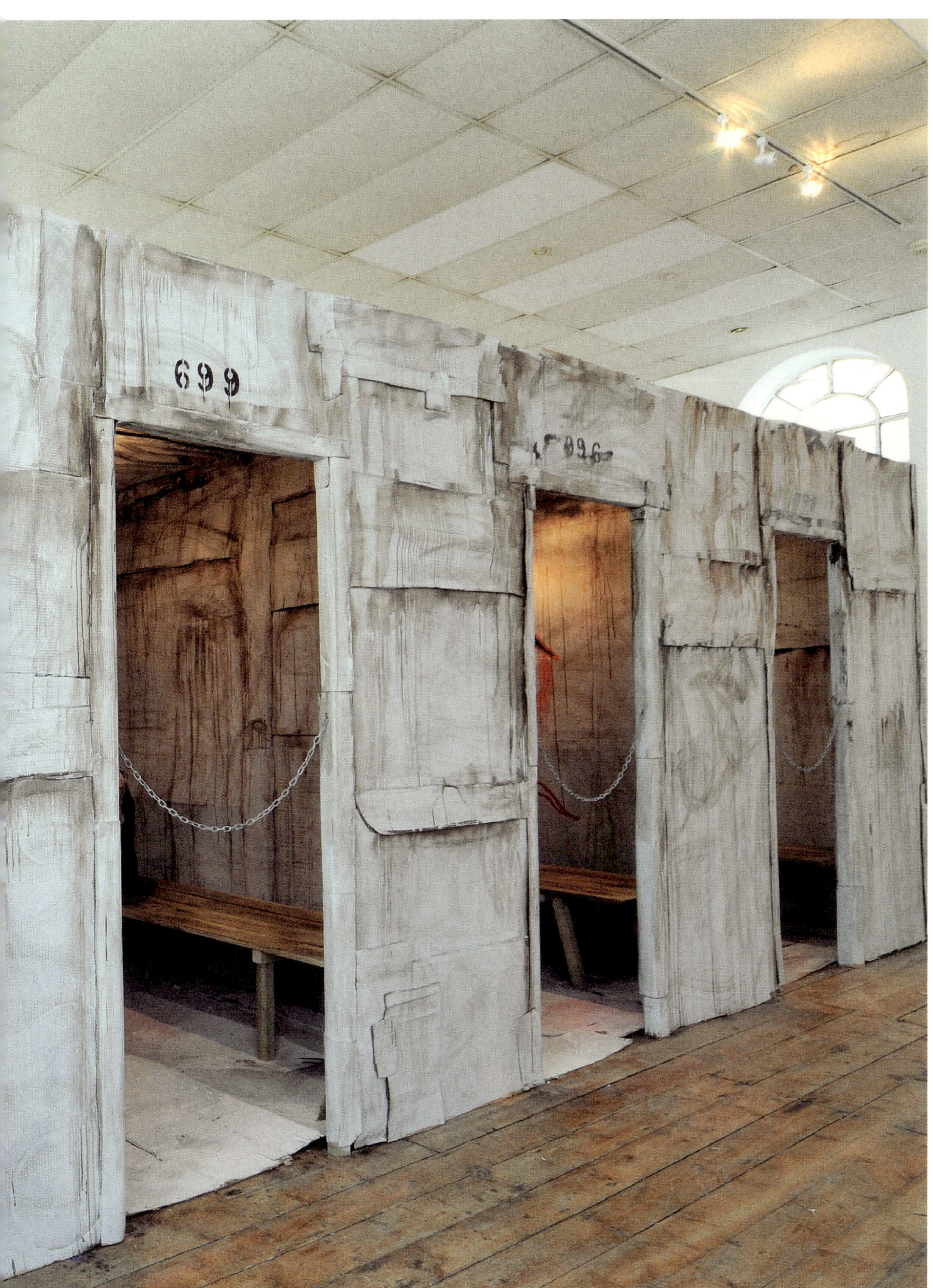

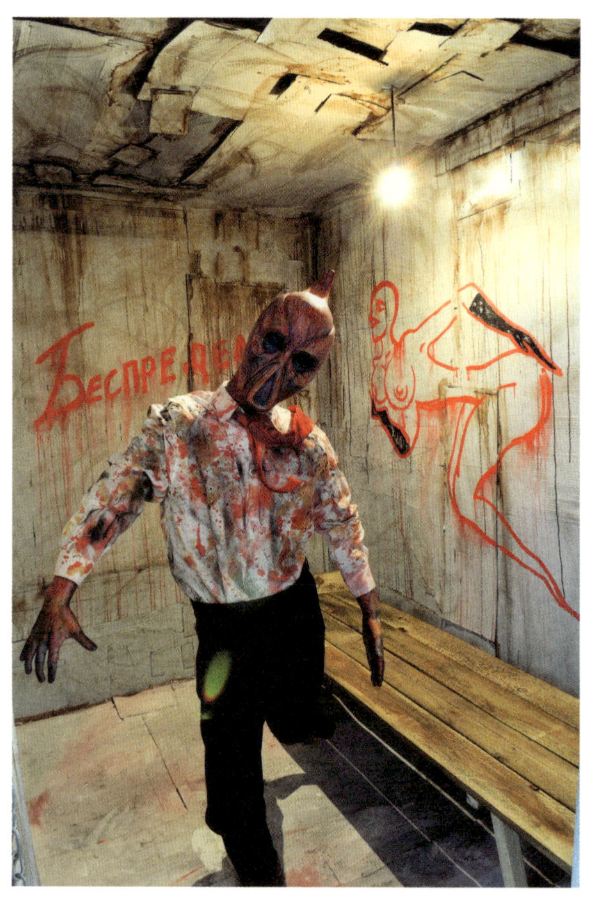

Беспредел

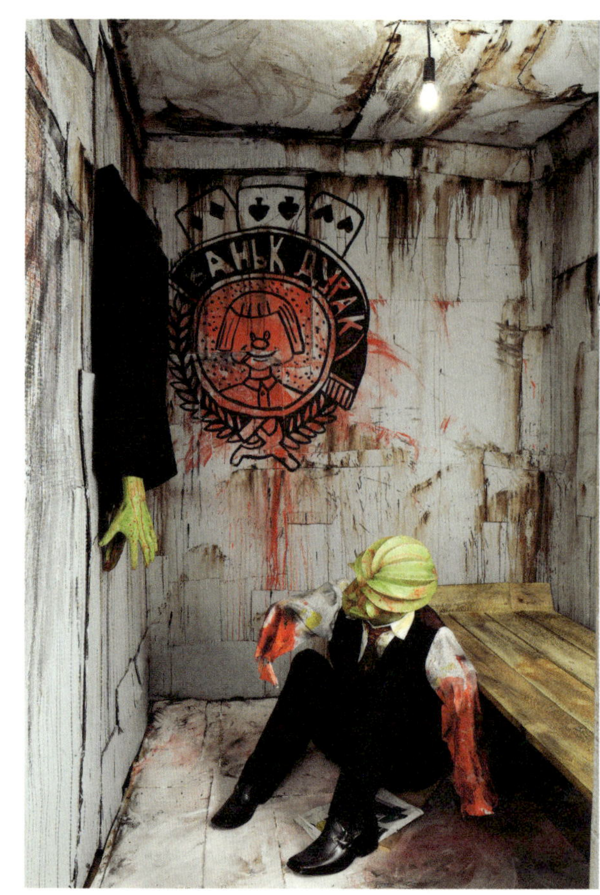

ВАНЬК ДУРАК

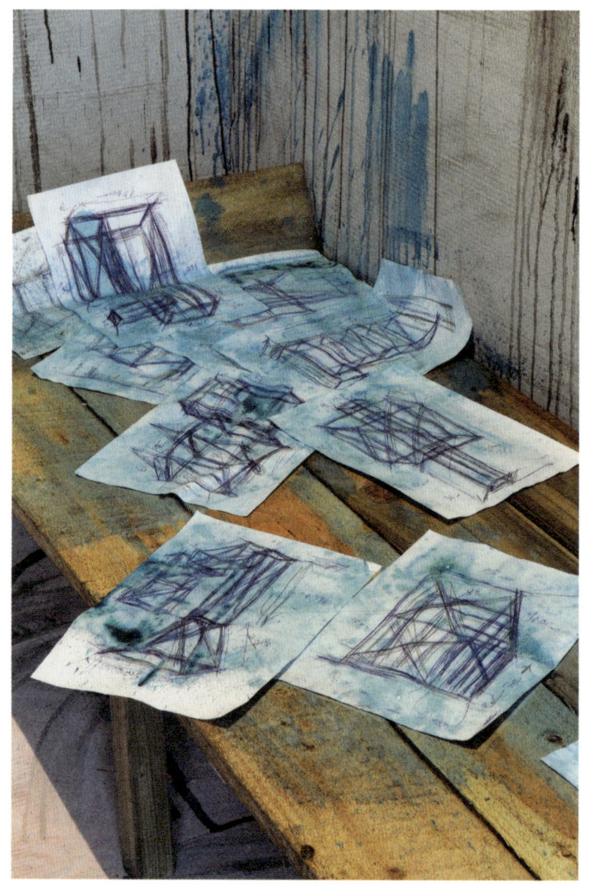

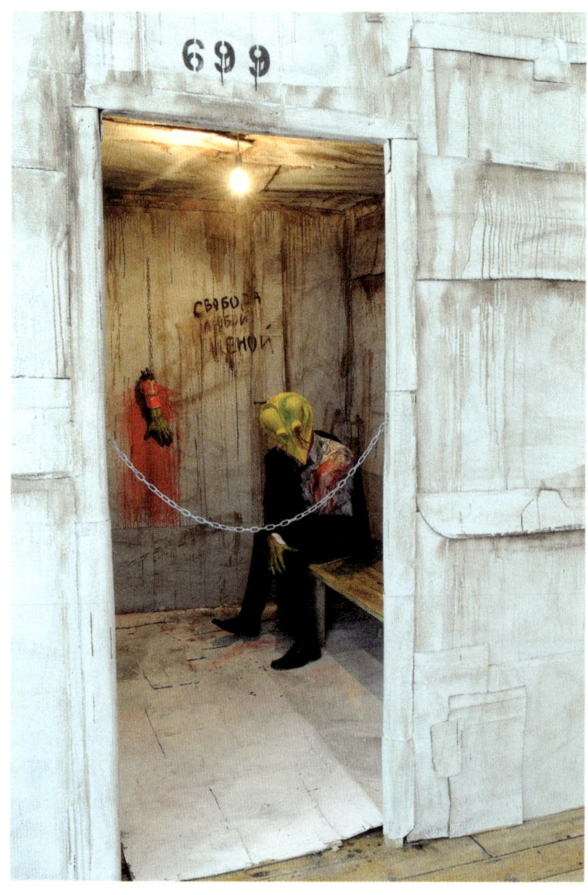

699
СВОБОДА
ЛЮБОЙ
ЦЕНОЙ

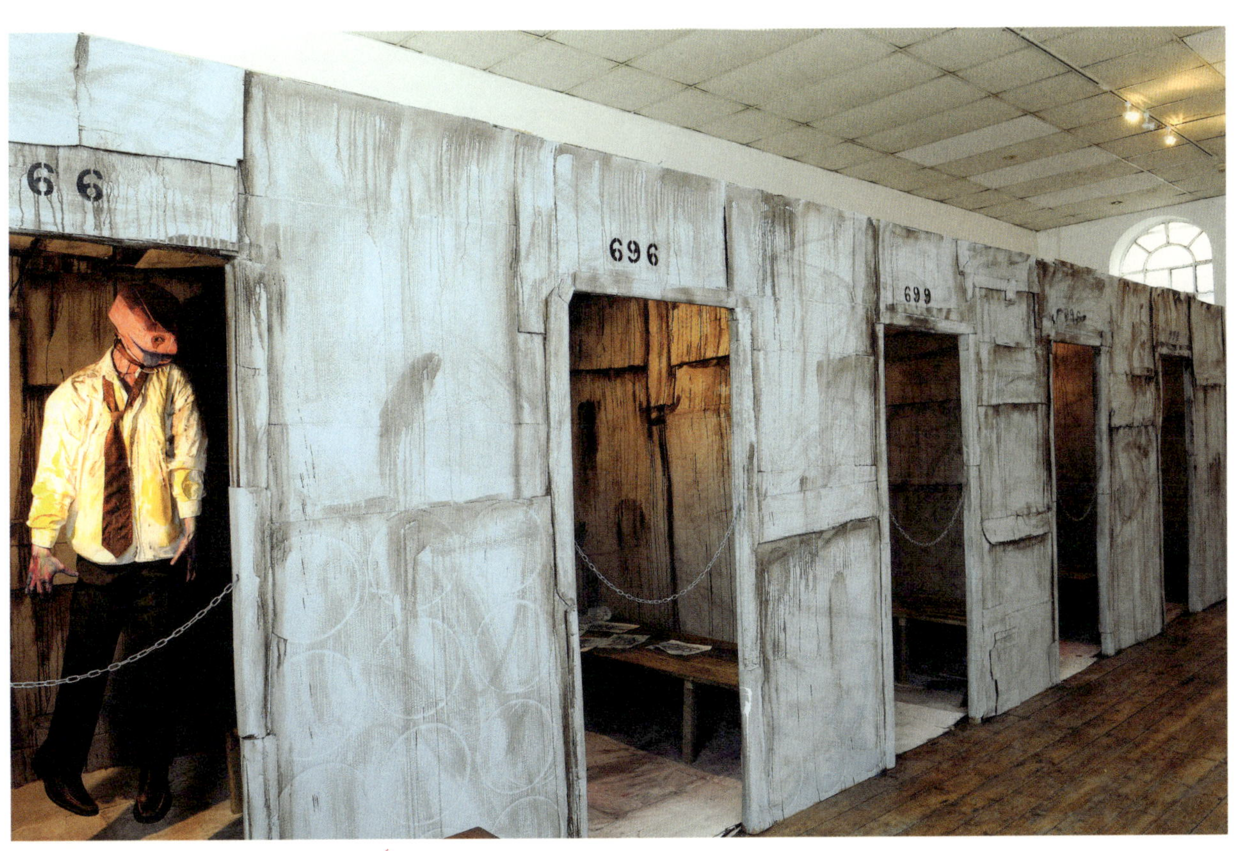
66
696
699

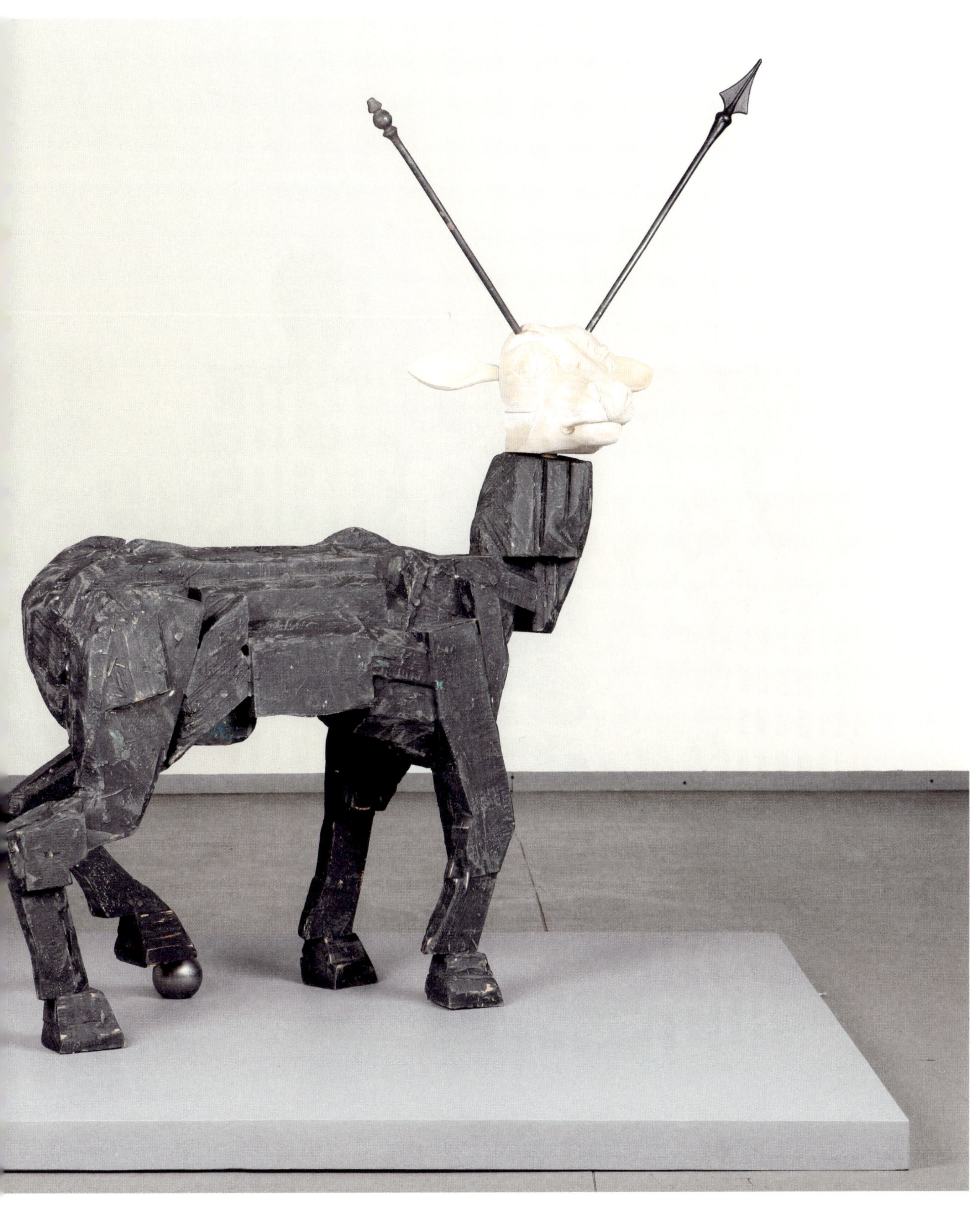

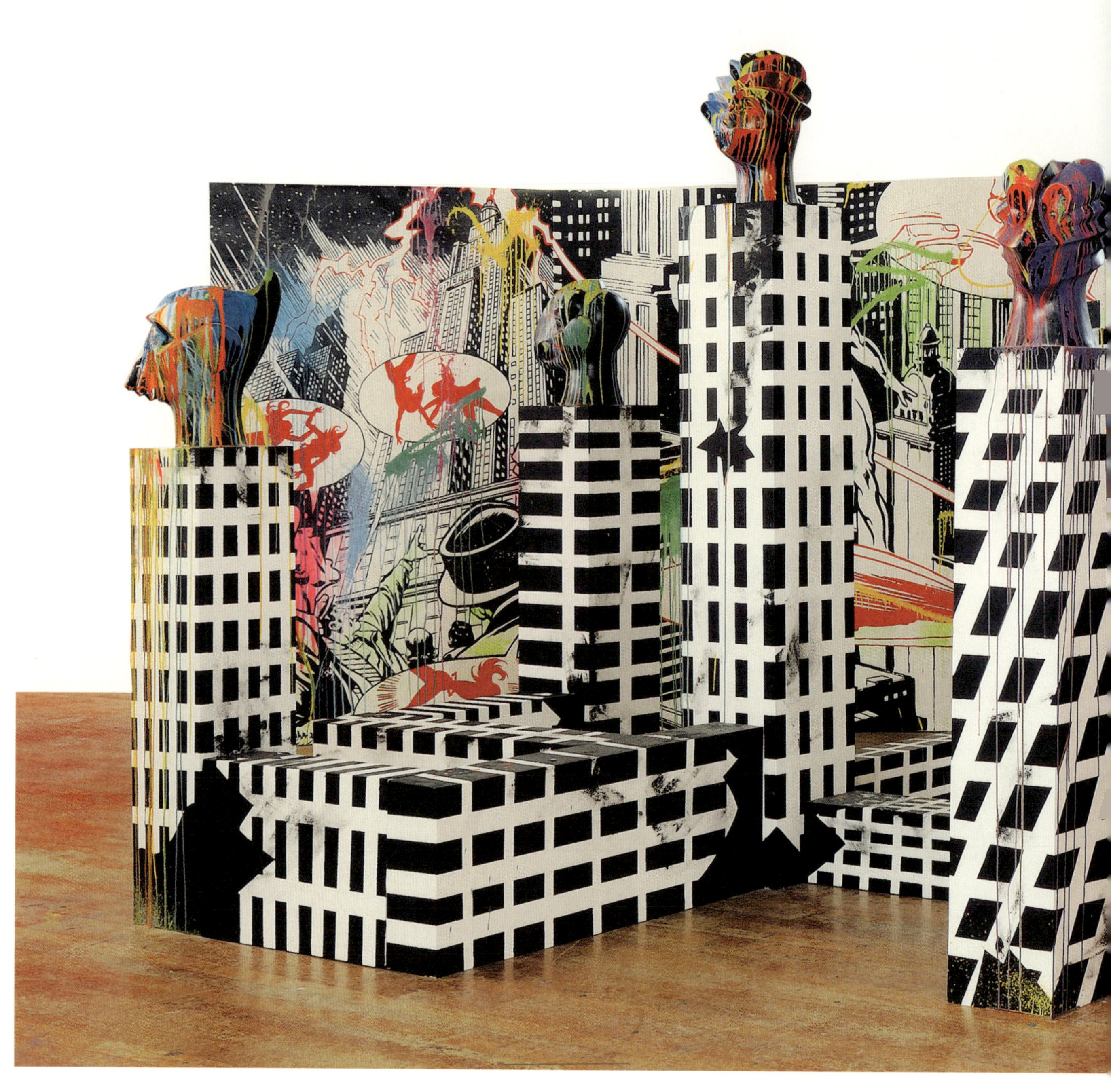

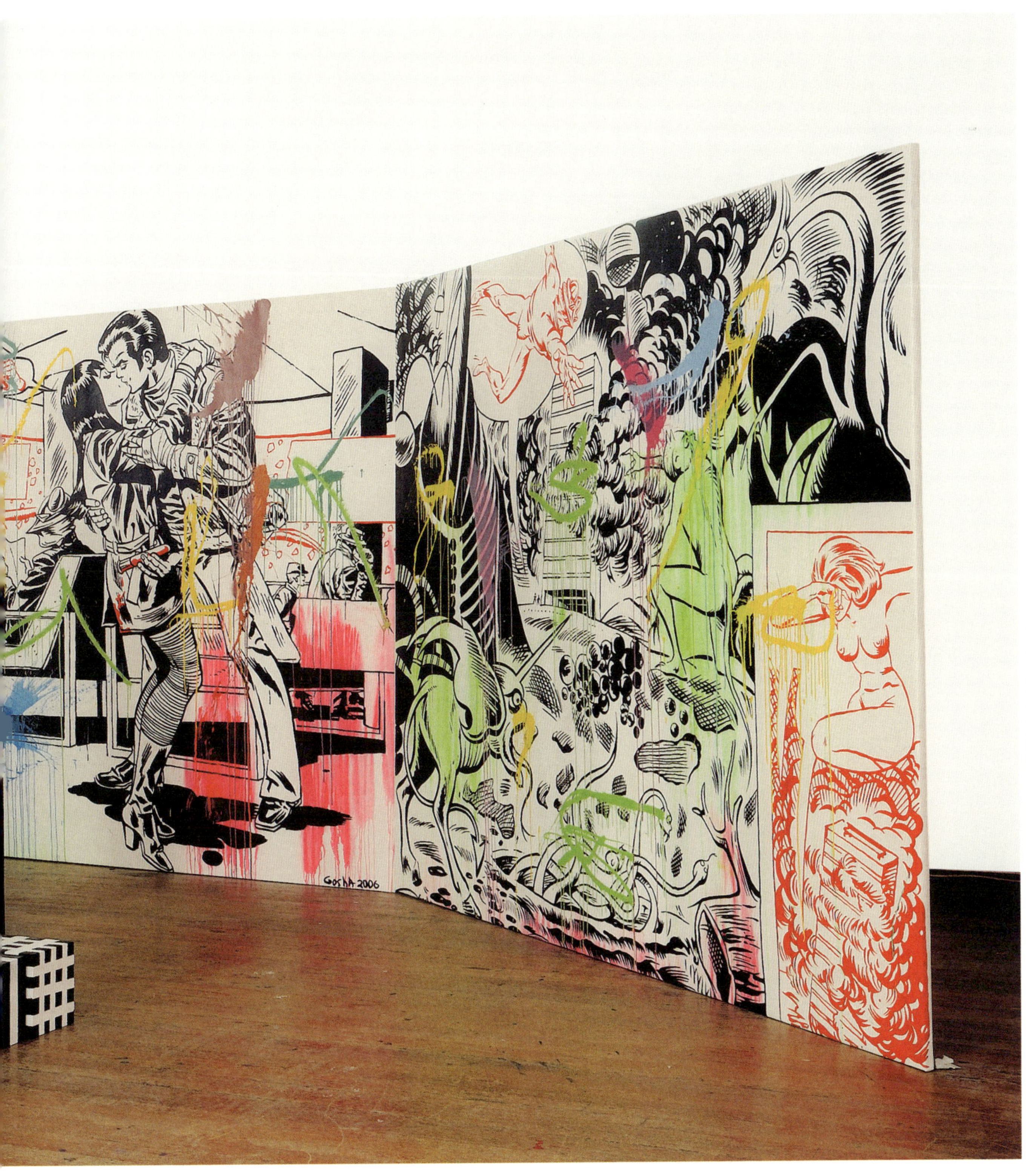

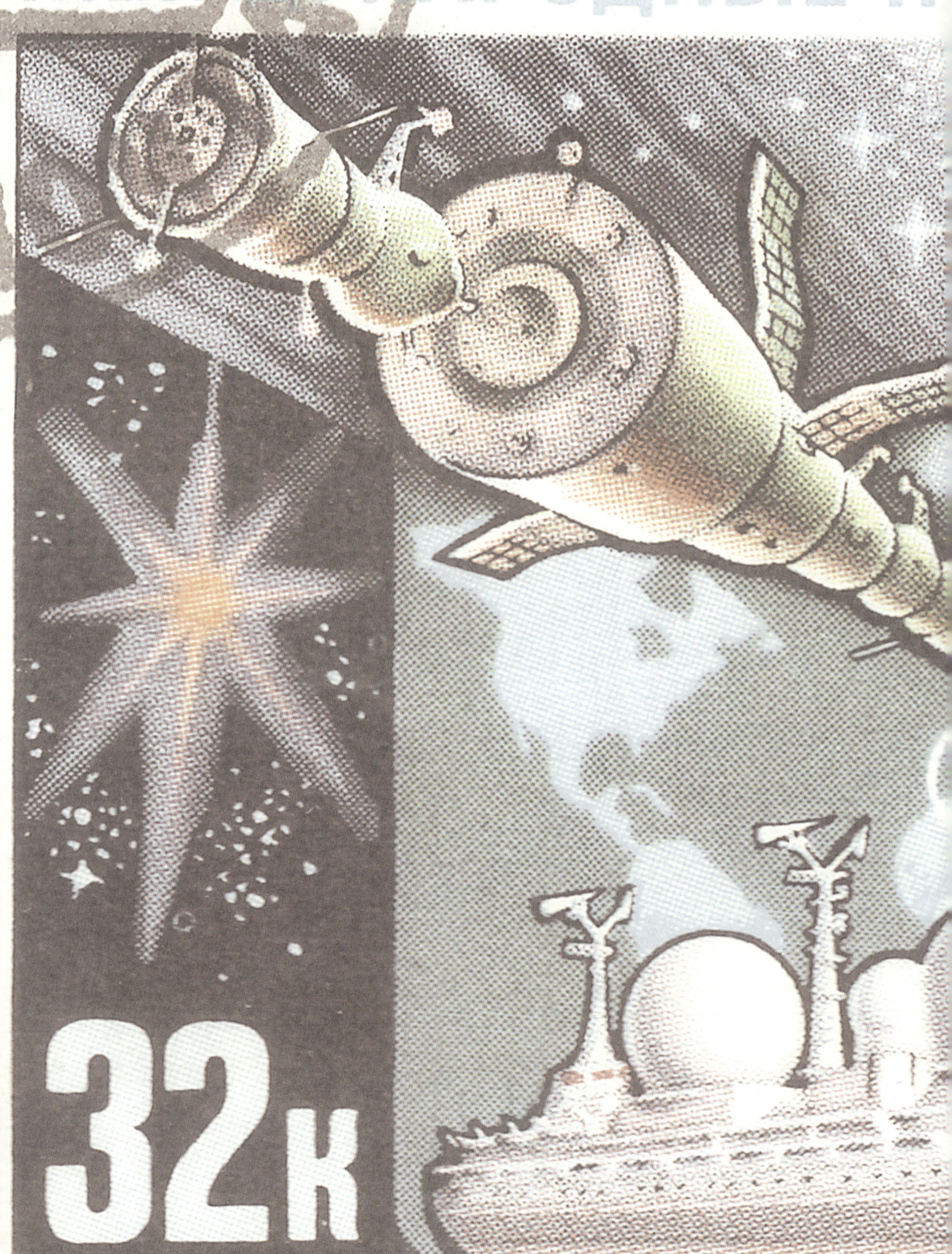
32к

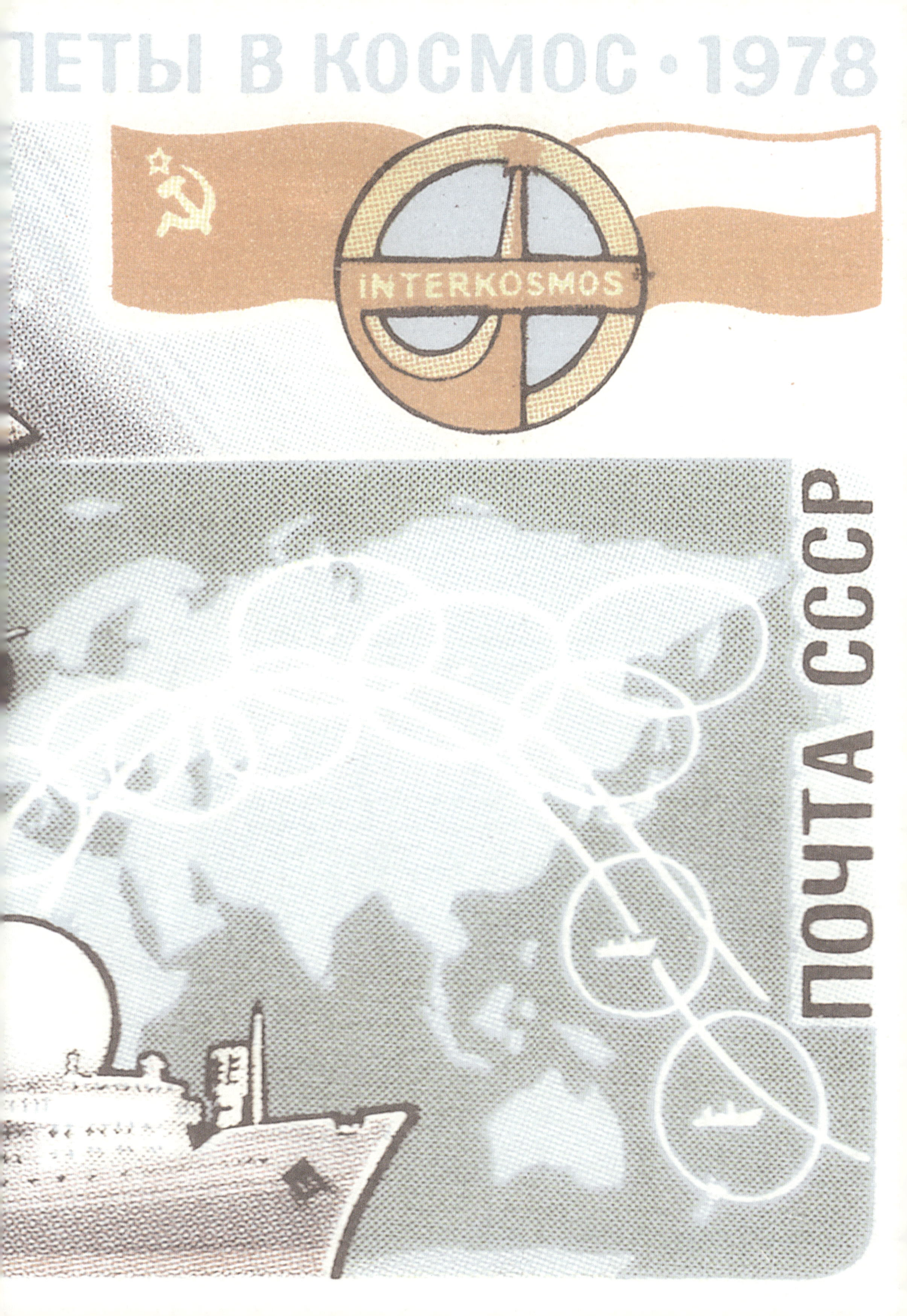

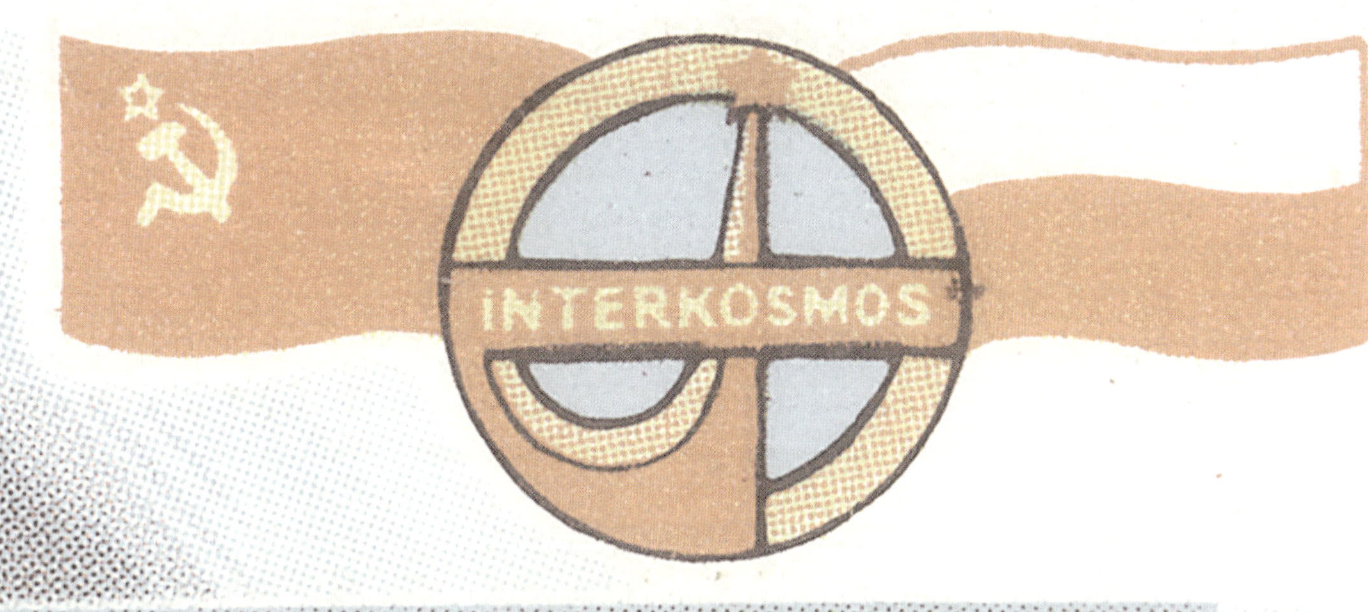
ЕТЫ В КОСМОС · 1978
INTERKOSMOS
ПОЧТА СССР

SERGEY PAKHOMOV

A DIY, punk aesthetic runs through the work of Sergey Pakhomov, whether it be his outsiderish paintings, ranting microphone performances, or his notorious participation in underground cult films. Pakhomov utilises a lo-fi theatricality to present his own take on how to define the Russian tradition, defending a staunchly anti-commercial stance feeding on so-called vulgar, popular visual culture, and pointing to its embeddedness within a larger culture of the absurd.

Pakhomov's multi-part paintings on wooden panels, such as the vibrant *Russian Landscape* (2011), contain a faint echo of traditional altarpieces and fold-out icon paintings. But with their bold, expressionistic style combining text and image, they also mirror the immediacy of political posters and picket signs. Each of the ten panels illustrates scenes suggesting burning, violence and chaos, factory work and barren landscapes. These vignettes serve as a narrative backdrop, but the real star of the work is Pakhomov's exuberant use of arresting, irregular lettering that captions each frame like an engorged, almost irrational headline.

Repetition and the confection of a lunatic-like self-regard permeate much of Pakhomov's practice. *Ya Pakhom!* [I, Pakhom] (2012) is made up of 16 smaller fibreboard panels encrusted with irregular geometric shapes and unified by a motto in yellow – his name, ludicrously dancing around each frame to the point where signature, and value, become nonsense speech. Pakhomov's regard for the unsung and the irregular is highlighted in *382 Sins* (2012), in which strange blue shapes are framed by a litany of 'sin' written 382 times in undulating handwriting recalling the hand-made signs written and held up, like icons, in public spaces by society's outcasts.

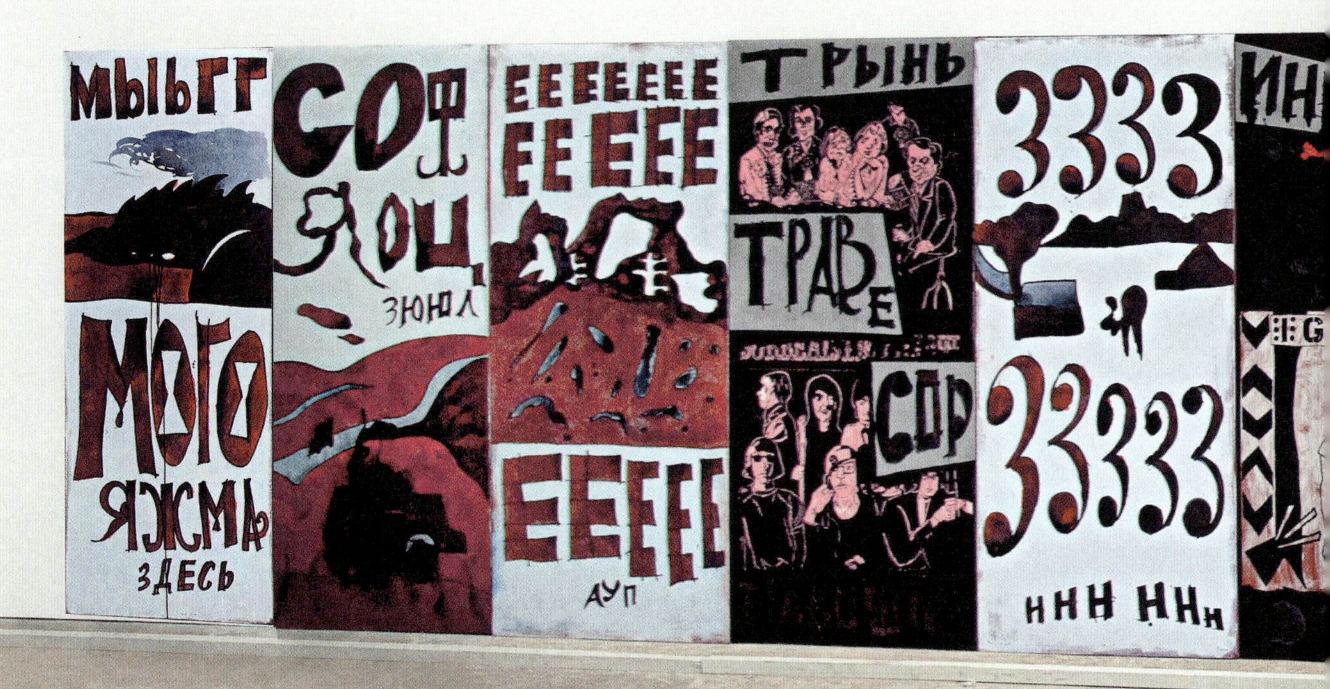

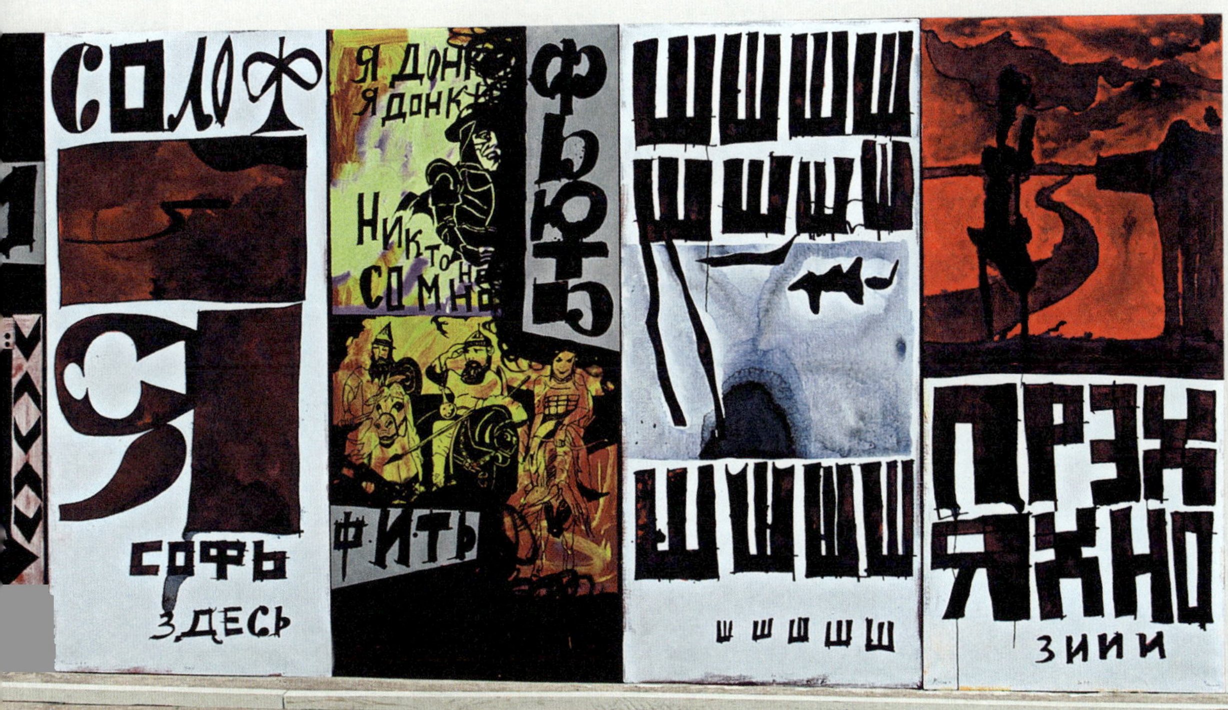
СОЛ
Я
СОФЬ
ЗДЕСЬ
Я ДОНК
Я ДОНК
НИК
ТО Н
СО МН
ФЬЮТ
ФИТЬ
ШШШШ
ШШШ
ШШШШ
шшшш
ПРЭЖ
ЯКНО
ЗИИИ

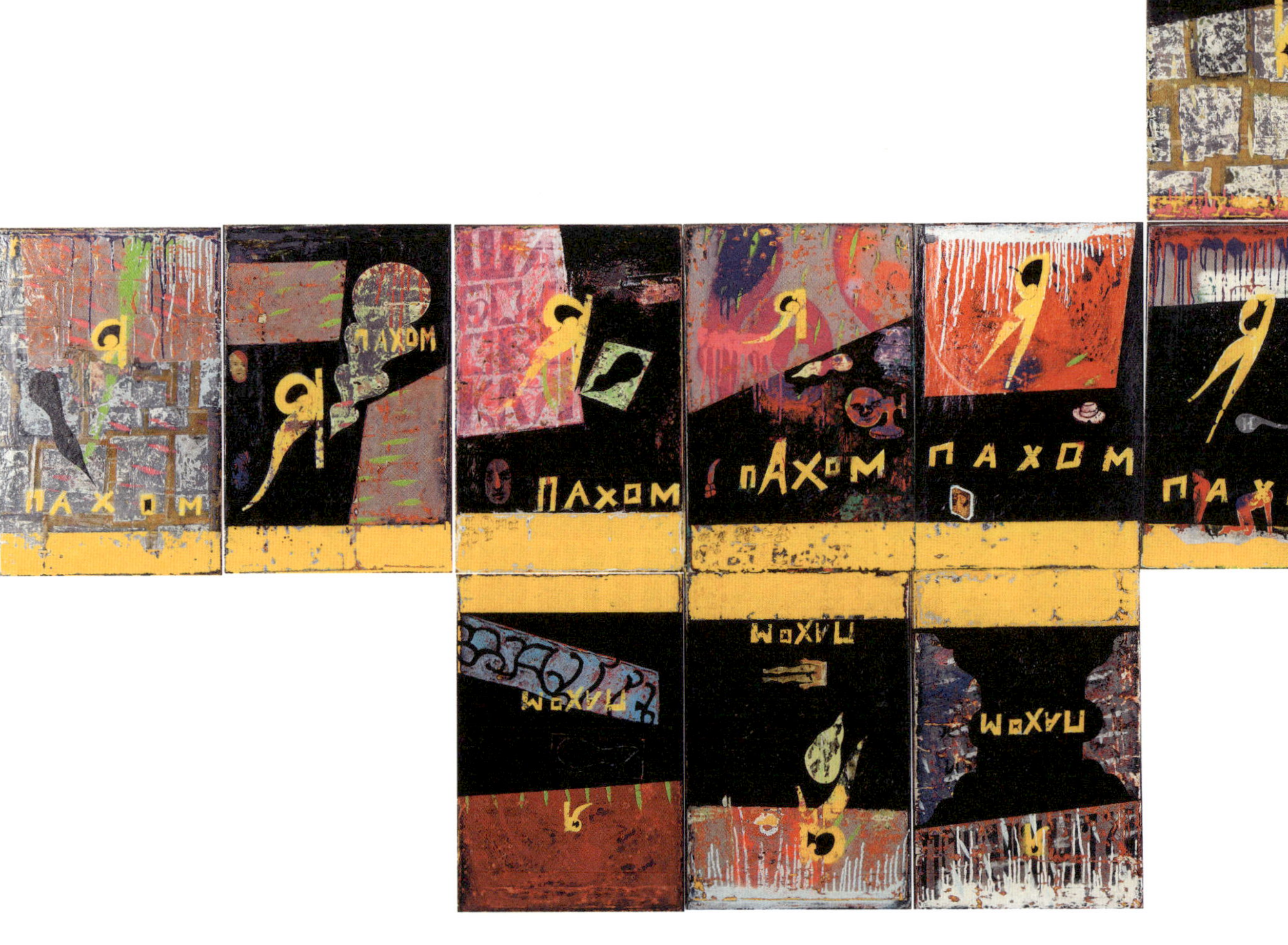

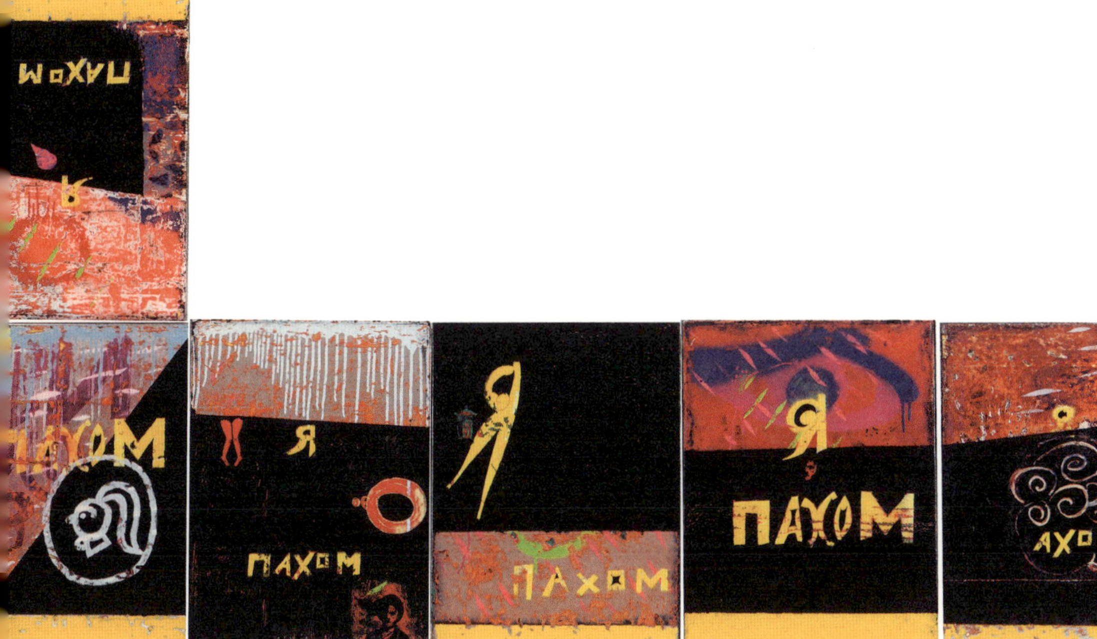

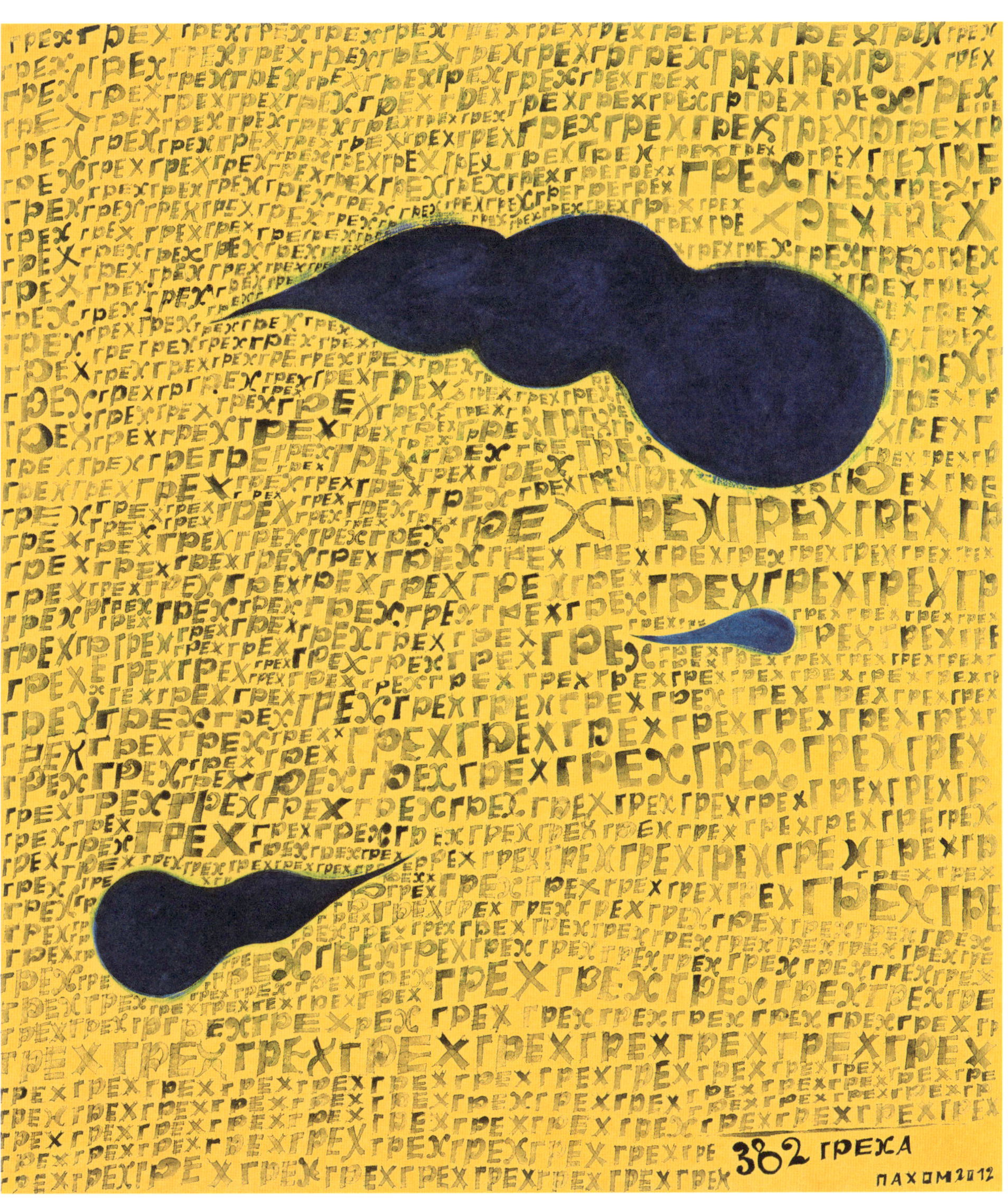
382 ГРЕХА
ПАХОМ 2012

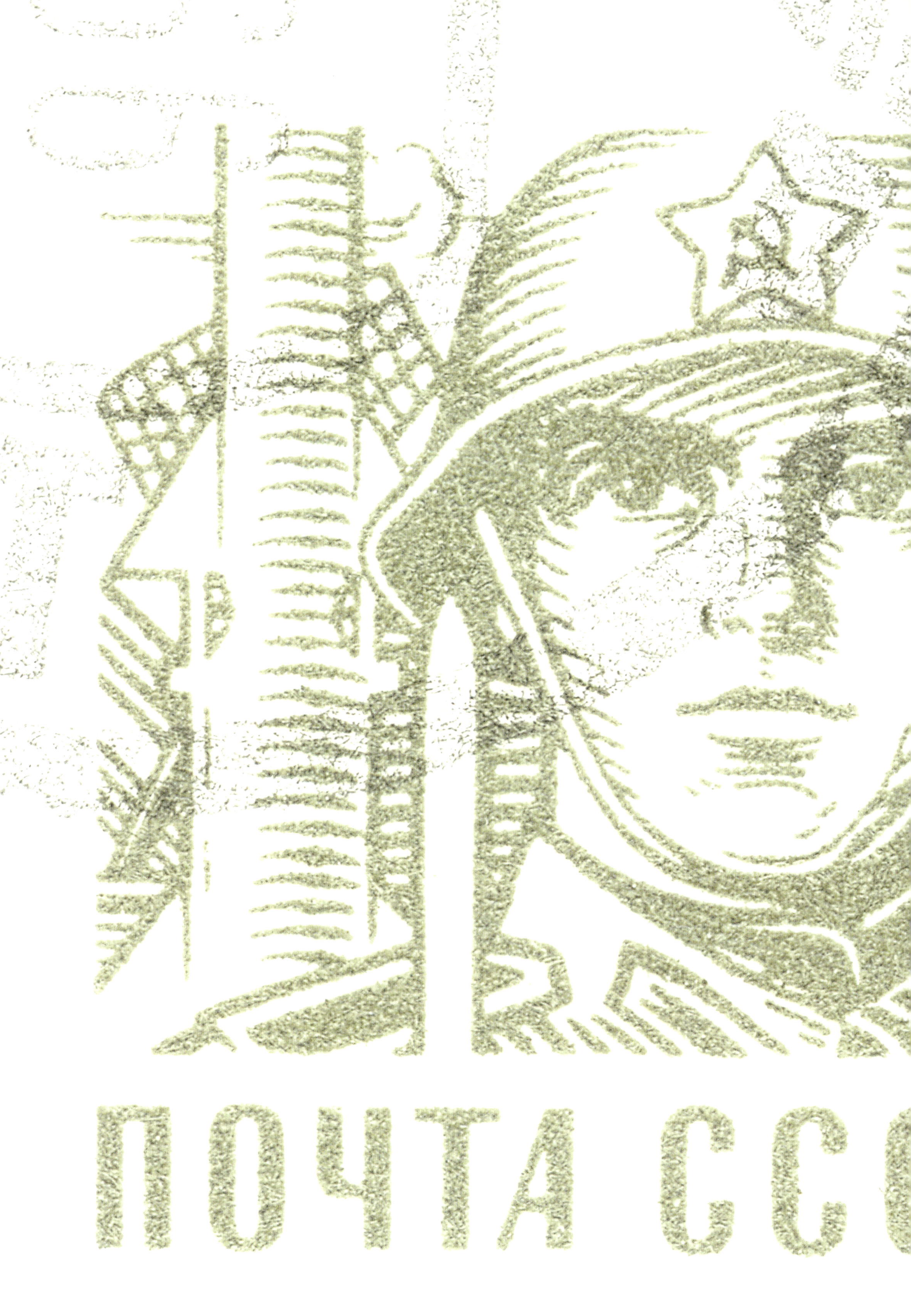

ПОЧТА ССС

Р 10 1966 коп.

ANNA PARKINA

Anna Parkina's collages and sculptures, aesthetically reminiscent of Constructivist and Soviet propaganda art, are visual juggernauts from which to contemplate the anxieties of contemporary Russian culture and society.

Parkina was born and raised in the Soviet Union, and lived in Paris and California before returning to post-Soviet Moscow. Marked by a slightly distant, inside-outside perspective, her collages revisit the medium and explore it through old and new images evoking both past and present in her native country.

Her work may visually reference the historical Russian avant-garde, but it is also her own edit of the status quo — a set of image- and text-based conceptual, inscrutable 'riddles'. Her collage works consist of abstract, geometric shapes, imagery taken from the mass media, cut-out printed type and hand-painted extras, completed by slightly cryptic titles. The result, despite the familiar nature of the genre and the ordinary quality of her materials, is both heady and mysterious.

Here, the everyday is re-configured and time suspended through a frenzy of layered, duplicated imagery and its suggestions — of nature, such as birds, and hands, but also of Soviet icons such as cars, instruments, buildings, trains, film still faces and sinister silhouettes of figures wearing fedoras.

Her sculptures convey a similar magnetic excess. *Thick Steam Above the Wing of a Sparrow* (2009) stands on a plinth as a defined solid but also nebulous shape. The way it fits together mixes the order of sharp, utilitarian craftsmanship with a chaotically abstract, non-specific purpose. Like her collages, it is like a puzzle, and it's easy to get lost looking into its engine of oddly patterned shapes and the hollows within.

AP-01

FIST TIMER, 2008
Oil and collage on canvas
50 x 40 cm

AP-02

TEATRIKS, 2008
Oil, collage, poster on canvas
60 x 50 cm

AP-03

HOLE IN HIGHWAY, 2008
Collage, pencil, ink, gouache, books, photocopy on paper, mounted on board
43.5 x 61 cm

AP-04

WHITE TURN TO BE BLACK, 2008
Oil, photocopy, coloured paper, book and poster on canvas
60 x 70 cm

AP-05

THE HOLLOW, 2008
Collage on paper, mounted on board
49.7 x 32.8 cm

AP-06

ZAMKI I SAMKI, 2008
Collage and gouache on paper, mounted on board
41 x 43 cm

AP-07

THE CASE IS OPEN II, 2007
Gouache photocopy and ink on paper, mounted on board
58 x 68 cm

AP-08

BLACKSCREANWRITARS, 2008
Collage, ink and gouache on paper, mounted on board
42.5 x 50 cm

AP-09

THICK STEAM ABOVE THE WING OF A SPARROW, 2009
Wood, paint
143 x 129 x 70 cm

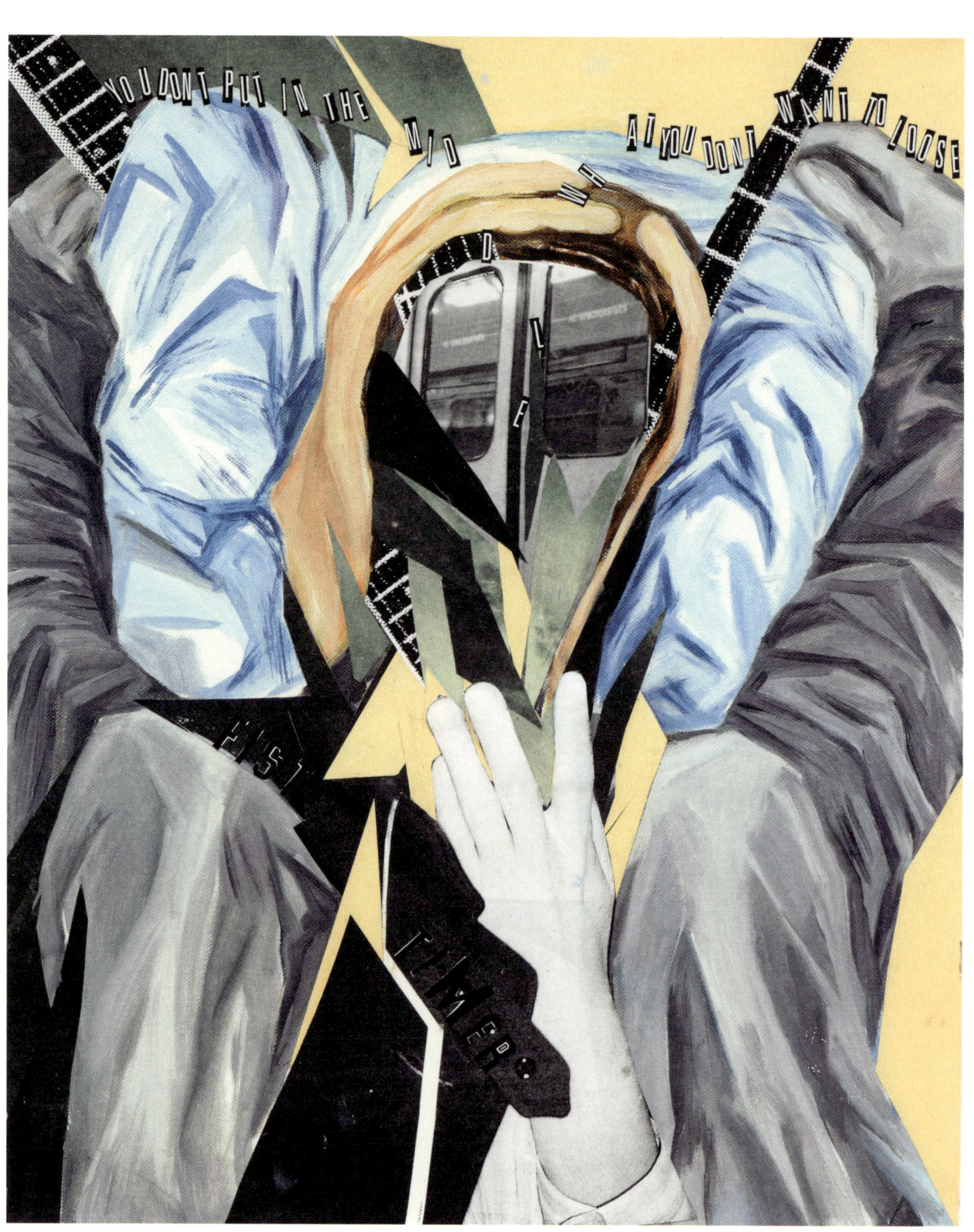

YOU DON'T PUT IN THE MIDDLE WHAT YOU DON'T WANT TO LOOSE
TIMER

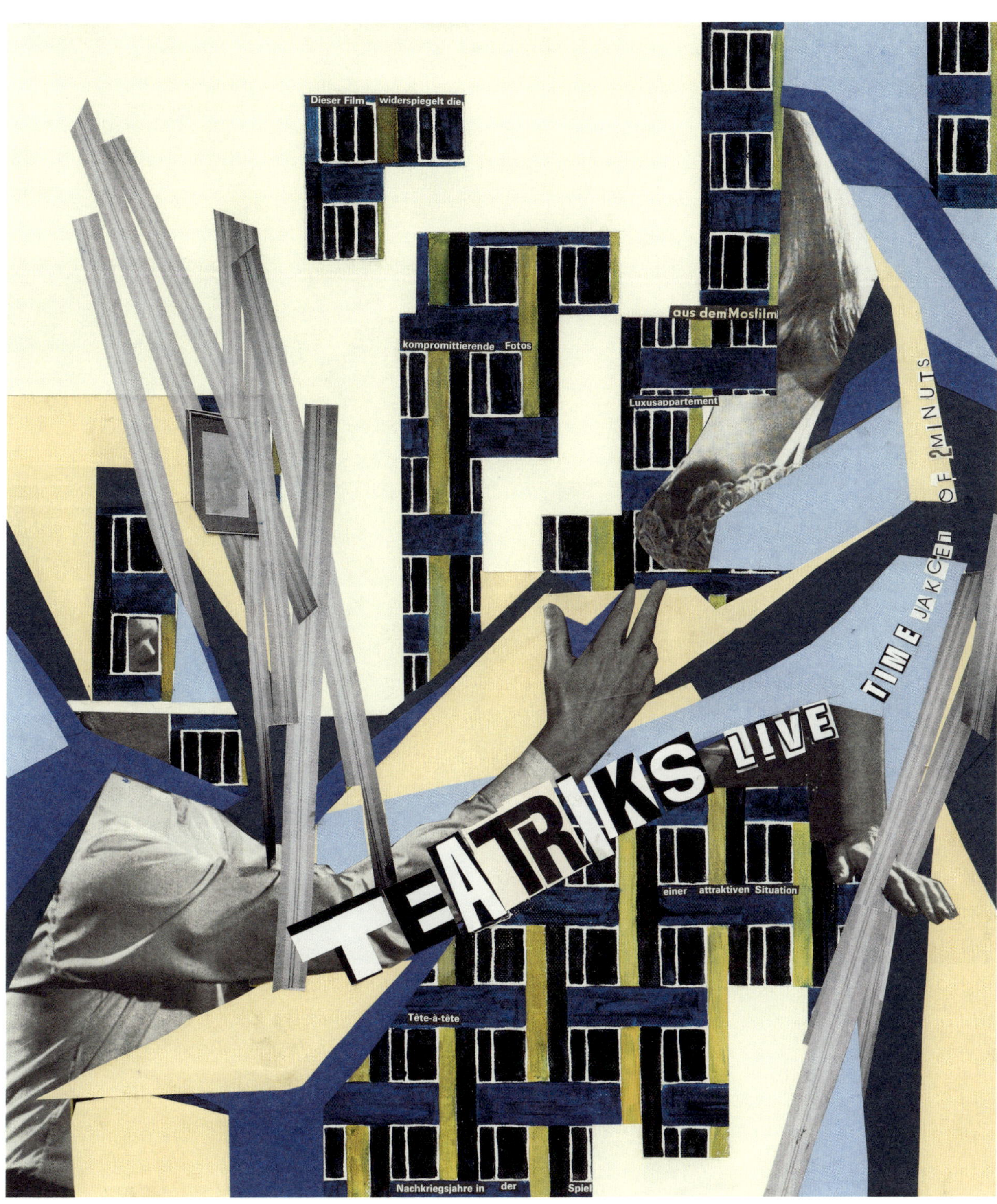

Dieser Film widerspiegelt die
kompromittierende Fotos
aus dem Mosfilm
Luxusappartement
TEATRIKS LIVE
TIME JAKCEN OF 2MINUTS
einer attraktiven Situation
Tête-à-tête
Nachkriegsjahre in der Spiel

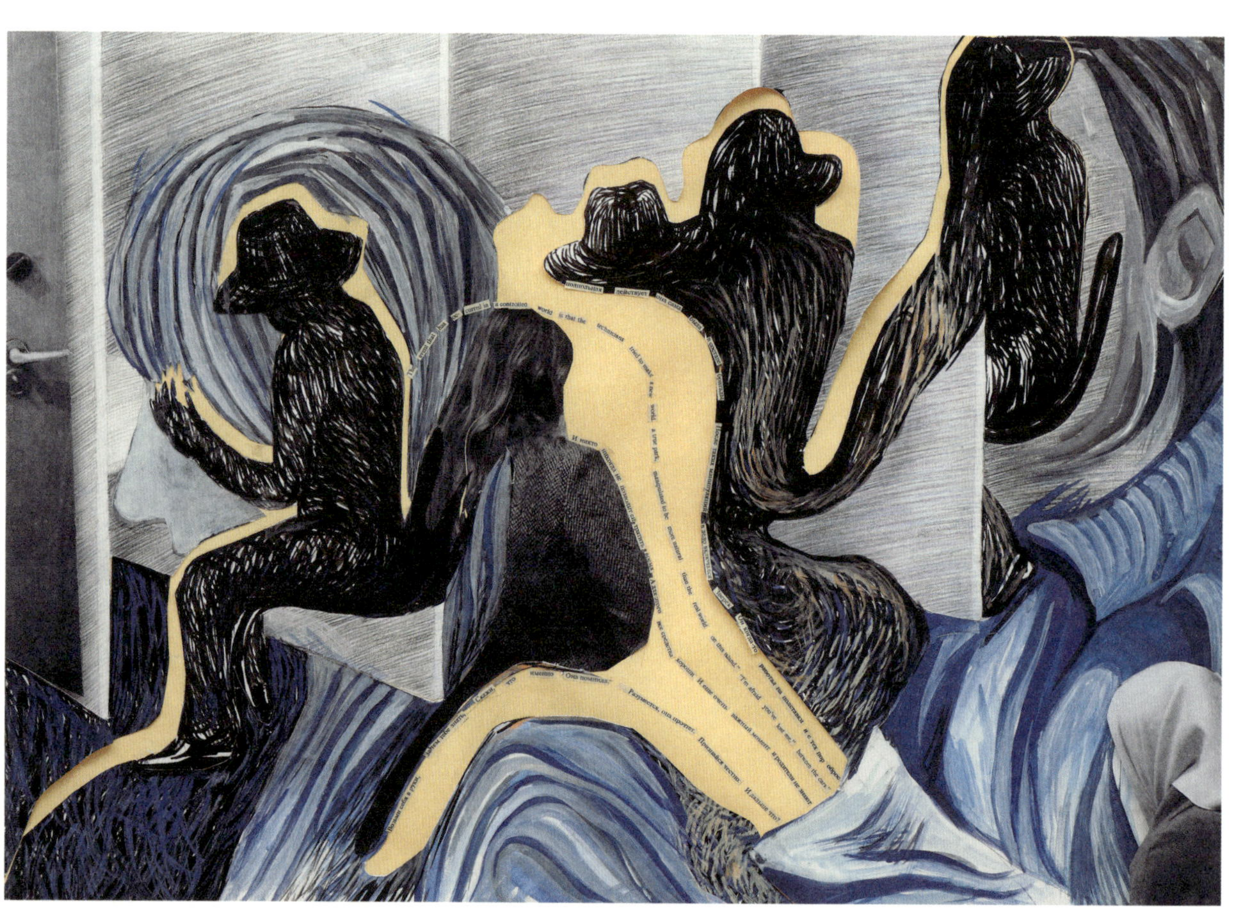

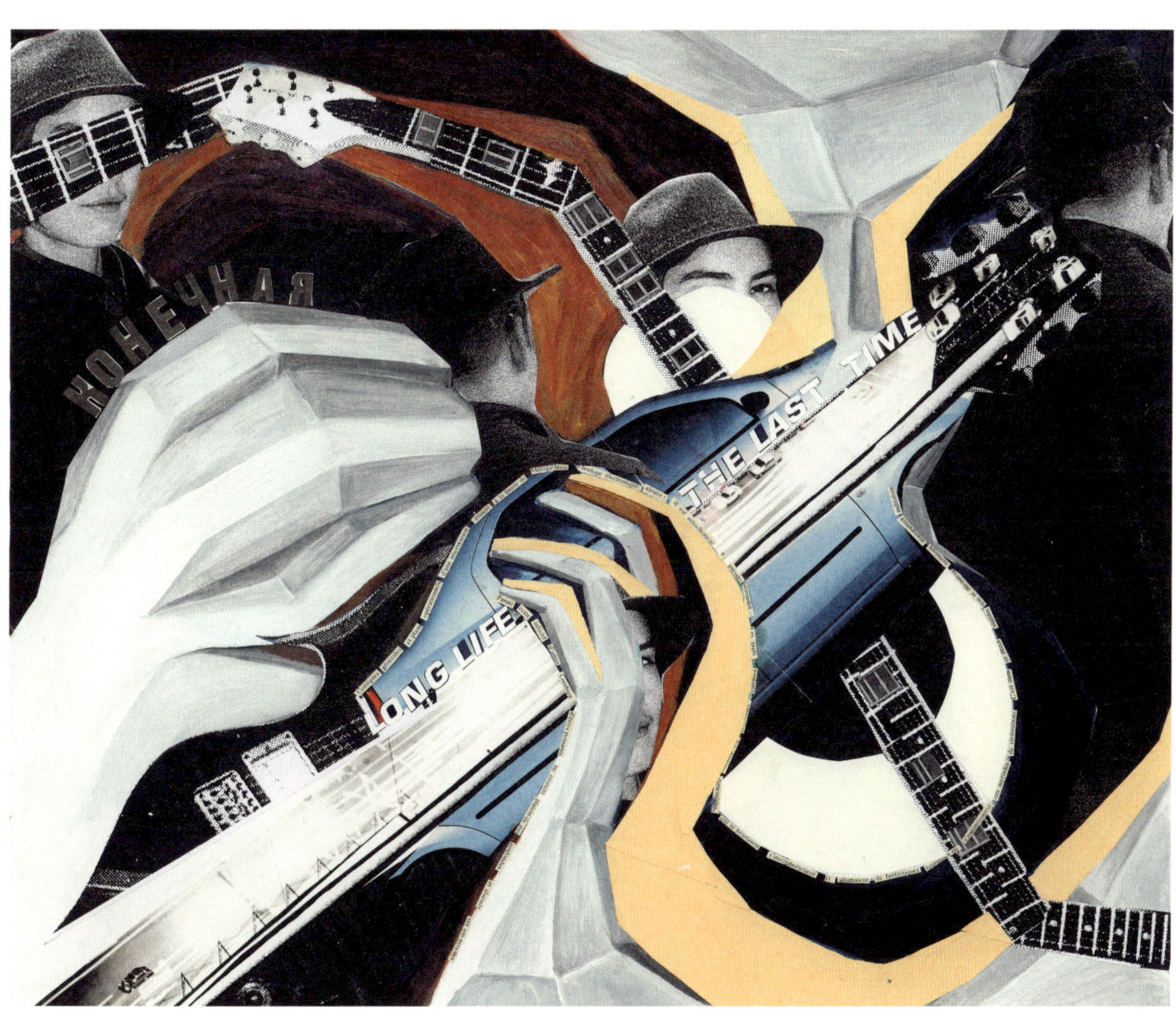
КОНЕЧНАЯ
LONG LIFE
THE LAST TIME

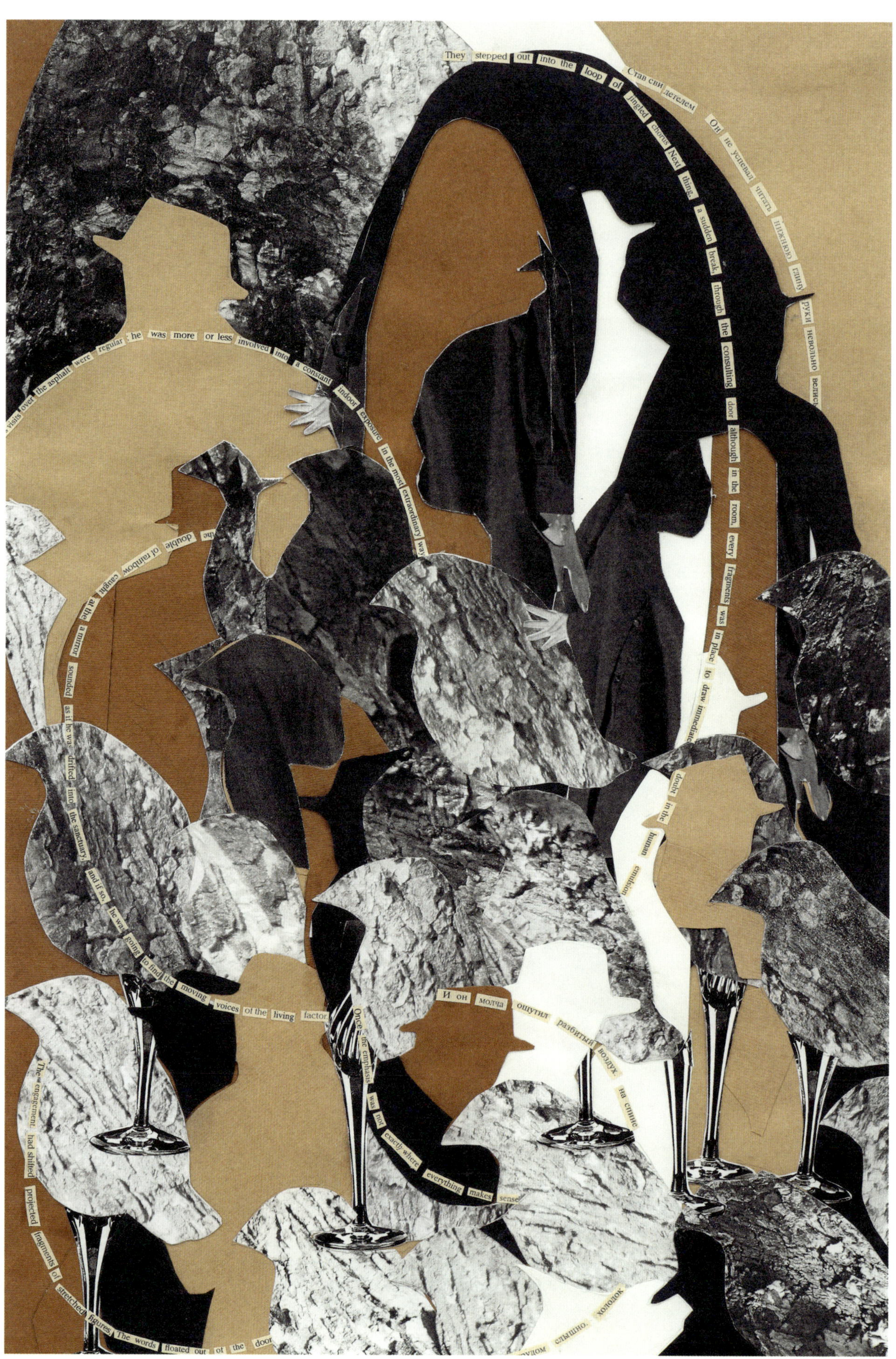

They stepped out into the loop of jingled chaos. Next thing, a sudden break, through the consulting door, although in the room, every fragments was in place to draw immediate doubt in the human emulsion
Став свидетелем Он не зацепил чтобы неждалл спину руки невольно велик
were regular he was more or less involved into a constant indoor exposure in the most extraordinary way
over the asphalt
visit
the double of rainbow caught at the mirror sounded as if he was drifted into the sanctuary, and if so, he was going to find the moving voices of the living factor.
И он молча ощутил разбитый воздух. на спине
Once the emphasis was not exactly where everything makes sense
The engagement had shifted projected fragments of stretched figures. The words floated out of the door
рудом слышно, холодок

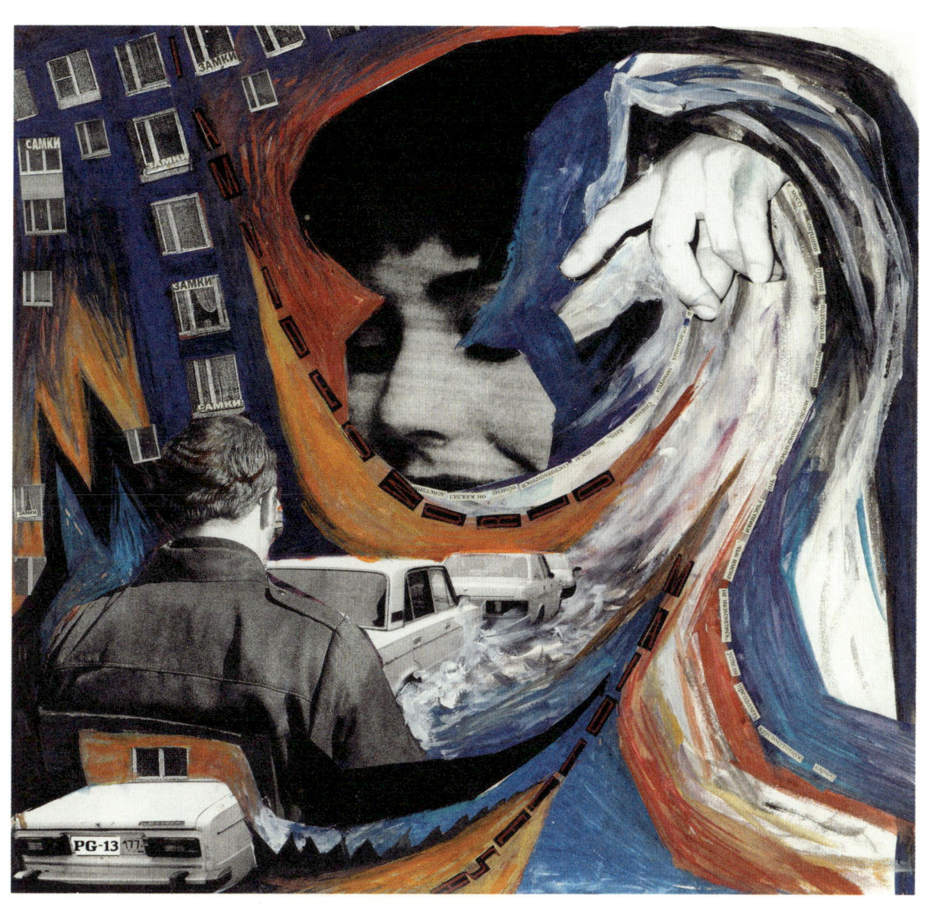

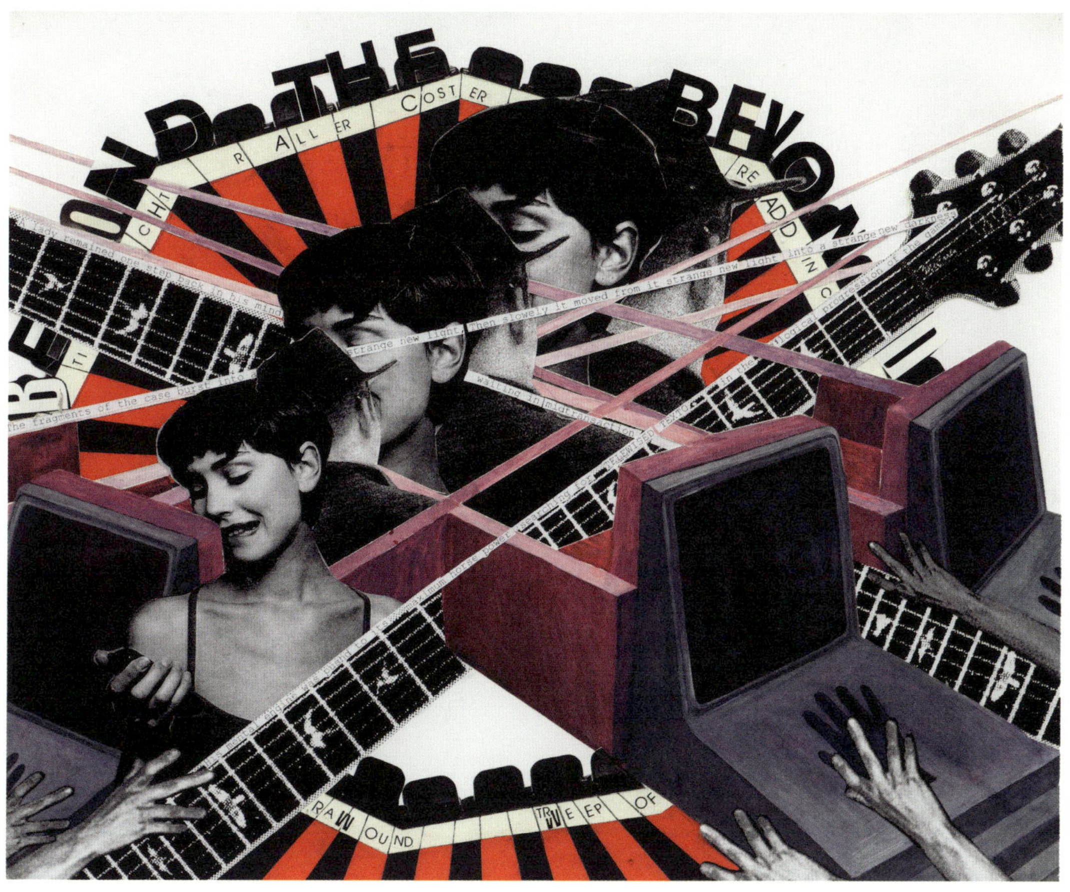
THE
BEYOND
COST ER
R ALL ER
RE
ADD

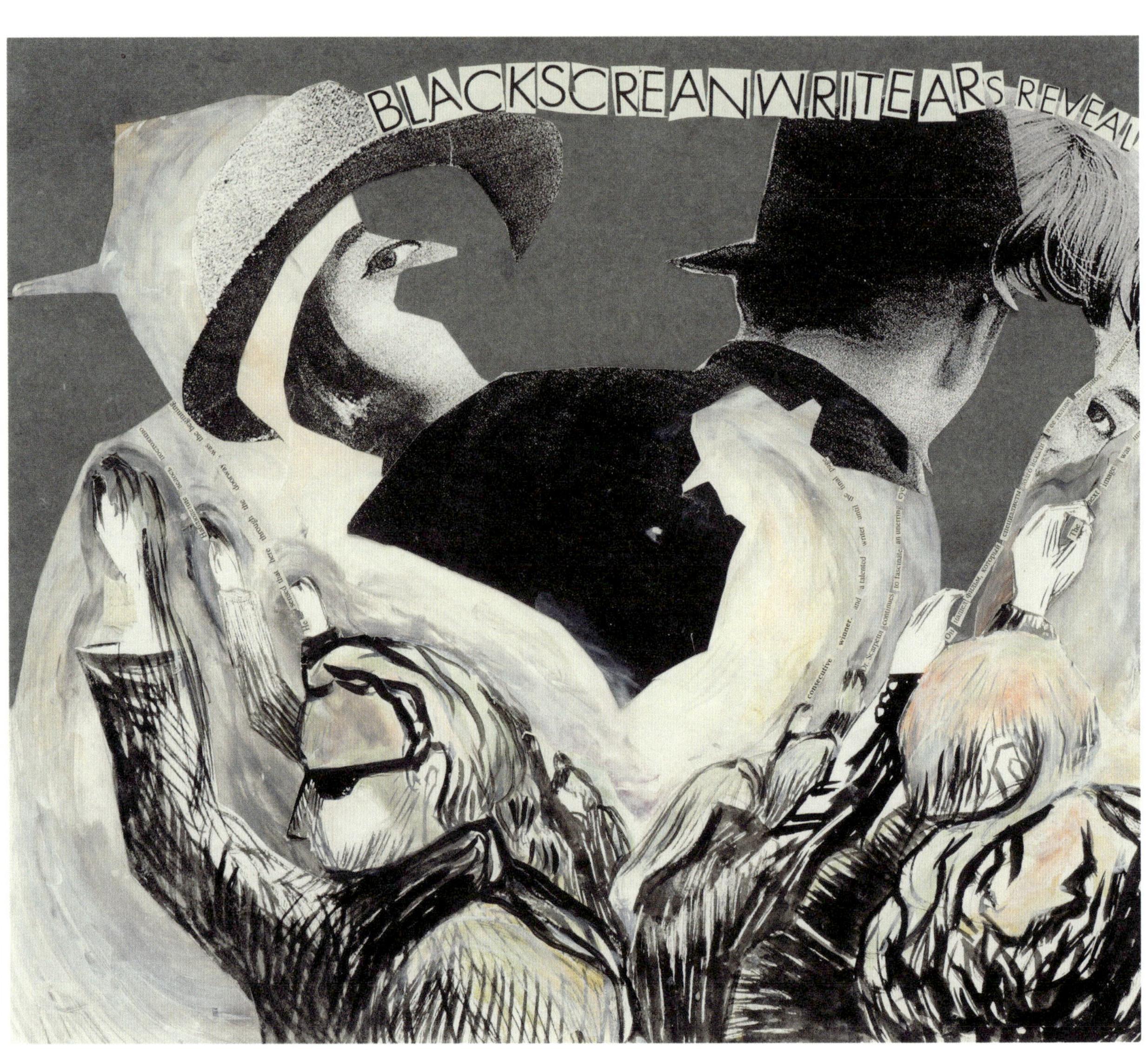
BLACKSCREANWRITEARs REVEAL

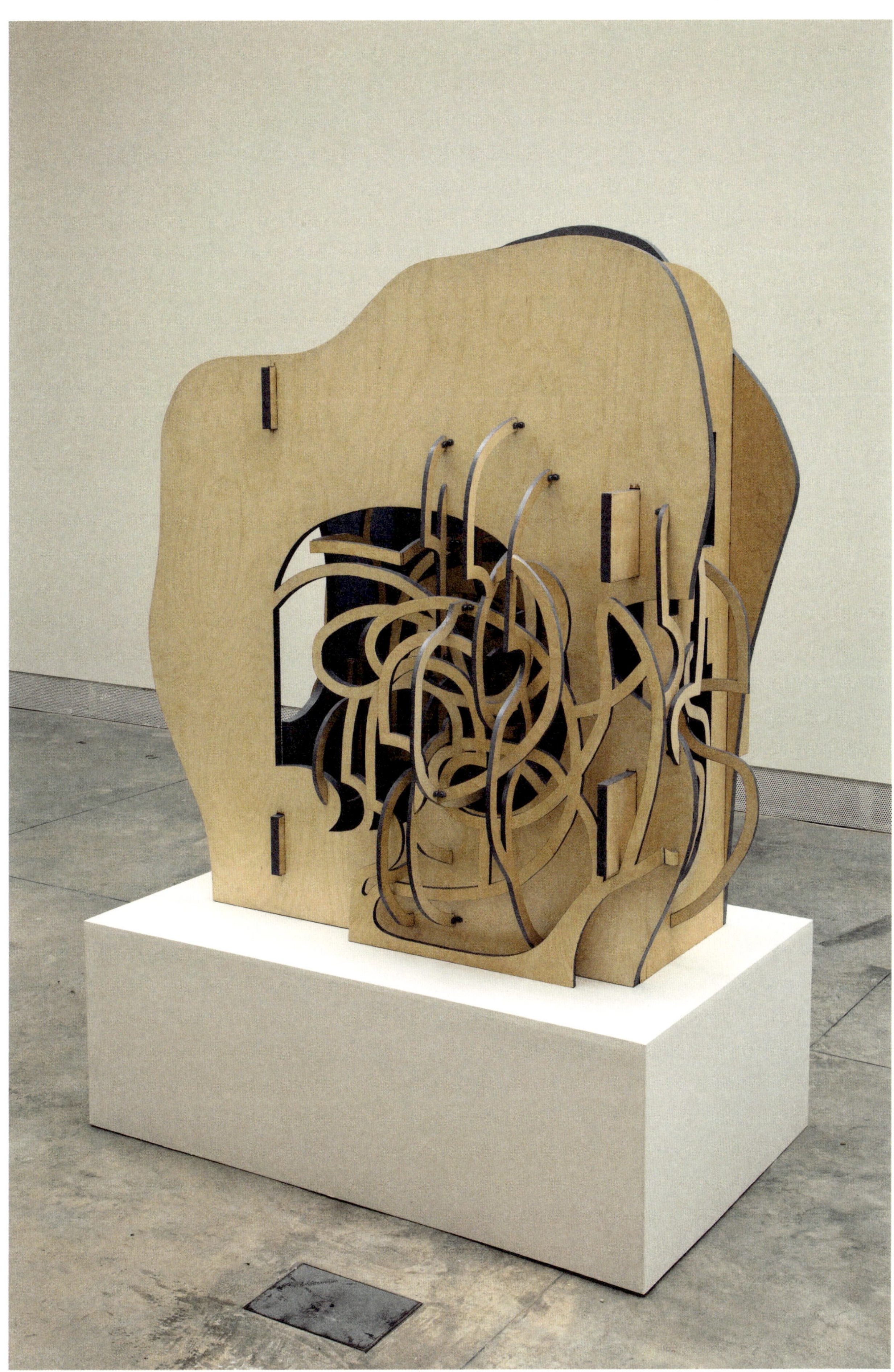

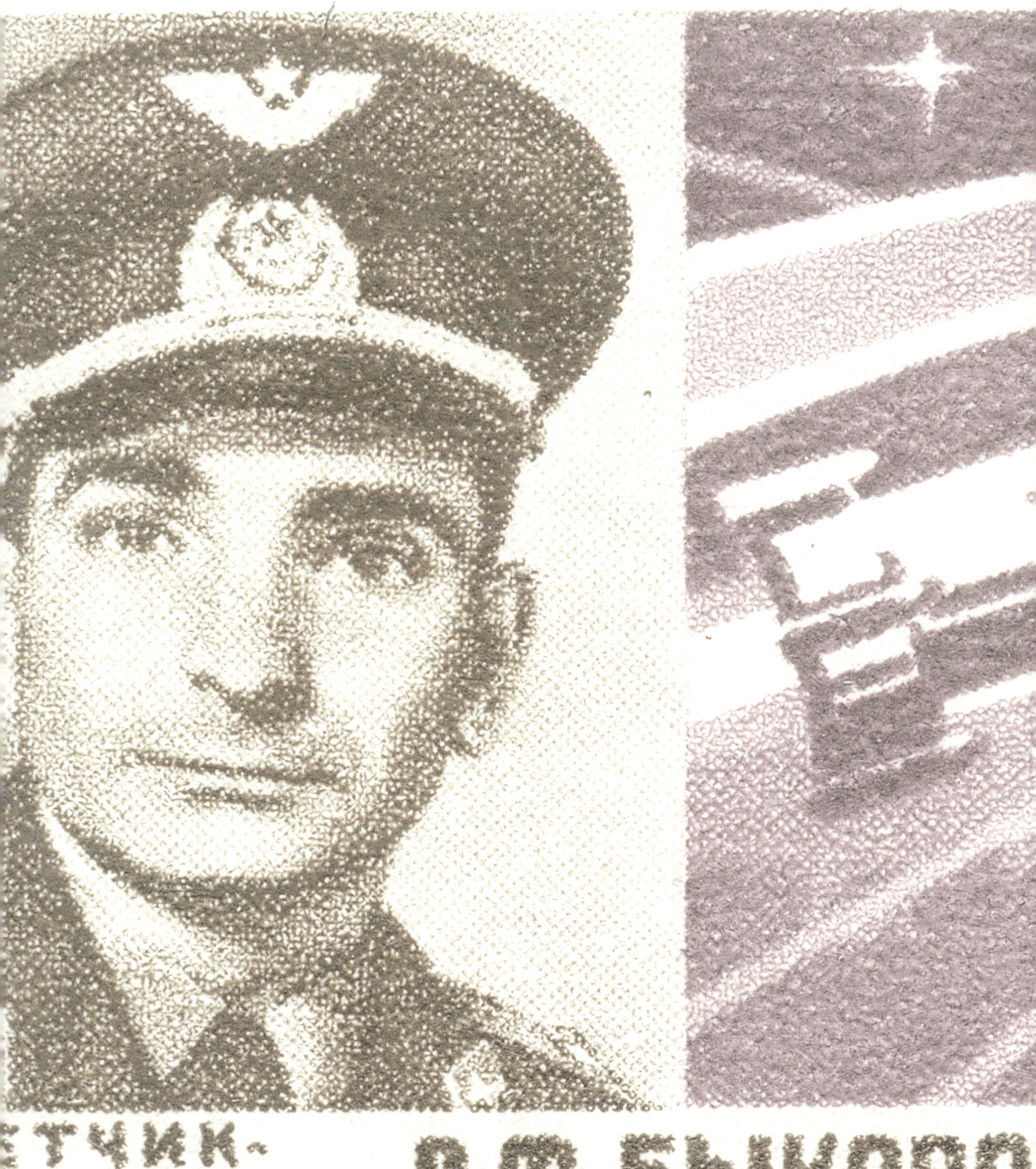

...ЕТЧИК-
...МОНАВТ   В. Ф. БЫКОВС...

МОСКВА
КОСМИЧЕ
КОРАБ
«ВОСТО
14·VI·196
СССР

YELENA POPOVA

With their transparent, softened geometric forms, Yelena Popova's paintings recall the graphics and aesthetics of both Russian Constructivism and Minimalism, and open up conversations about the materiality of painting today.

Popova's practice encompasses painting, video and installation, and all her work is tied together by an interest in exploring the concept of balance, whether in politics, representation, or in our relationship with machines.

"I'm not interested in making single objects, but in creating a complex network of facts, fictions, emotions, gestures, materials and images, which could relate to the world outside it," the artist explains.

For a recent project she made paintings and video inspired by the metaphor of the discus thrower; the elliptical curves and repeated, rhythmic shapes on her linen canvases articulate the kind of balance, external and internal, expressed through fixed rotation. Popova's films, which deal with overt imbalances such as Cold War topics and radioactivity, seem the perfect counterpoint to her 2D work, the flipside of the same theme.

Balance of Probabilities (2011) is a multi-part installation of paintings on linen that plays with similar ideas. The canvases in a range of sizes combine graphic pattern and unpredictable shapes with a delicacy of touch and thin gradients of pale colour that sometimes even show the grain of their linen surfaces. Precariously arranged on each other or held in place with makeshift pallet supports and even a doorknob, the paintings convey a sense both of dangerous asymmetry and of harmonious interconnectedness.

YP-01

BALANCE OF PROBABILITIES, 2011

Mixed media on linen, wooden domestic
objects, brass doorknob
Dimensions variable

YP-02

PARADE OF THE OVERBLOWN HERO, 2011 - 2012

13 parts, mixed media on linen, MDF peelings
Dimensions variable

YP-03

UNTITLED, 2011

Mixed media on linen
150 x 90 cm

YP-04

OVERBLOWN HERO, 2011

Mixed media on linen
170 x 110 cm

YP-05

UNTITLED (BATS), 2011

Mixed media on linen
55 x 48 cm

YP-06

UNTITLED, 2011

Mixed media on linen
75 x 55 cm

YP-07

UNTITLED, 2011

Mixed media on linen
75 x 55 cm

YP-08

UNTITLED (SHINY FRISBEE), 2011

Mixed media on linen
120 x 90 cm

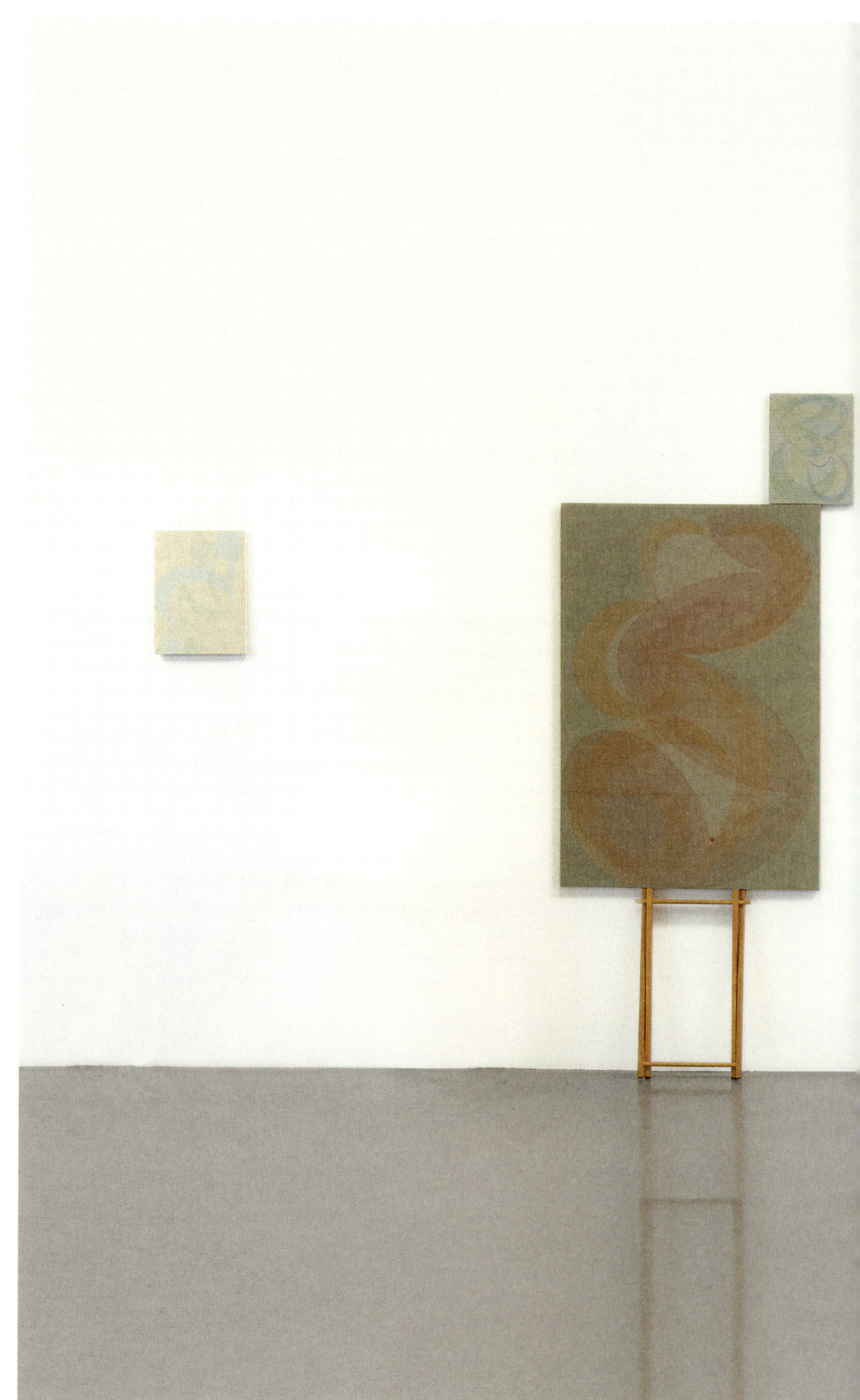

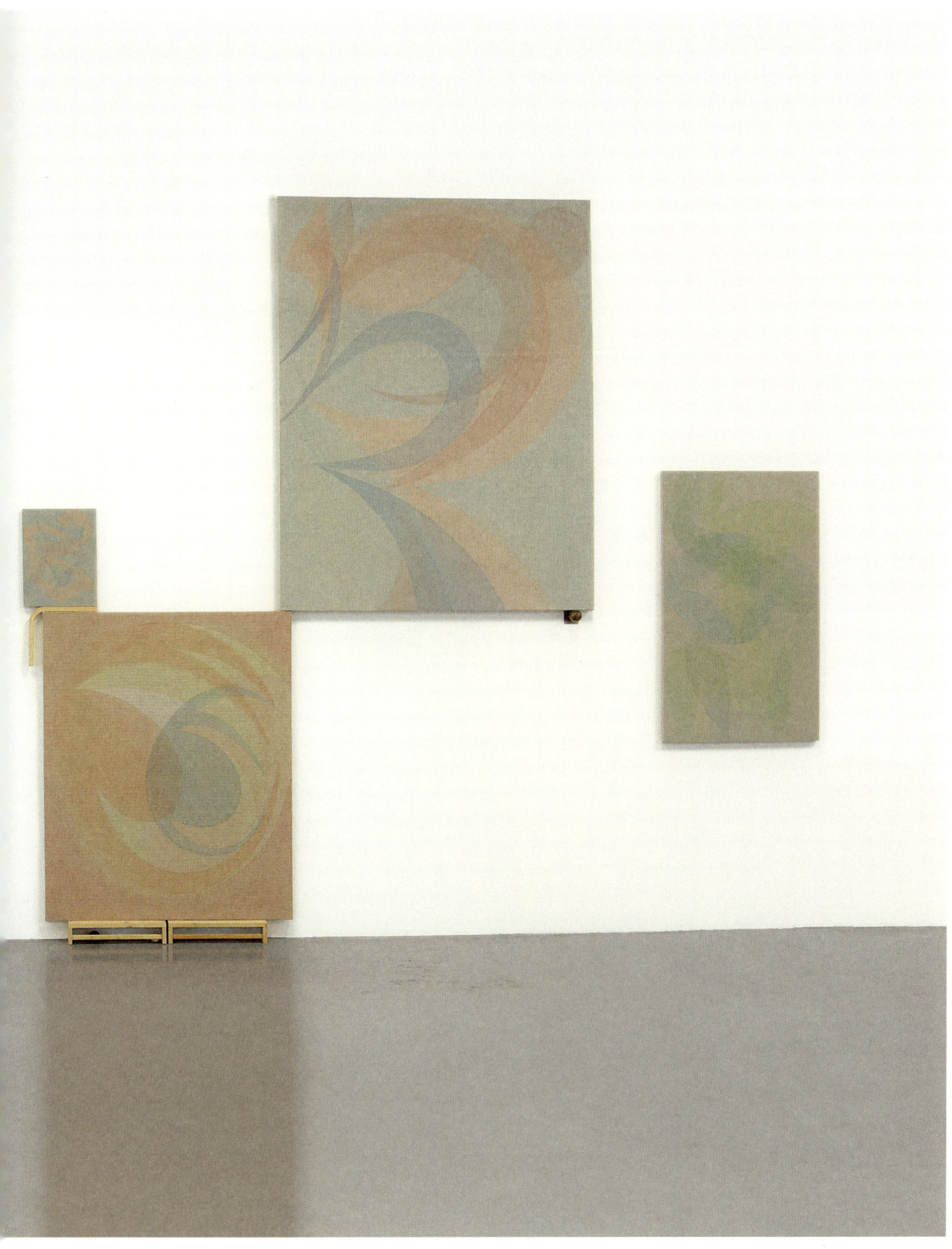

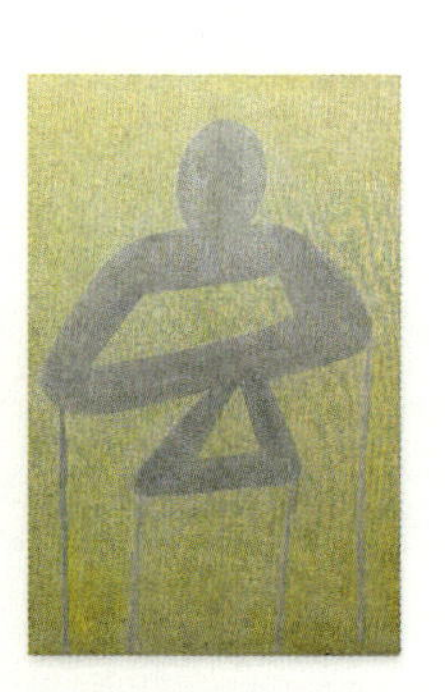

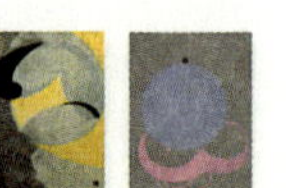

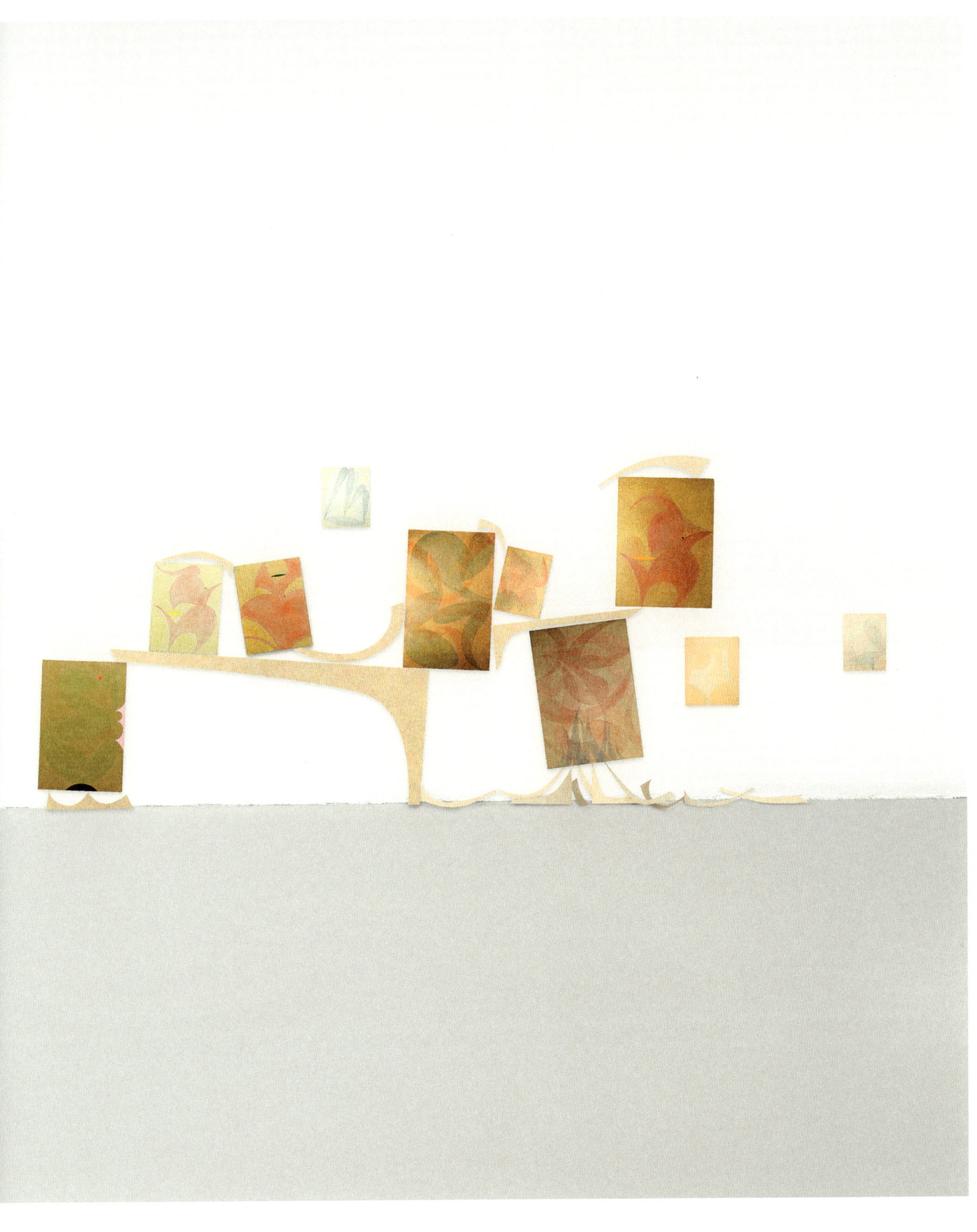

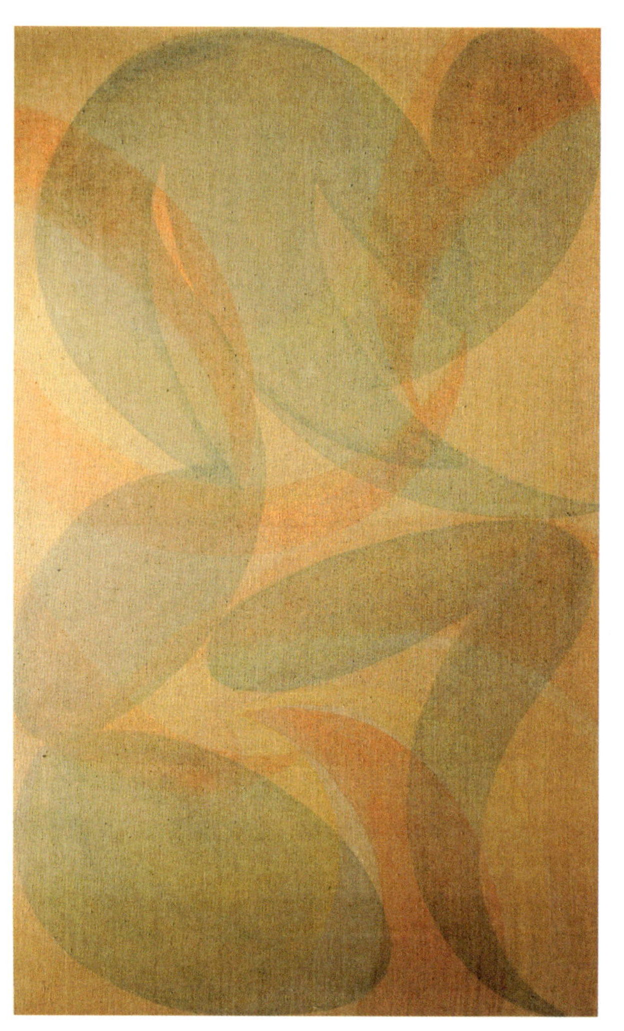
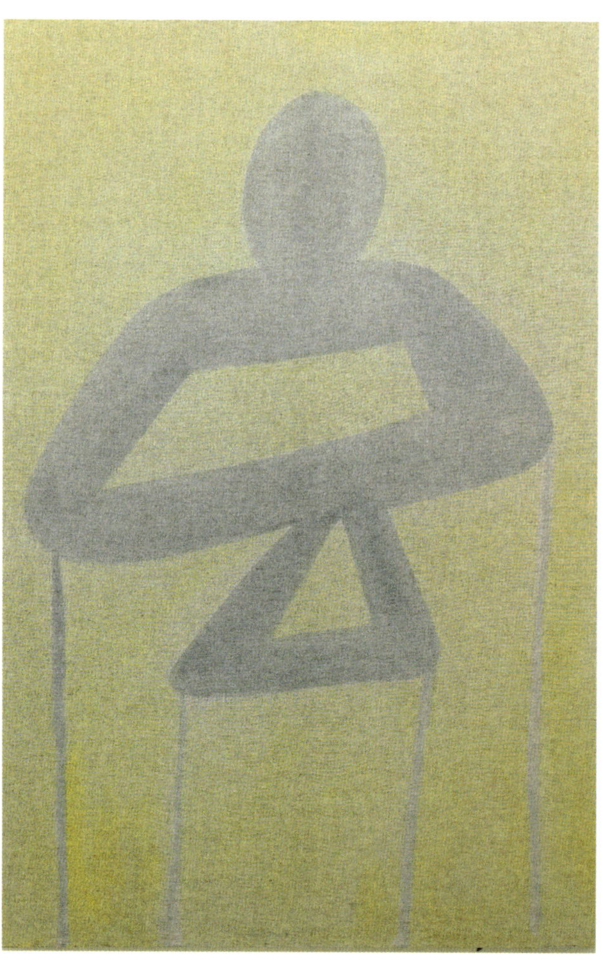
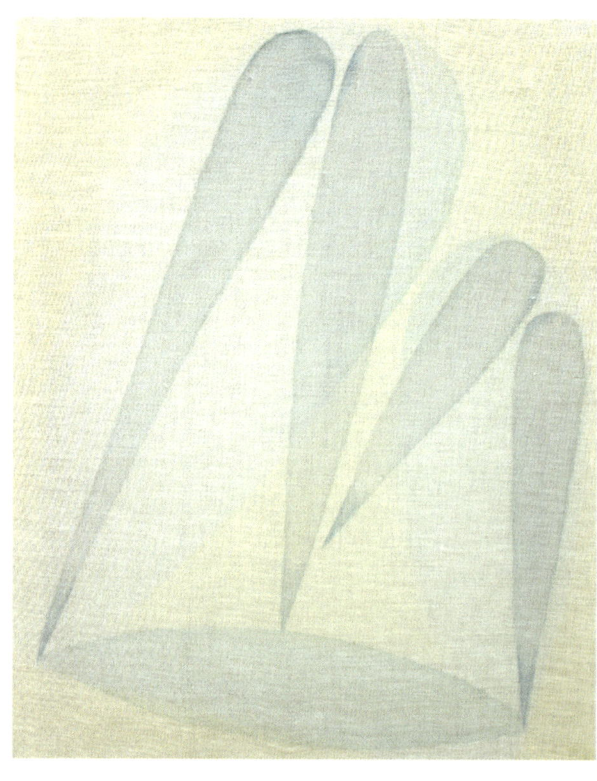

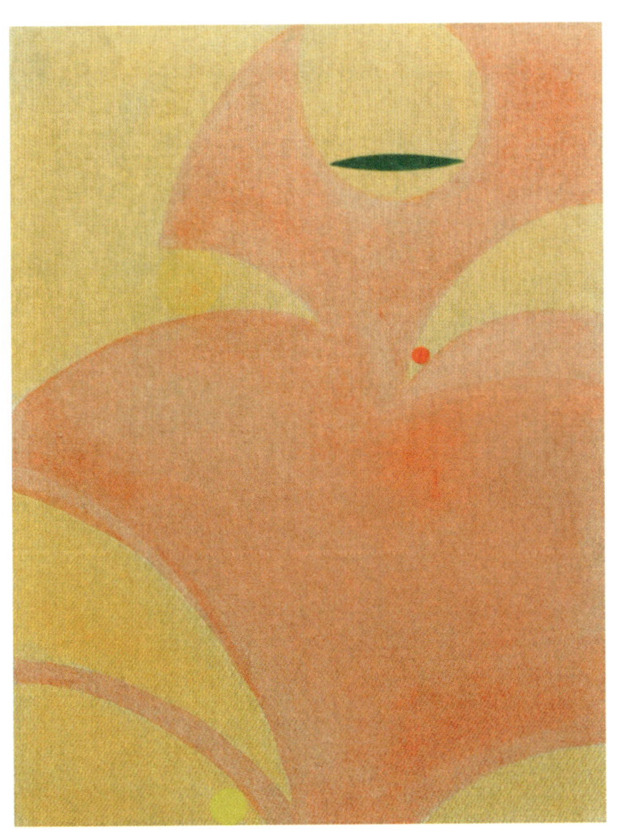
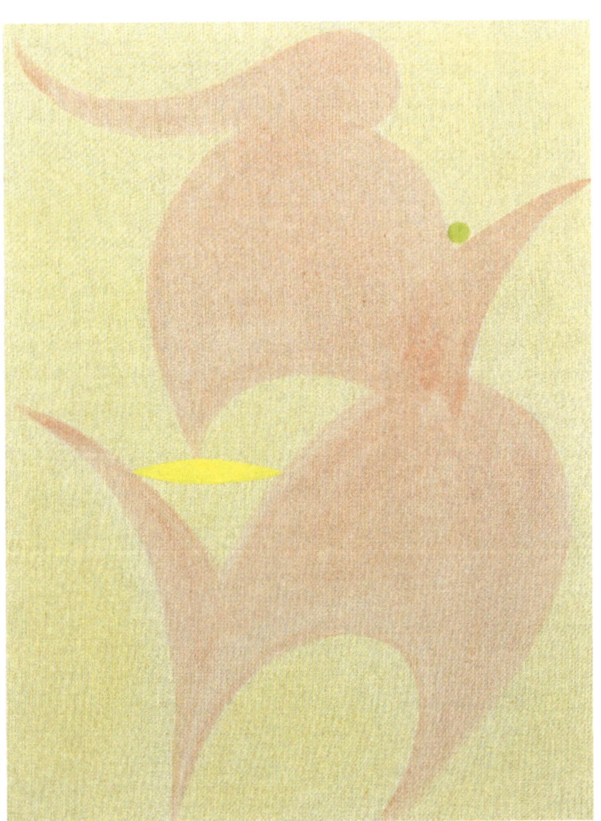
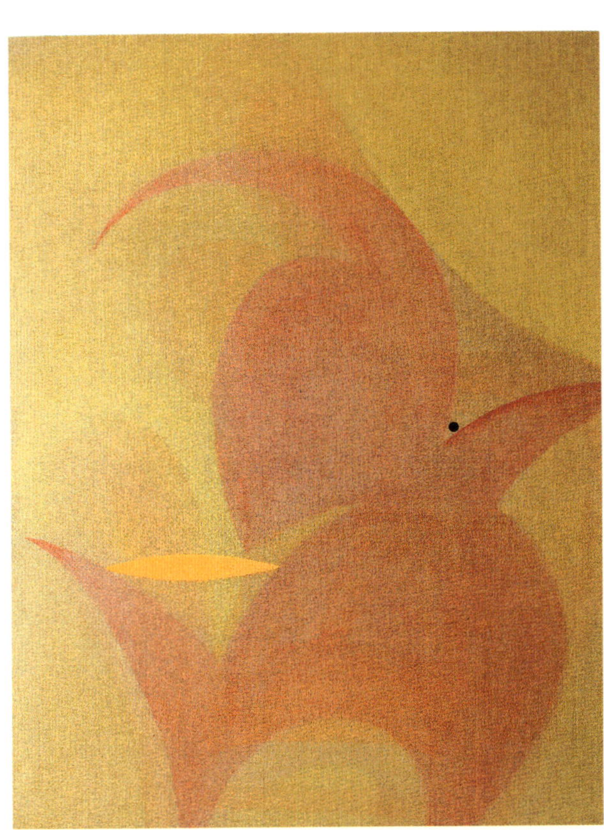

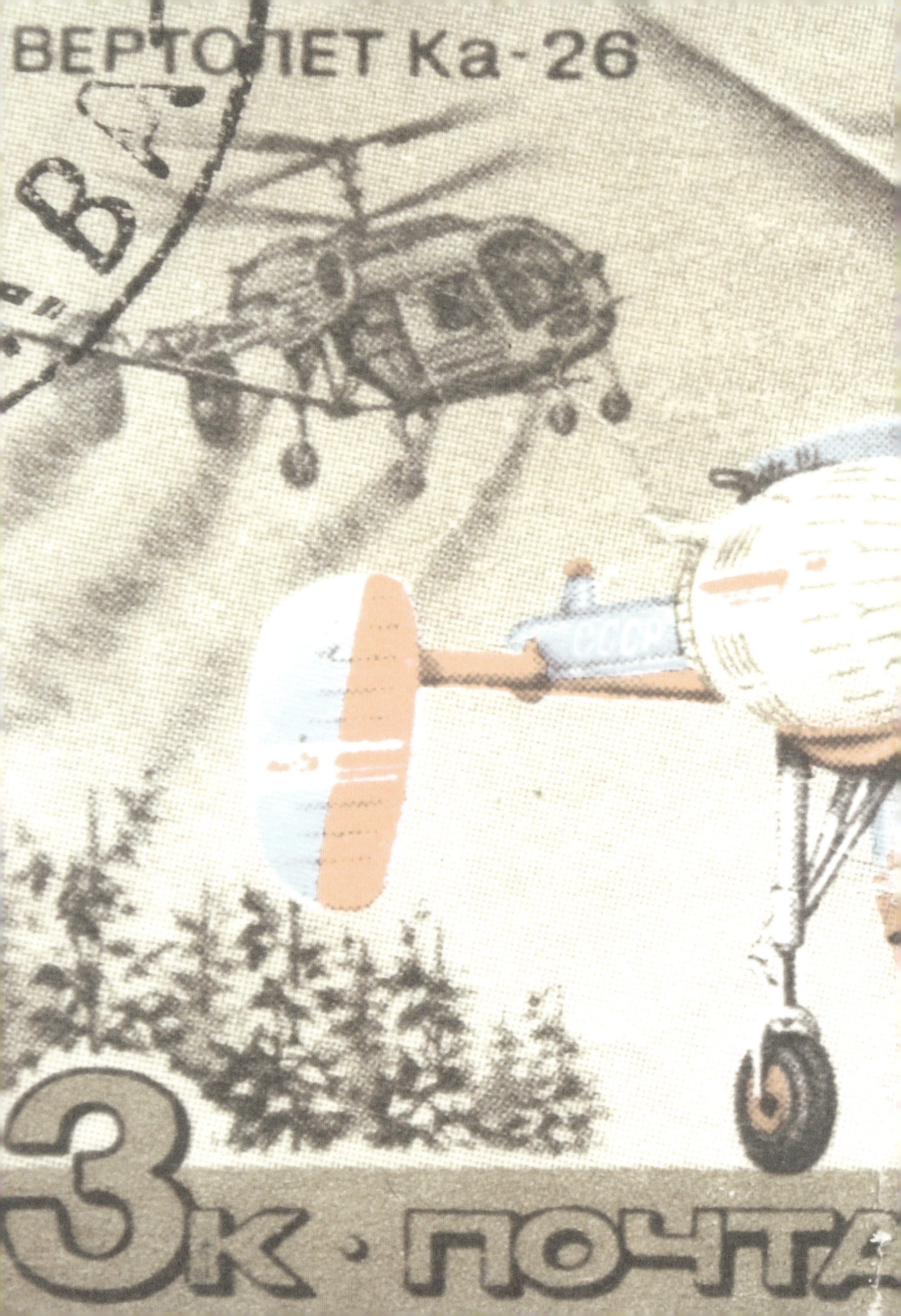
ВЕРТОЛЁТ Ка-26
СССР
3 к. ПОЧТА

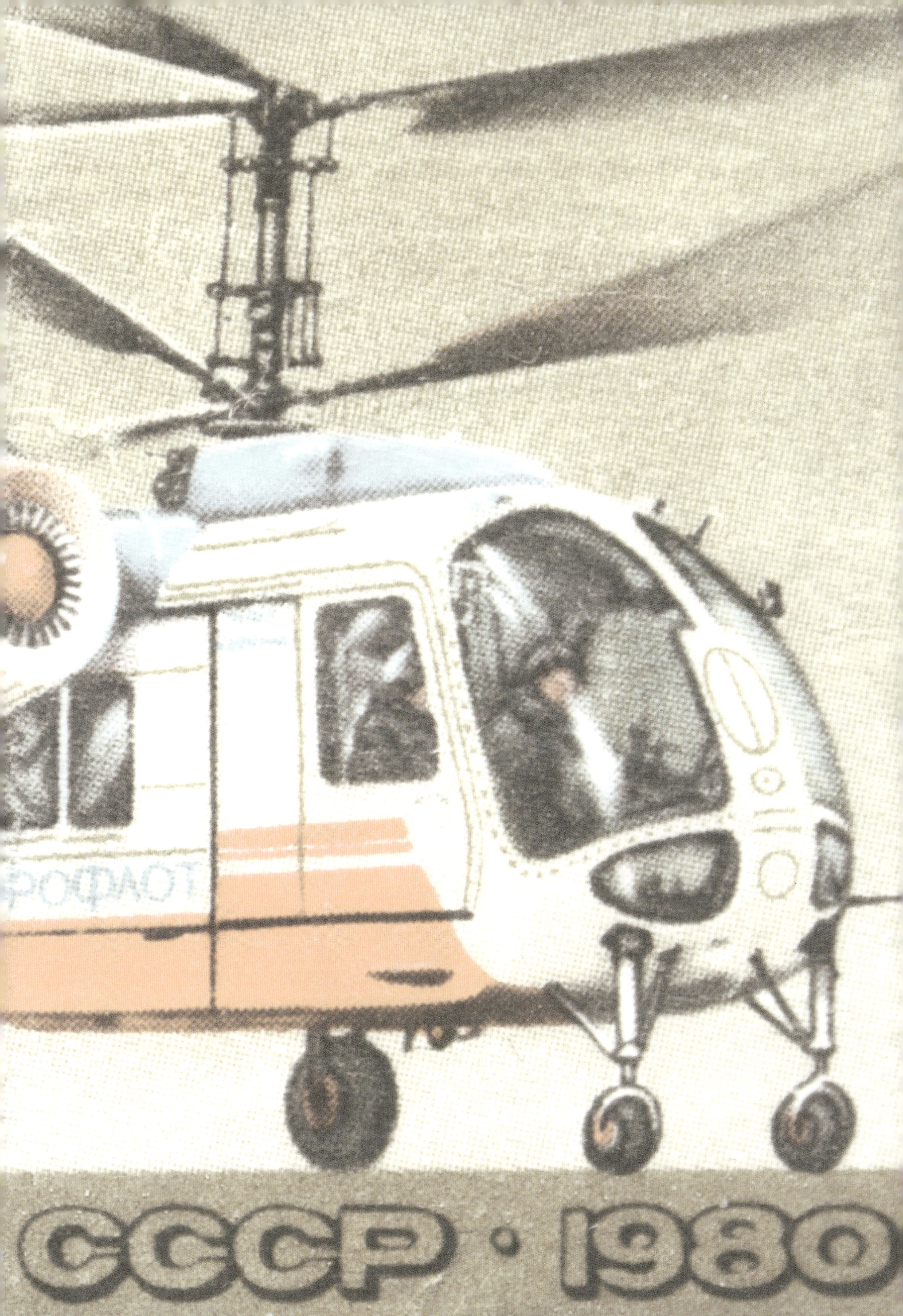
РОФЛОТ
СССР · 1980

ROMAN SAVCHENKO

Like steam, smoke and vapour trails, the abstract shapes in Roman Savchenko's ballpoint pen drawings depict formations that appear to be self-generated, ominously curling out of themselves.

Savchenko, whose practice also encompasses performance and dance (under the name Roman Ass), provokes a visual tension from what might first appear to be no more than simple, Rorschach-like randomness found in a sketchbook. Many of his drawings are dominated by floating shapes lashing out from the centre of otherwise empty brown sheets of paper. His obsessively patterned motifs are often outlined in a darker colour and placed asymmetrically over contrasting, painted pseudo-architectural edges, with which they almost fuse or combust.

Verging on the figurative in their dynamic, comic book-like detail, the shapes can tempt the viewer to project a kind of meaning or logic onto them, despite an awareness of their doodle-like quality.

Cloud (2010) is a large-scale mixed media drawing depicting a sprawling, horizontal mass made up of individual, rolling clusters and sharp lashes pointing downwards. Lightly painted in patches, it's been mostly worked over with swirling ballpoint pen strokes; the paper's worn, wrinkled surface is evidence of this repetitive action and suggests the drawing as a document of the artist's performance-like process.

The cloud, self-contained, looming and dark, stands as an obvious symbolic presage of an impending storm, but it reflects a moment of tension and transition in more ways than one. It's on the brink between abstraction and figuration, and between referencing a pre-existing visual culture and birthing its very own language.

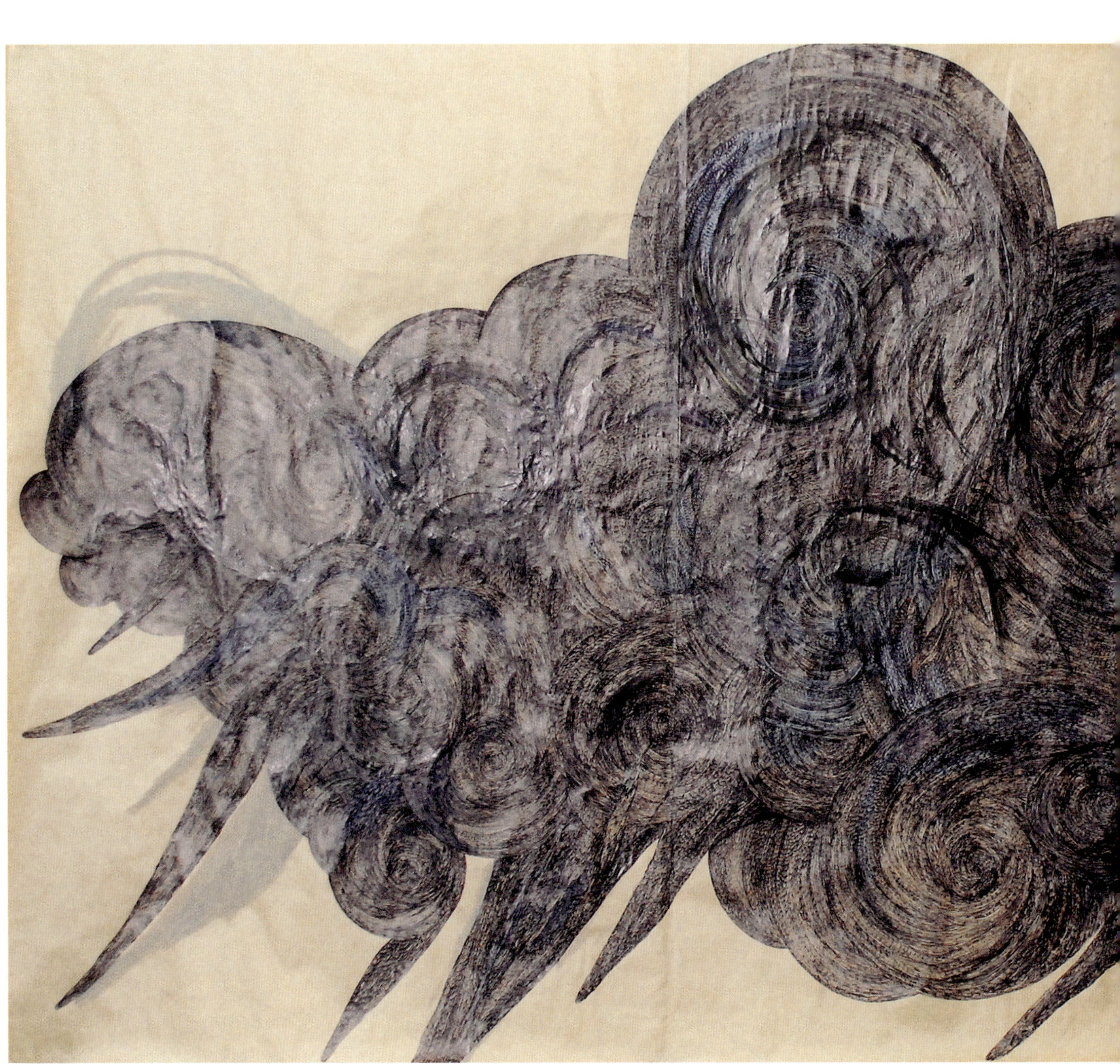

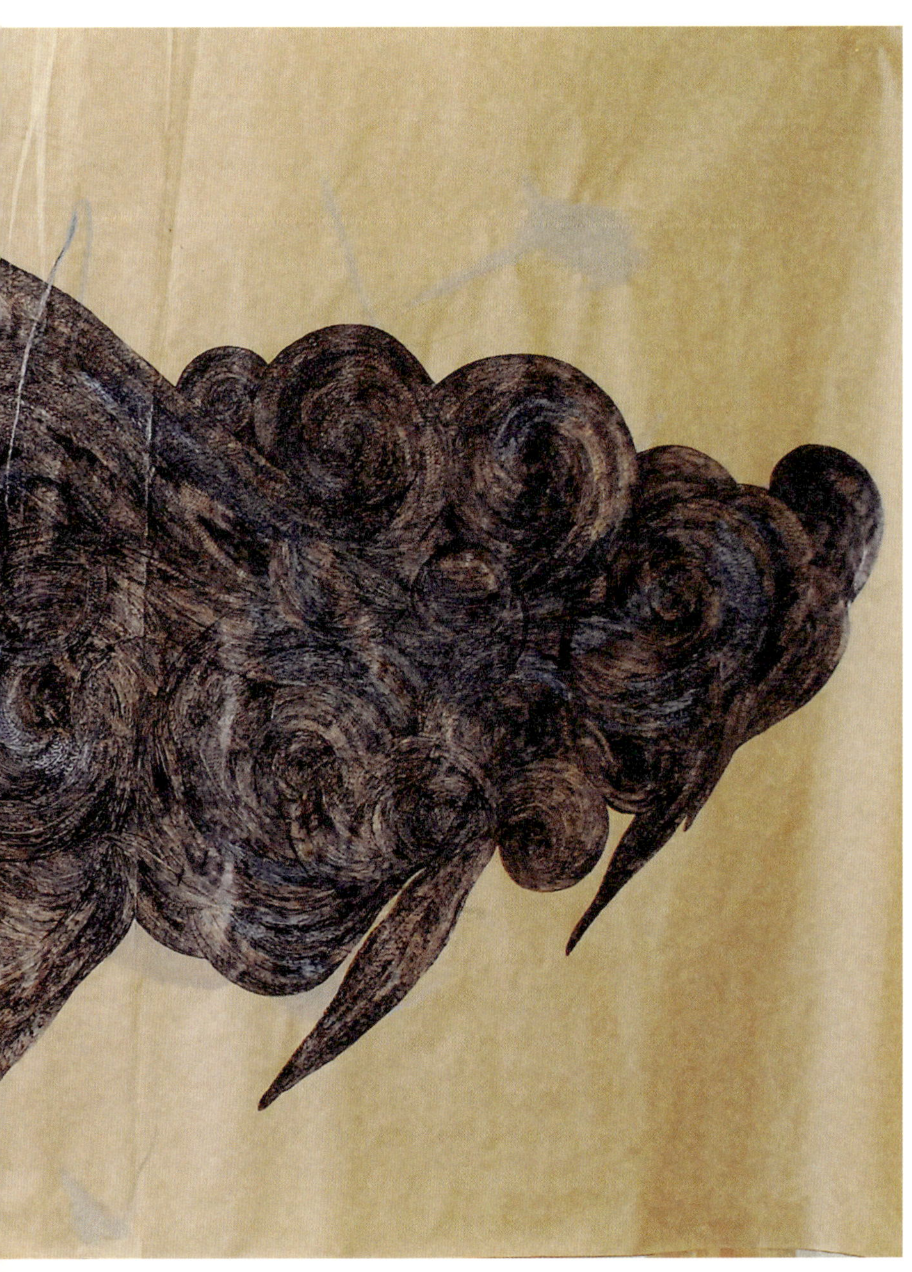

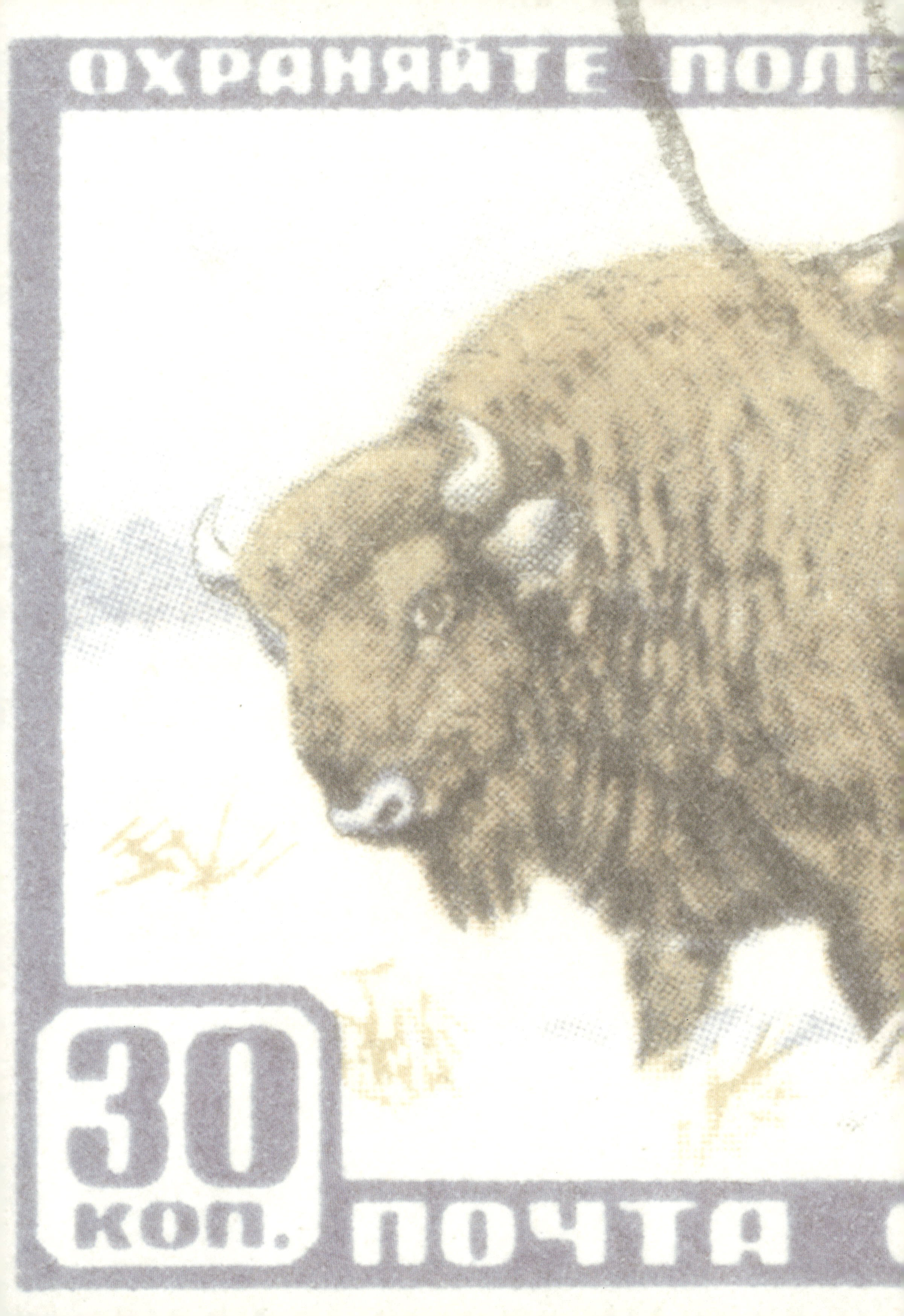

ОХРАНЯЙТЕ ПОЛ
30
коп.
ПОЧТА

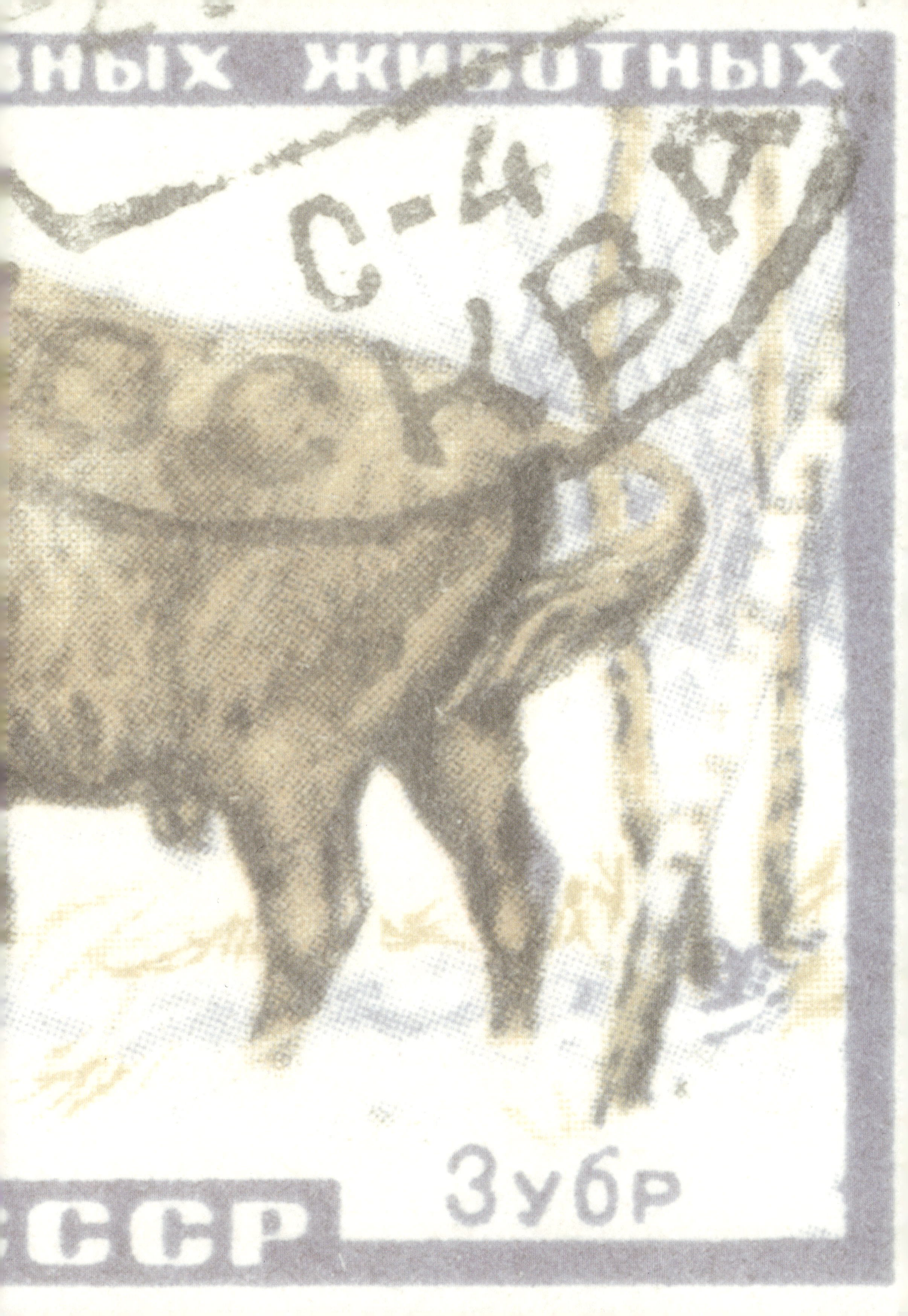

зных животных
ССР
Зубр

DASHA SHISHKIN

Driven by line, Dasha Shishkin's colourful drawings display an inventiveness and confidence not limited to fluid draughtsmanship. Her large-scale compositions on Mylar are inhabited by a psychedelic multiplicity of scenes and characters, bordering on the comical and the grotesque – a glimpse into a strange, parallel world where pre-assumed rules don't apply.

Crowded into vertiginously patterned interiors, her blank-faced figures of elegantly clad and high-heeled women sit cross-legged, stand behind counters, talk among themselves as in a ball or ponder alone, lingering in erotically charged poses as if morphing into each other in a dream fantasy that seems to take life's superficiality as its subject.

In interviews Shishkin has explained that she doesn't think of her works as paintings, but strictly as drawings; she considers the colour, whether it be paint or pastels or anything else, to be a kind of filling, not defining.

But colour is a crucial element shaping the form of her pictures, laying down a neon, sugary context and constant energetic distraction from the odd nonchalance of her carnival players, as seen in the large-scale *What Does It Matter To Her Ever Creating Womb If Today Matter Is Flesh And Tomorrow Worms* (2012).

Survival Takes A Good Memory (2012), another large-scale drawing, highlights the sinuous quality of her lines and their visceral precision truly through the bold colour blocks, like a coloured-in surrealist children's book or Schiele on acid. *Not Sad, Just Sighing* (2012) depicts another oneiric performance by a familiar high society debutante cast, here even more cartoonised and claustrophobically embedded within a dizzyingly patterned gallery arcade; beyond the Dior gowns and chic pencil skirts, a desert.

Some have seen similarities between her work and the visionary, idiosyncratic action tableaux of outsider artist Henry Darger; her penchant for traditional low-brow art supplies, manneristic repetition and for phallic accessorizing (for starters, take a look at her figures' noses and nipples) certainly reveal a similar fragility and fantastical obsessiveness.

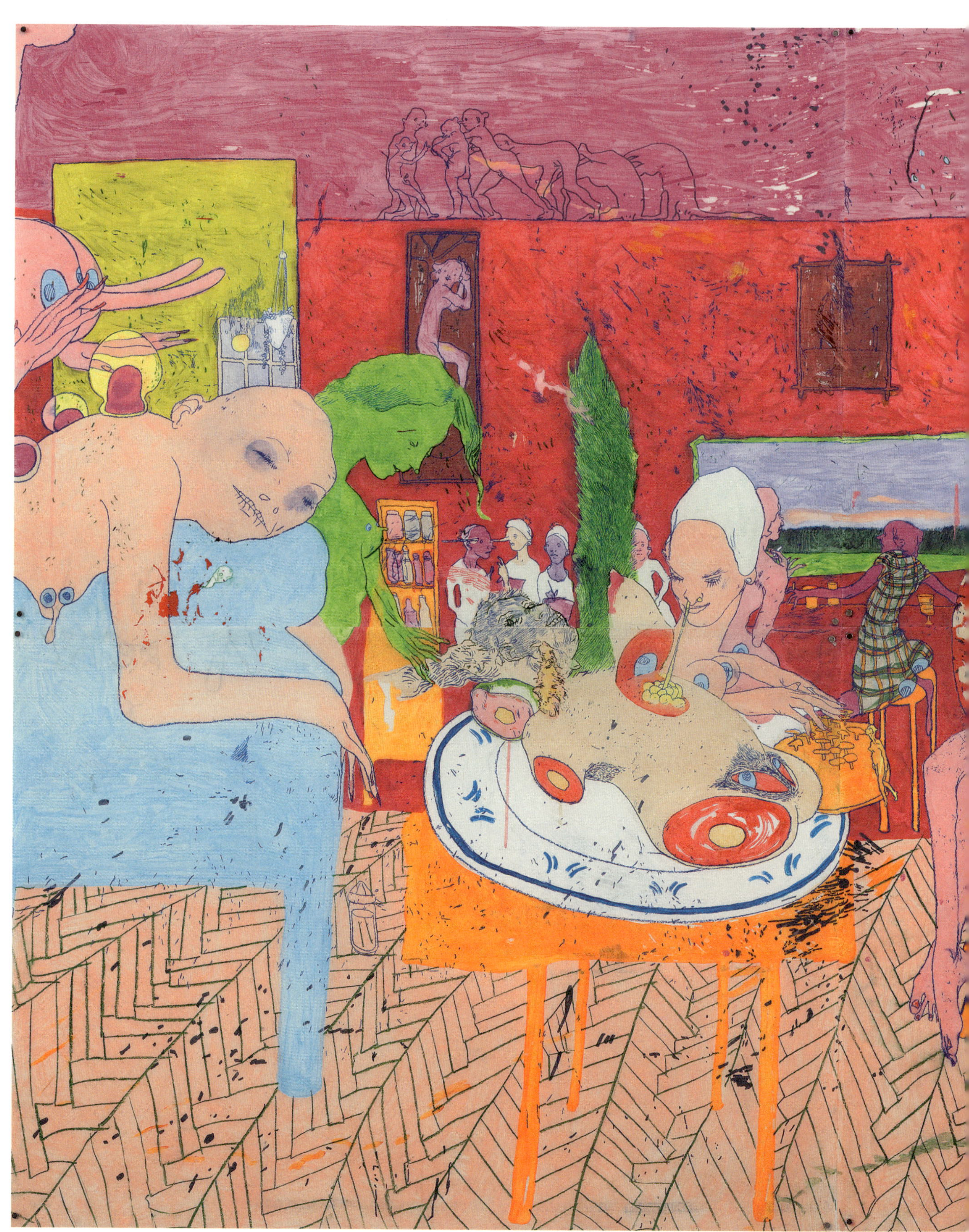

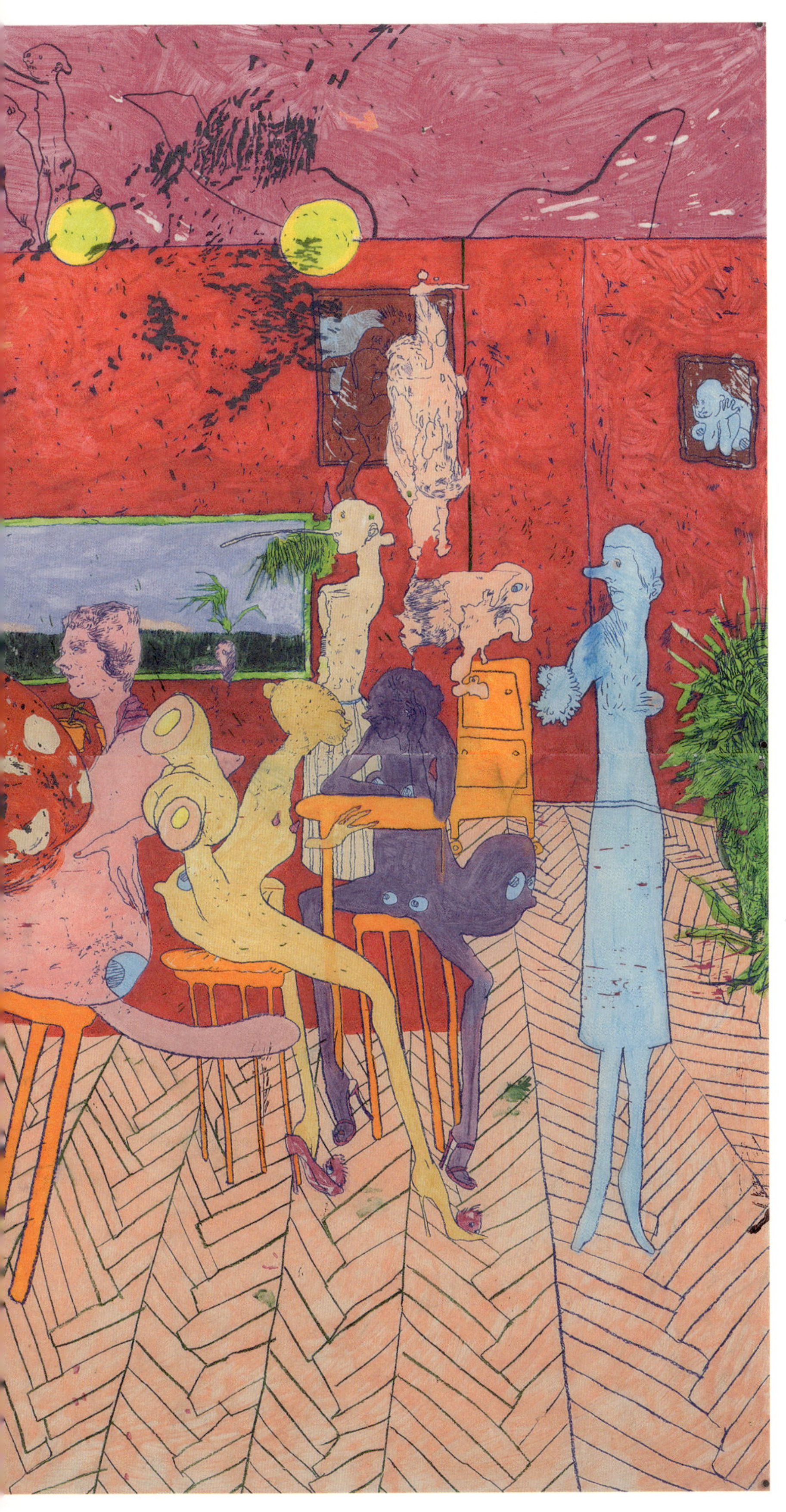

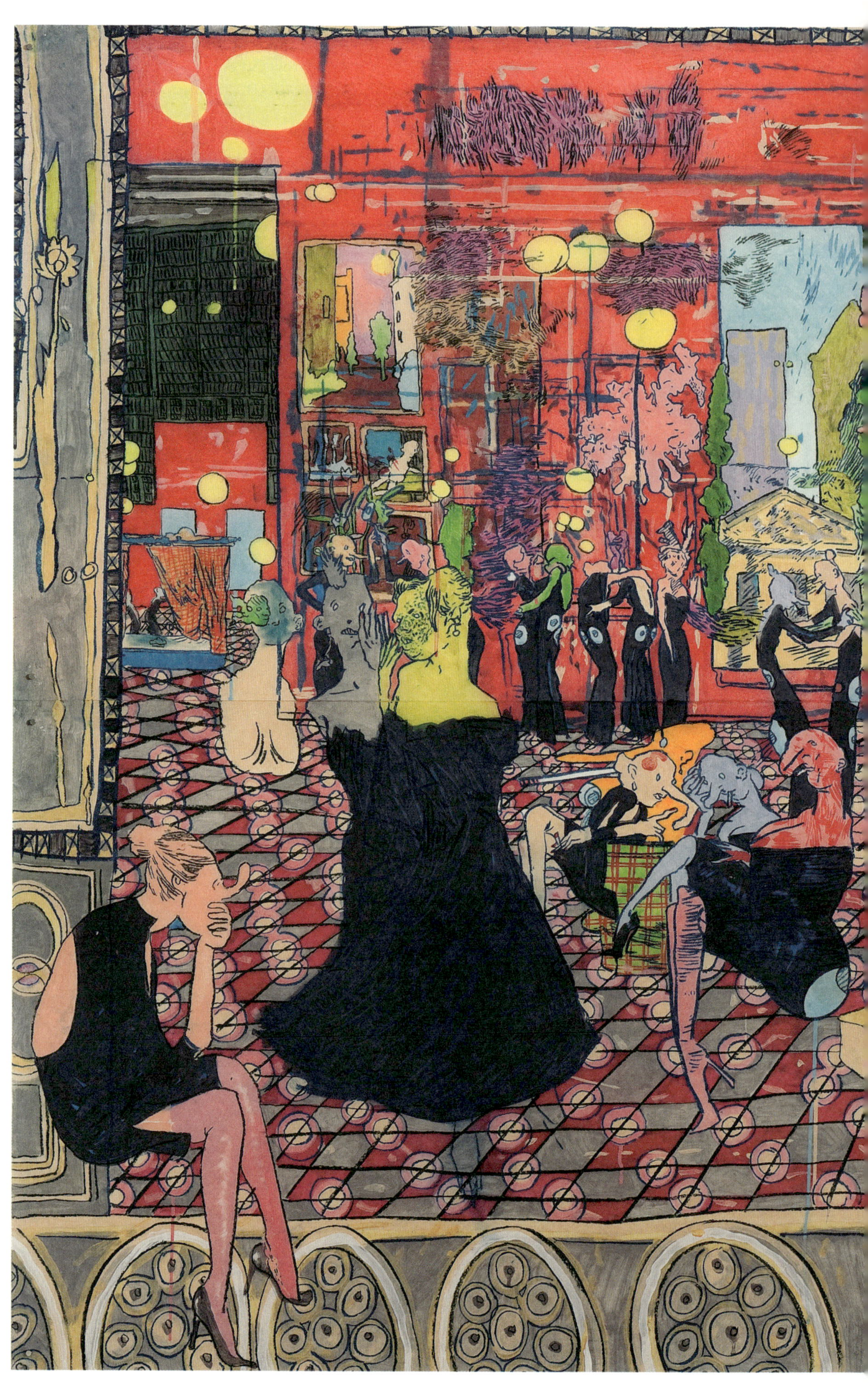

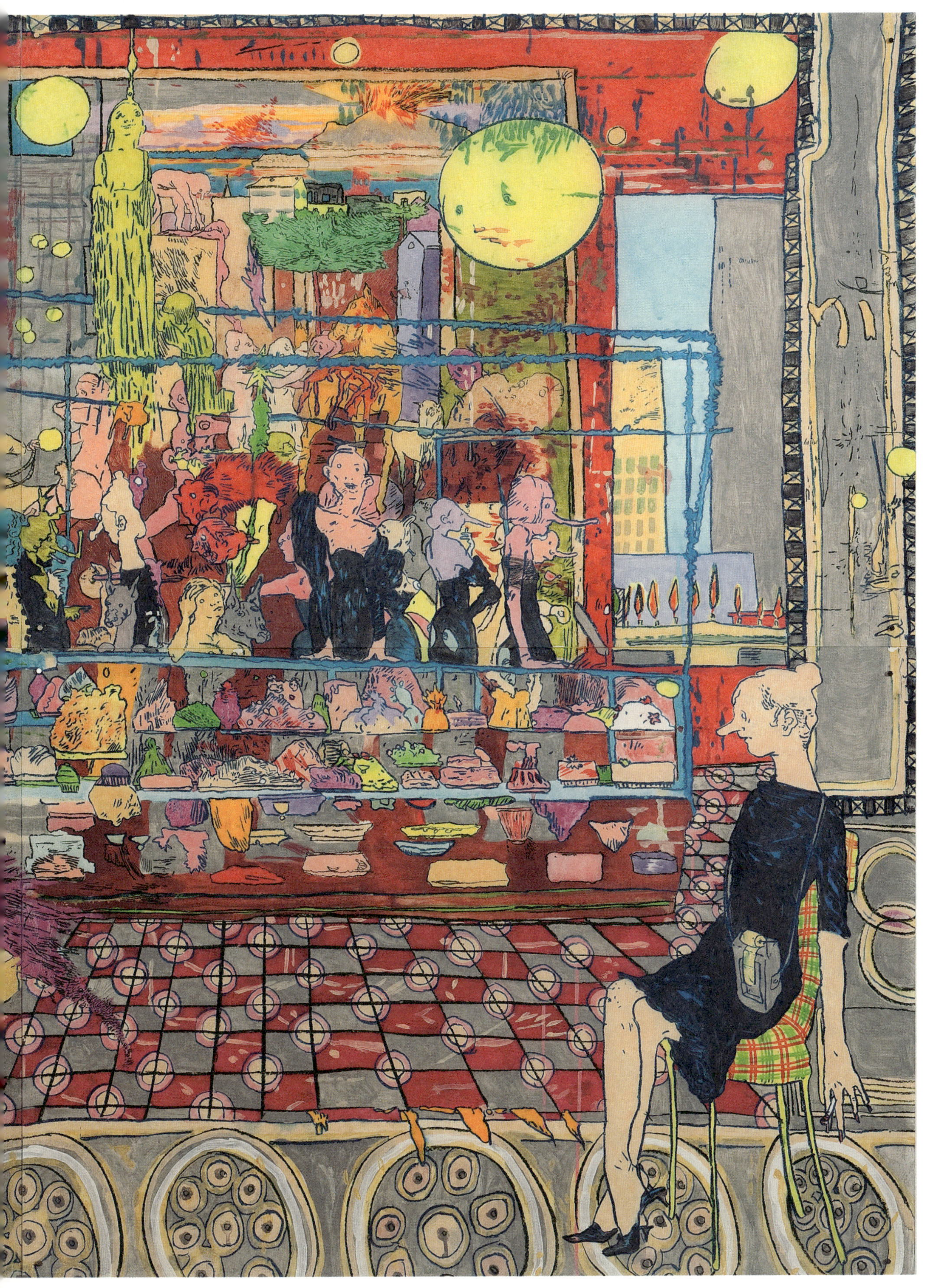

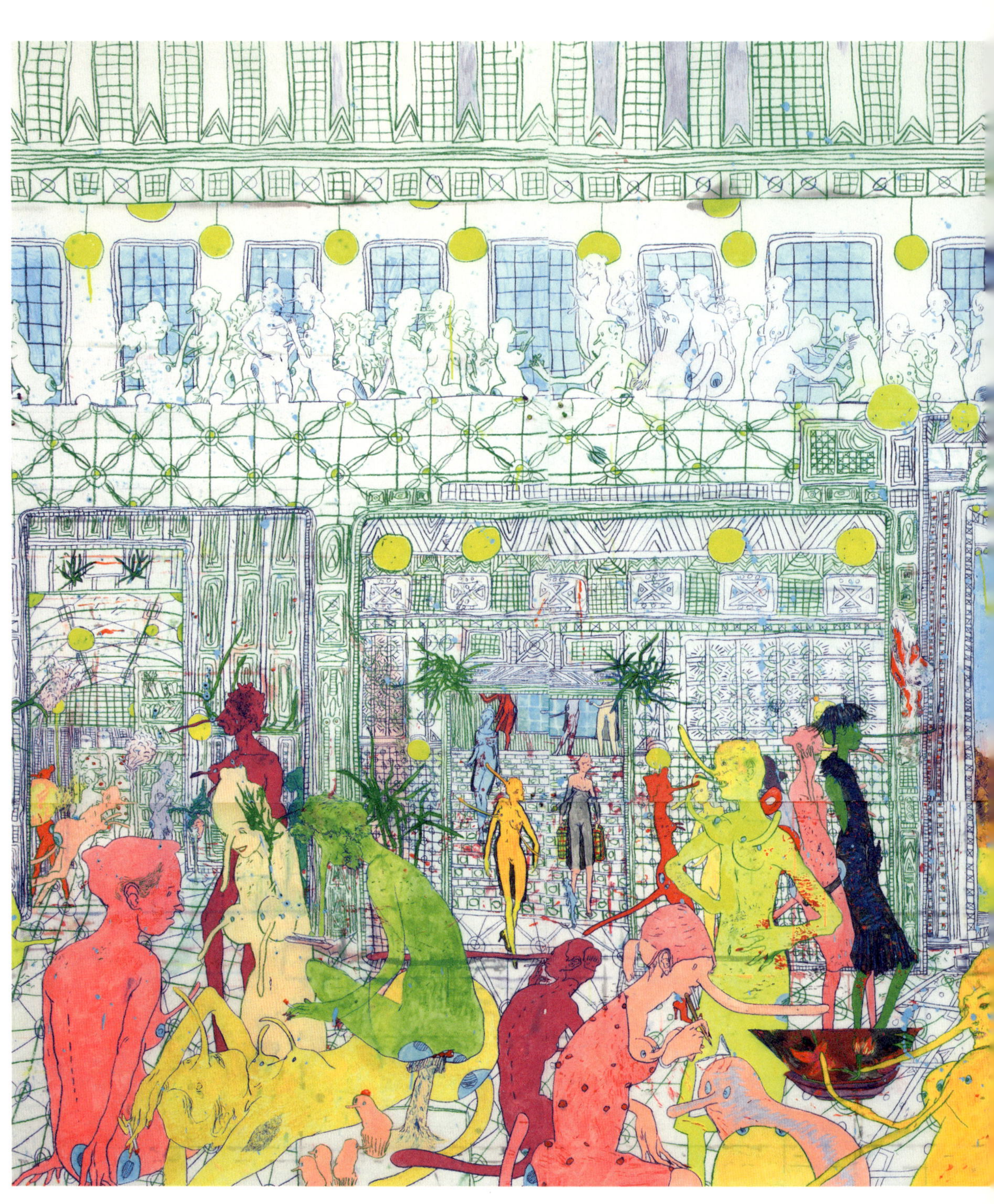

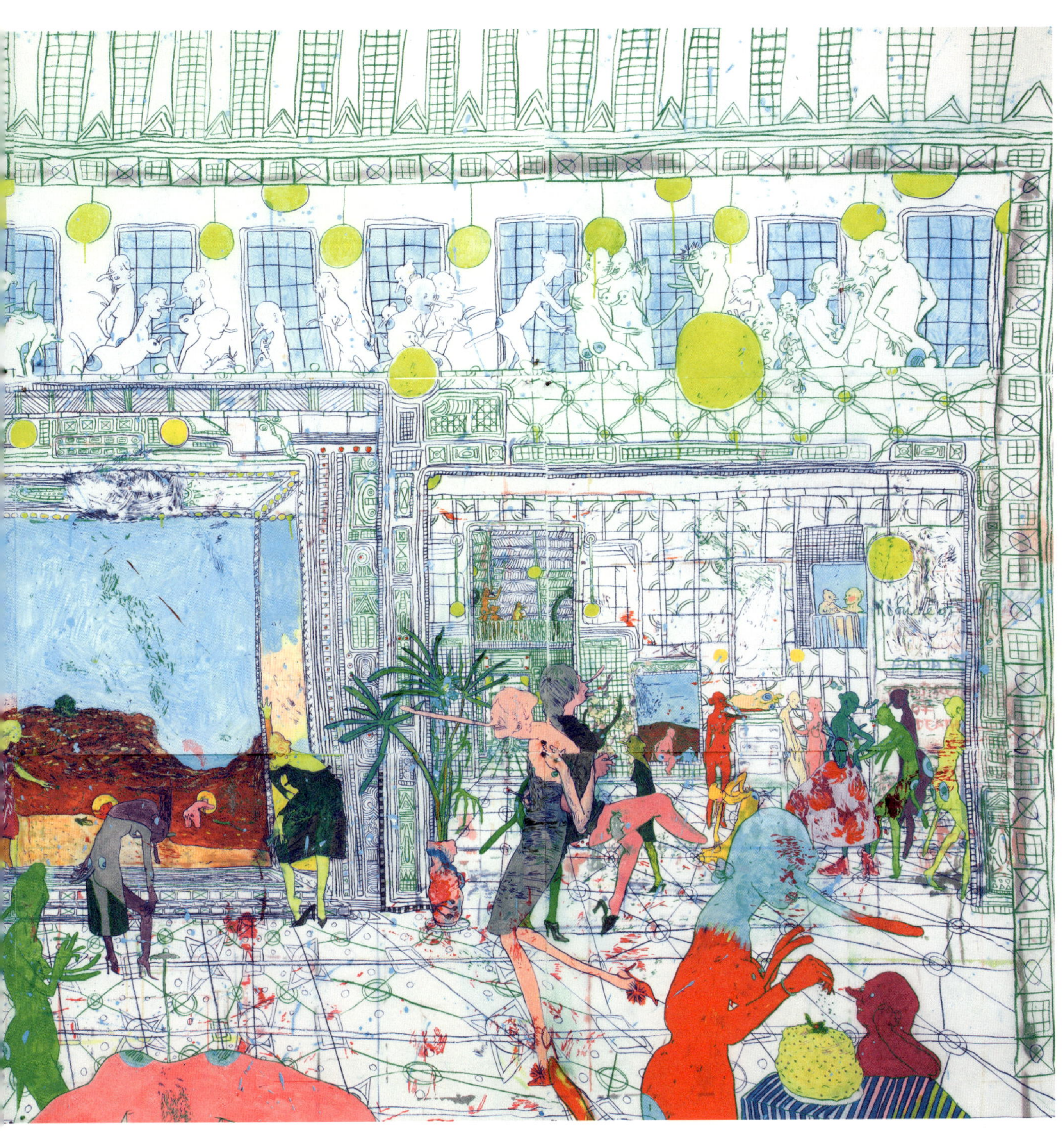

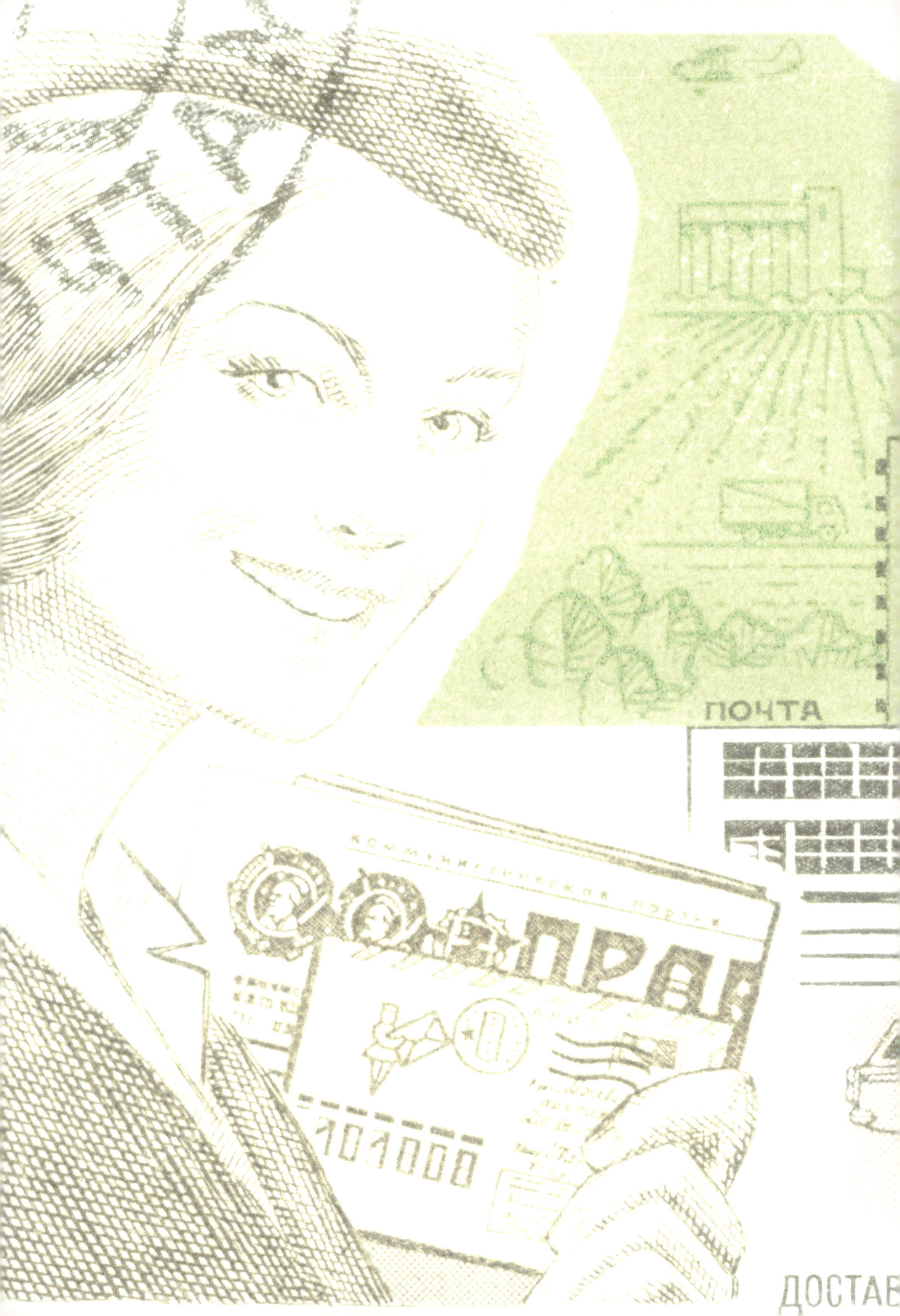
ПОЧТА
ПРА
101000
ДОСТА

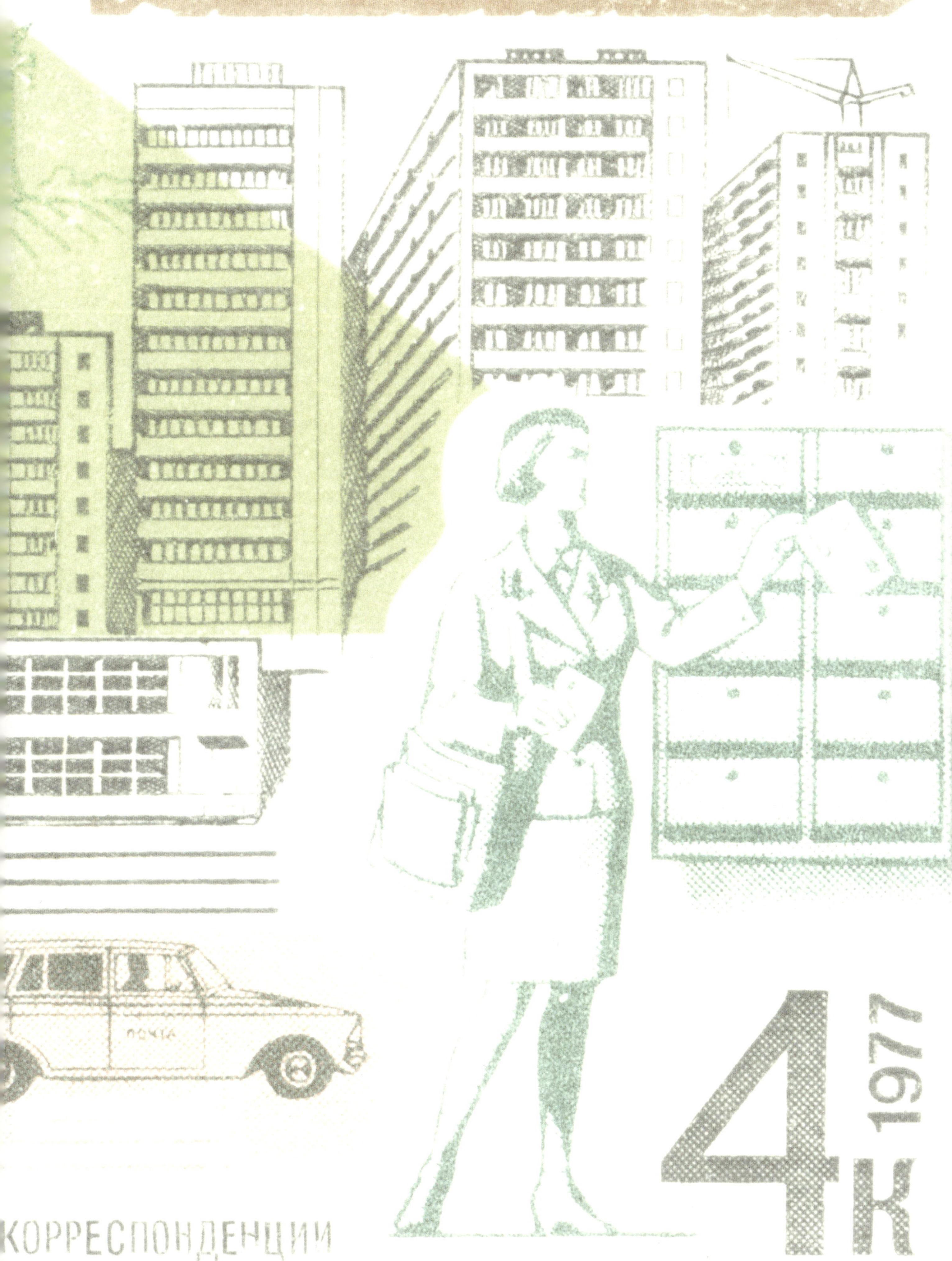
ПОЧТА СССР
1977
4
к
КОРРЕСПОНДЕНЦИИ
ПОЧТА

TAMUNA SIRBILADZE

Tamuna Sirbiladze's paintings, fast, expressionistic canvases depicting abstract shapes and naked female figures in the midst of bodily functions, convey an intimate, unavoidable physicality.

Born in Georgia and based in Vienna, Sirbiladze could be said to be channelling some of the Viennese Actionists' subversive spirit. She paints unromanticised images of faceless women naked, bleeding, defecating and vomiting, a kind of scrapbook of acts that are not particularly taboo now but aren't the most obvious subjects for artists to explore in their works. There's a raw frankness to her characters that goes beyond their crude, puerile figuration; they at once conflate the imagery of pornography and primeval ritual within scenes that hint at the diaristic and at a wide range of emotional states.

There is always something ordinary, something humorous, something melancholy and something sinister in her paintings. *Map 4 – Got Too Much LA Sun* (2005 - 2008) shows the body of a naked woman on a beach, completely sunburnt and crimson (even her head and pubic hair), bending over an abstract shape with arched arms and legs, but still wistfully looking over to the blue waves and the sky on the horizon.

Map 3 – Being Left There (2006 - 2008) is a more modest depiction of a figure kissing the air to the right, but more sinisterly holding a cartoonish, hot pink bone behind her back, like a club. *Map 2* (2006 - 2008) and *Map 3* include unflinching paintings of a woman's buttocks during the act of defecation and penetration, across which text has been painted in bright neon colours, like graffiti.

The exact meaning of these arresting works is left open, blurred and made even more ambiguous by their often poetic titles. Sirbiladze is also the widow of artist Franz West, and the two often collaborated on projects.

TS-01

MAP 1, 2005 - 2008
4 parts, all: Acrylic and oil on canvas

TOGA COULD NOT REMEMBER
200 x 185 cm

FEMME INFIDELE
200 x 180 cm

DRUGES
150 x 190 cm

HORSE SHITS ON THEIR ROSES
240 x 180 cm

TS-02

MAP 2, 2006 - 2008
4 parts, all: Acrylic and oil on canvas

UNTITLED
190 x 200 cm

ANDRO
200 x 185 cm

DRUG PICNIC
180 x 160 cm

WHEN HIS BOLDNESS REFLECTED
TWILIGHT ON HER HAIR
200 x 200 cm

TS-03

MAP 3, 2006 - 2008
3 parts, all: Acrylic and oil on canvas

PICKLED ASS
200 x 200 cm

VAN GOGH
200 x 140 cm

BEING LEFT THERE
200 x 200 cm

TS-04

MAP 4, 2005 - 2008
5 parts, all: Acrylic and oil on canvas

GOT TOO MUCH LA SUN
200 x 185 cm

SUICIDE PAINTING
200 x 200 cm

ADIDAS STILL LIFE IN THE TENNIS COURT
200 x 180 cm

IN SAHARA
200 x 185 cm

KOTZEN
220 x 155 cm

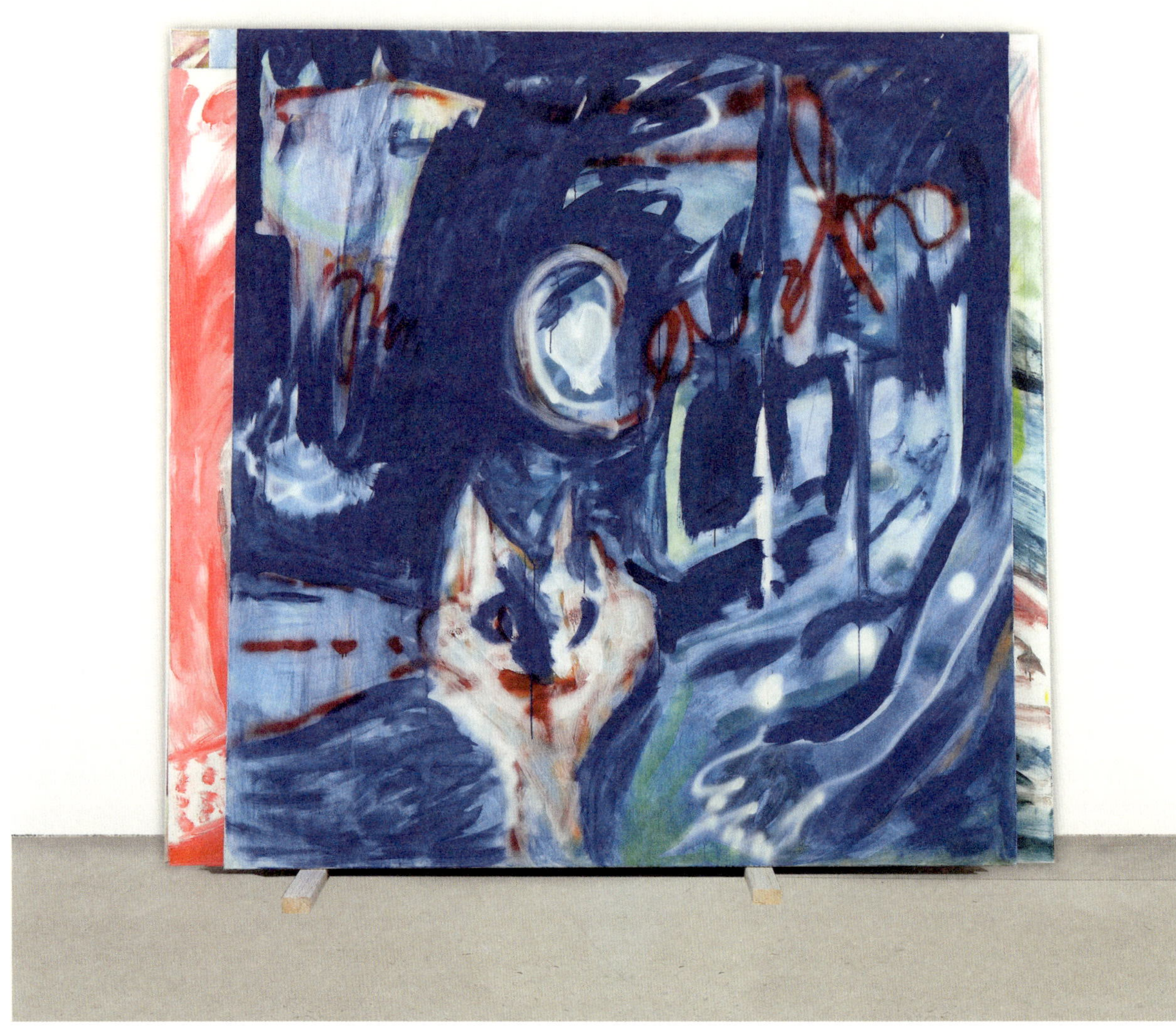

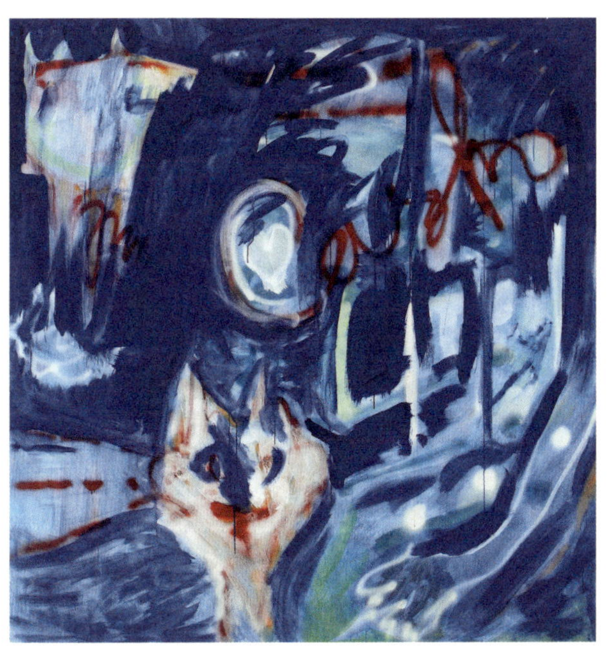

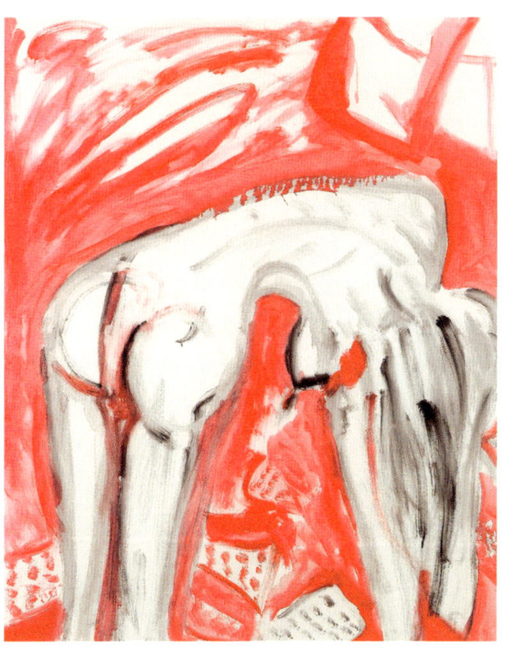

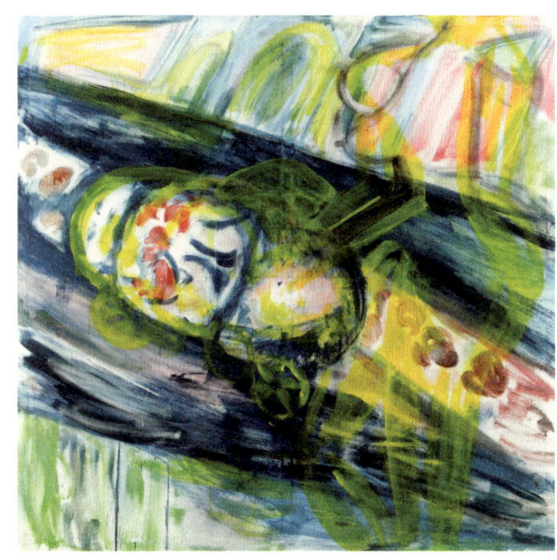

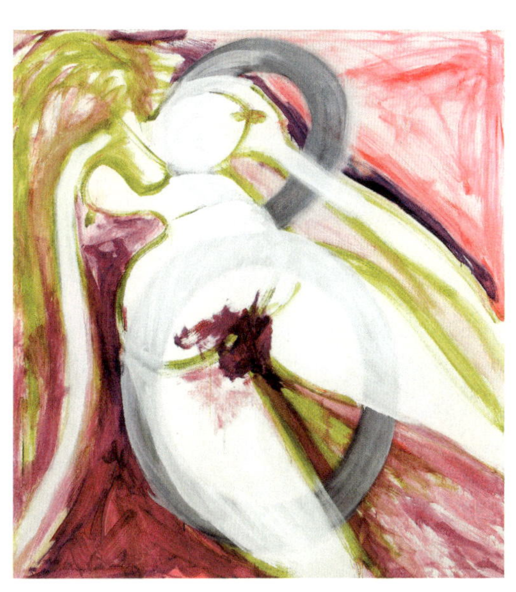

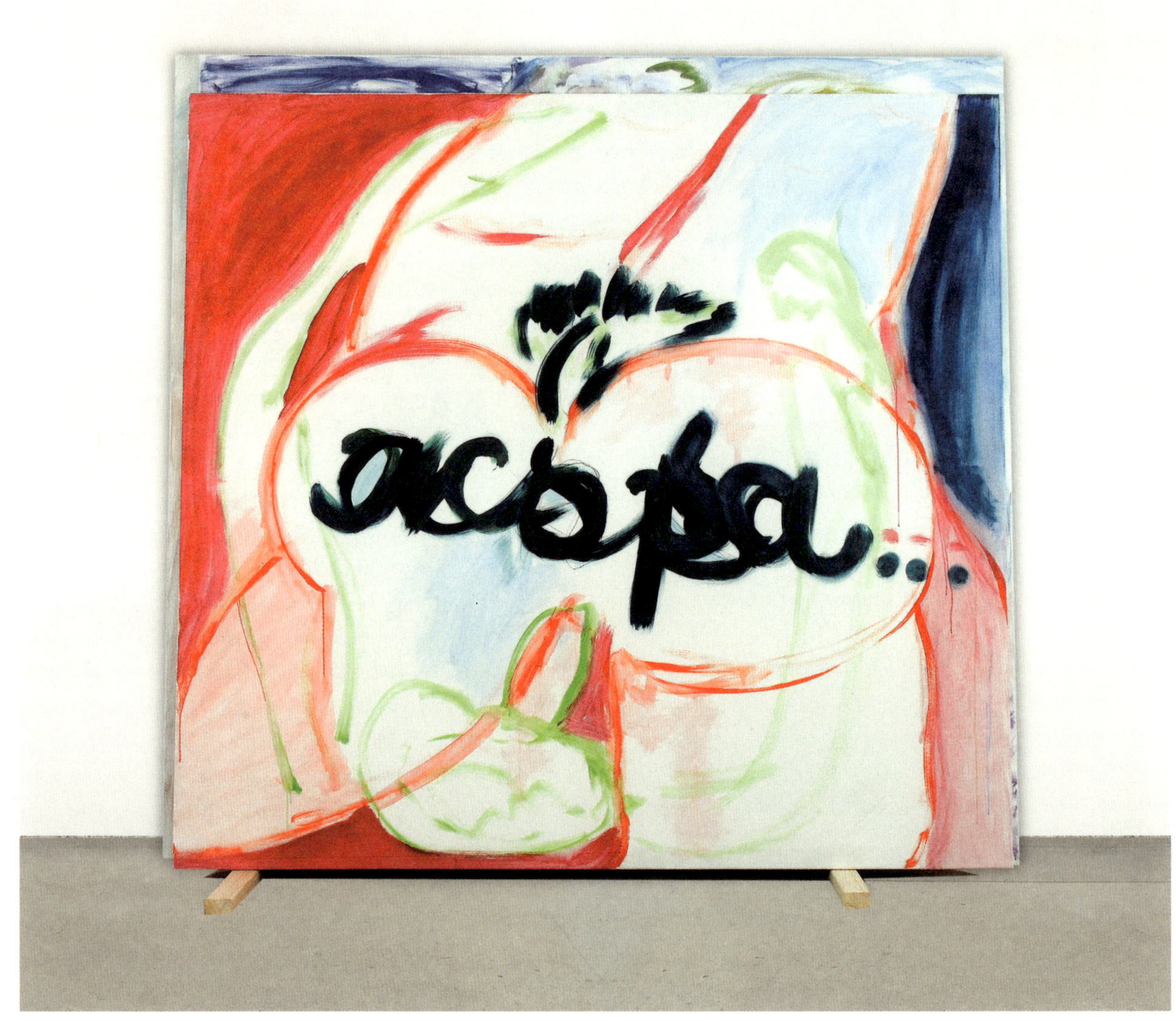

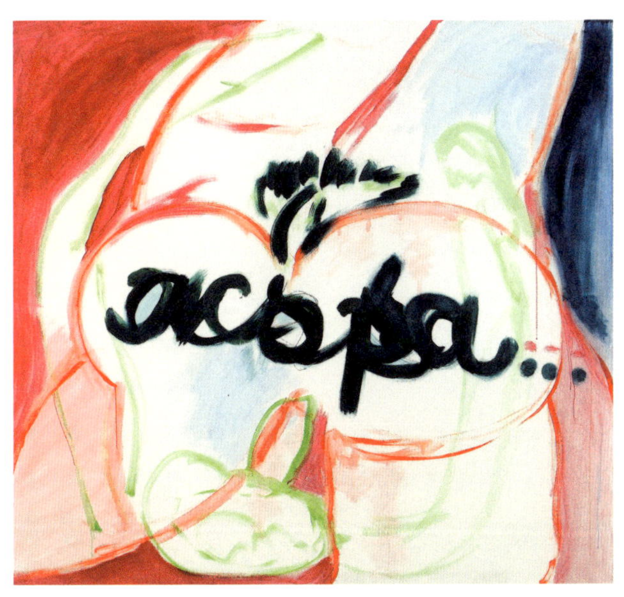

acapa...

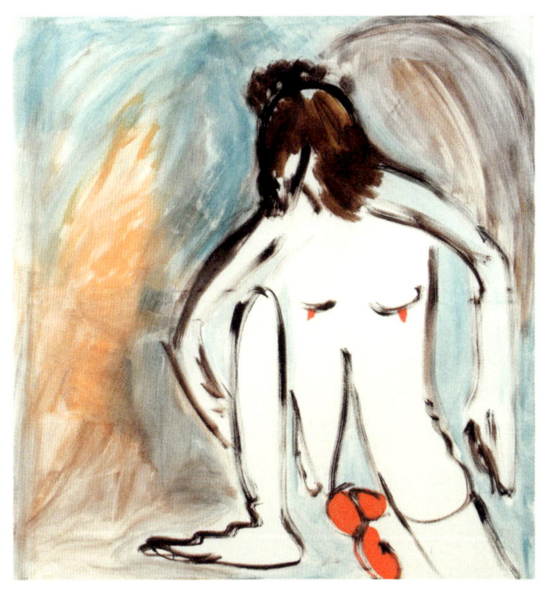

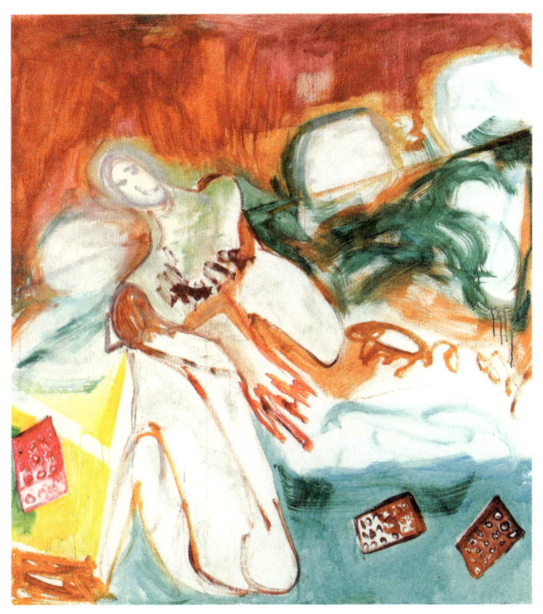

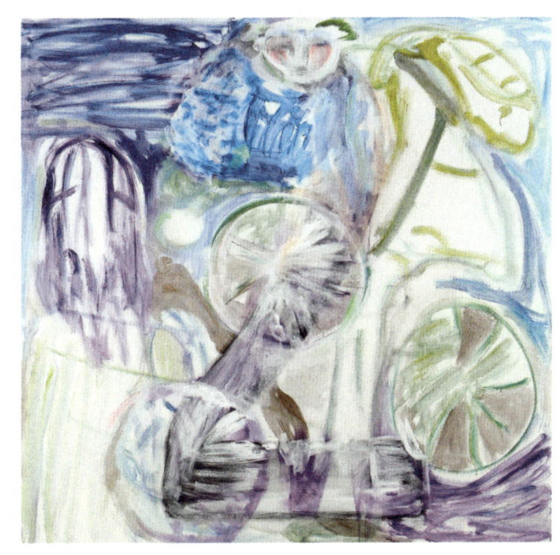

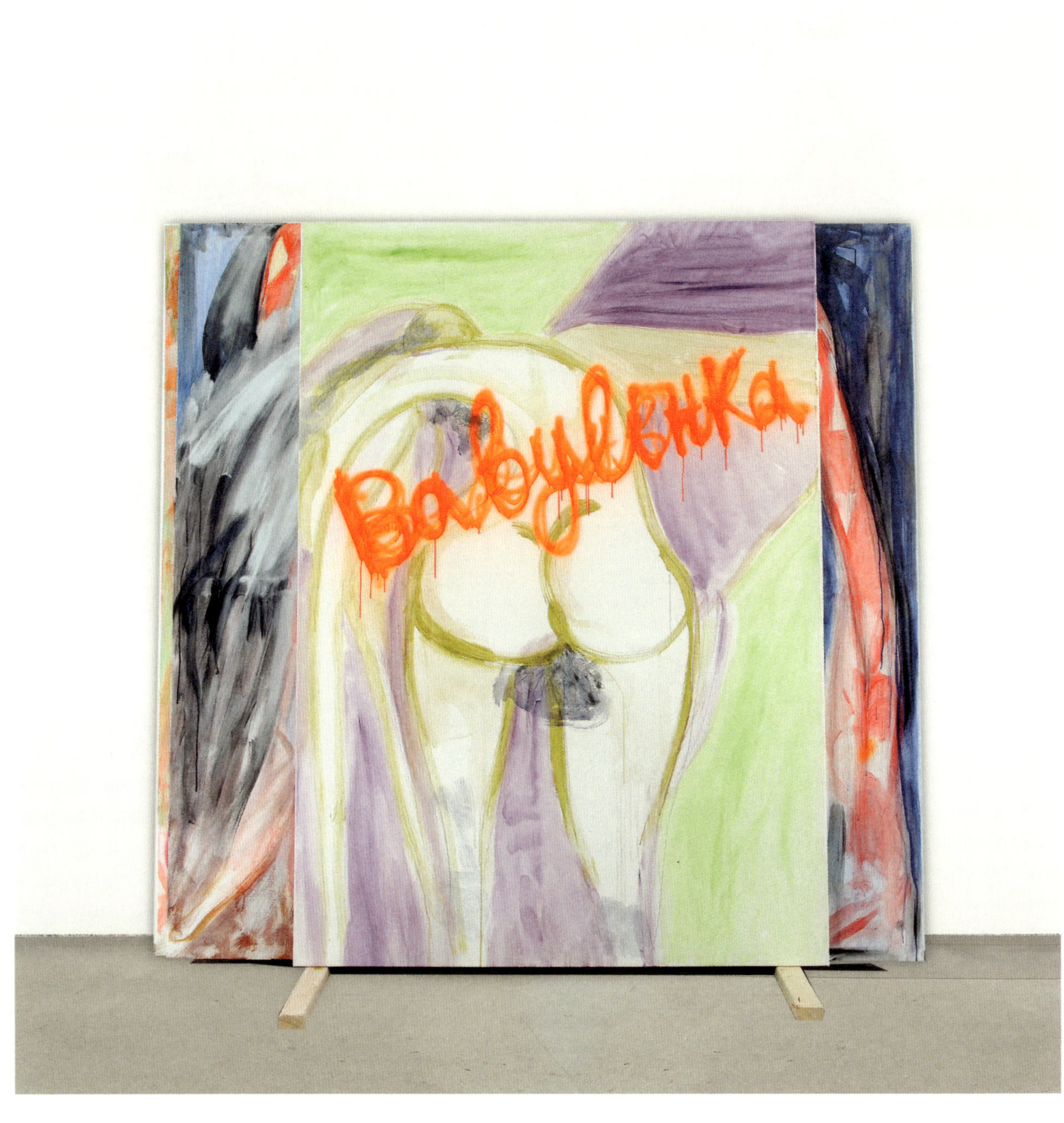
Бабуленка

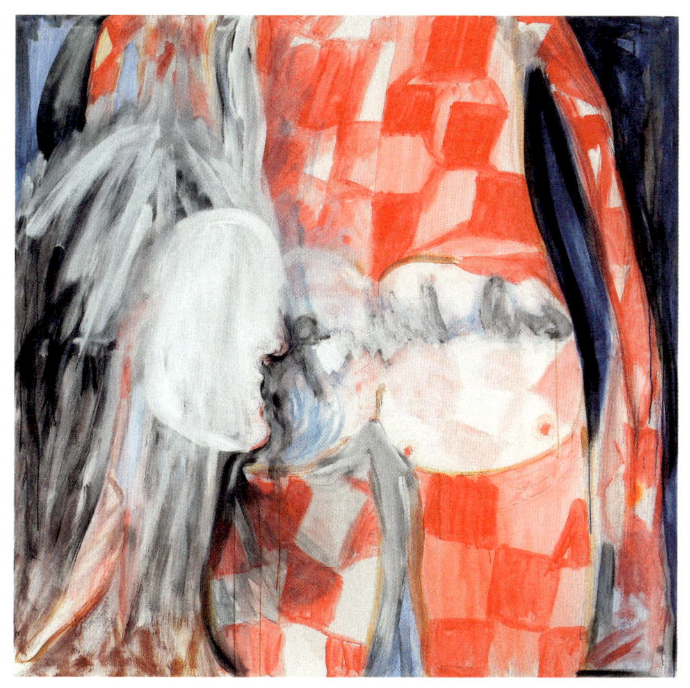

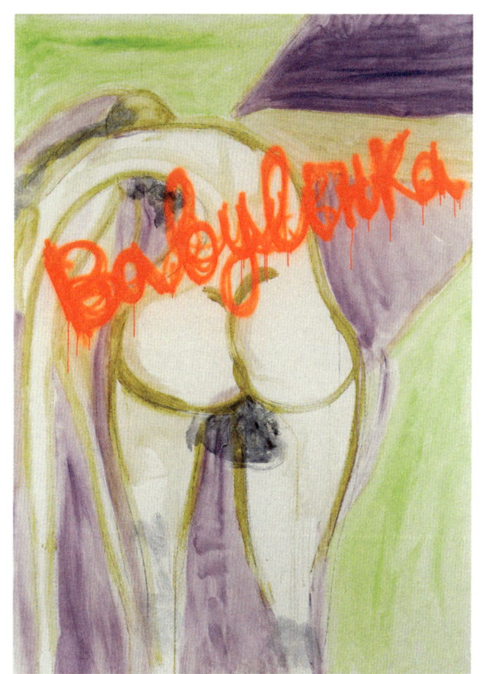

Бабуленка

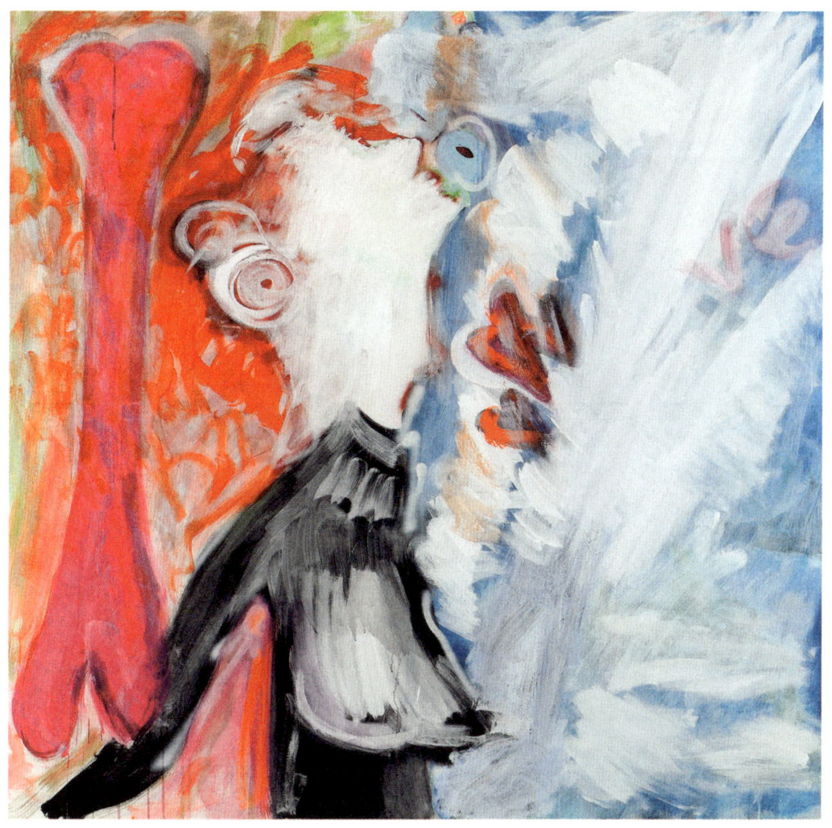

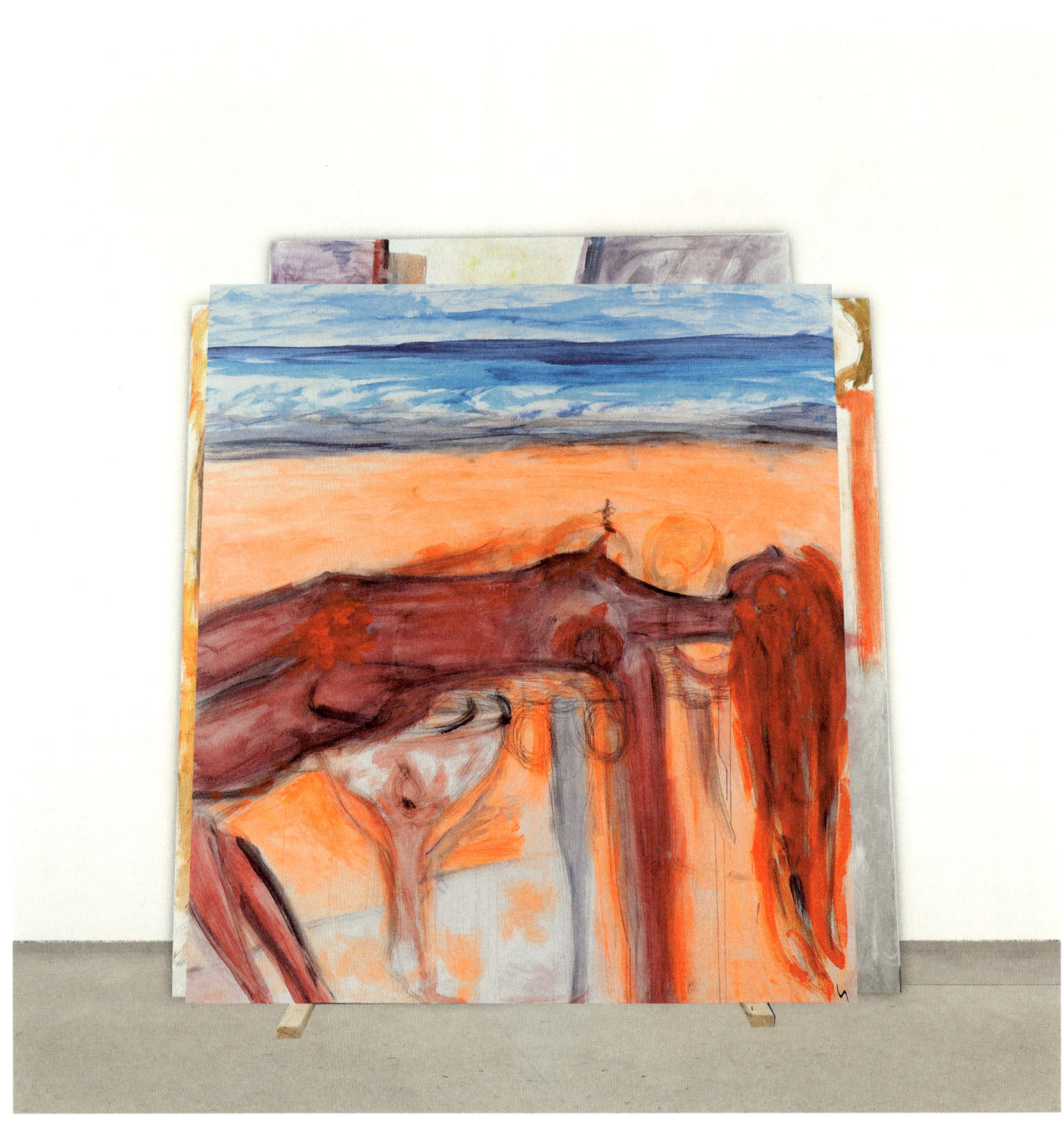

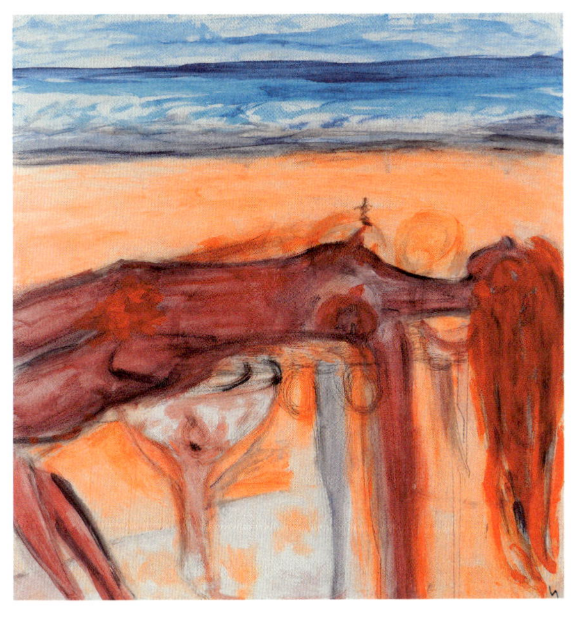

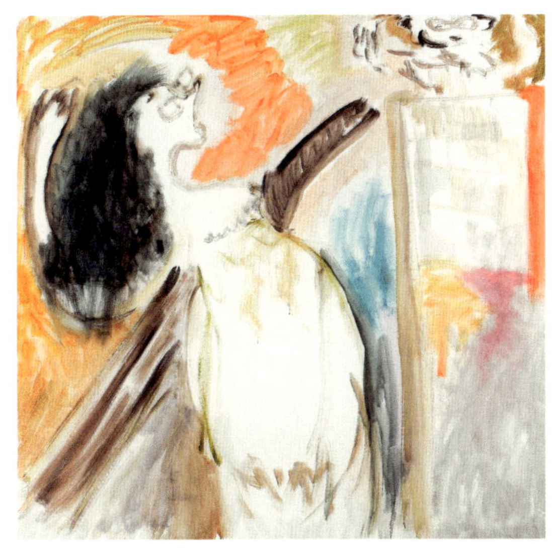

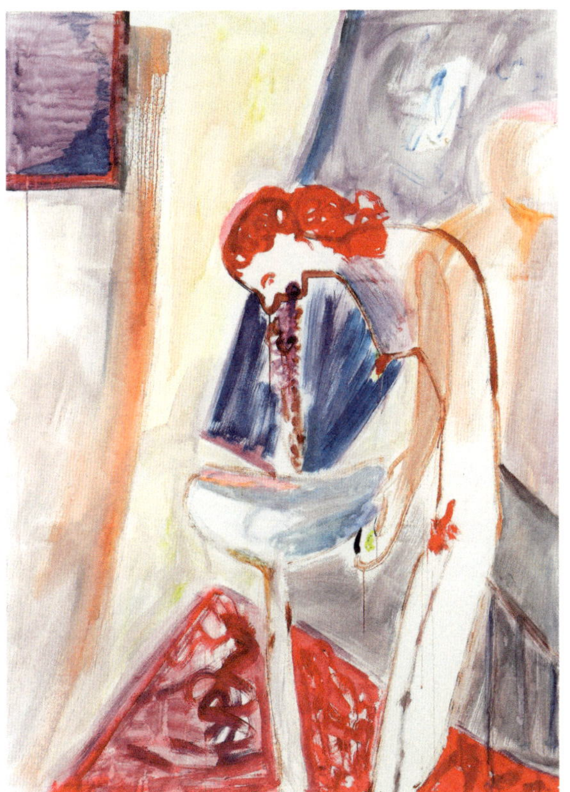

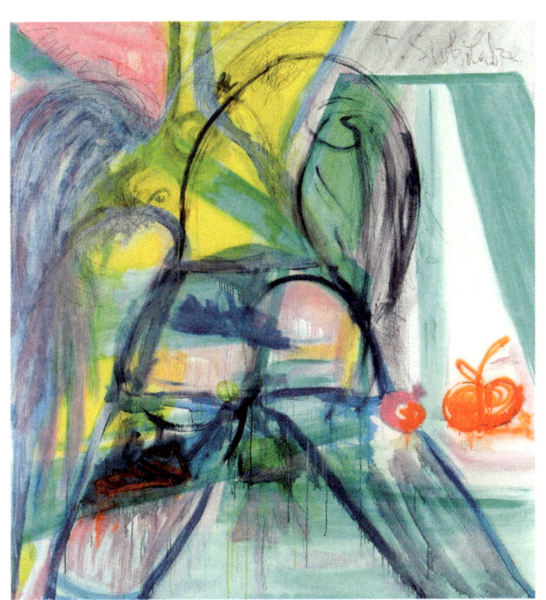

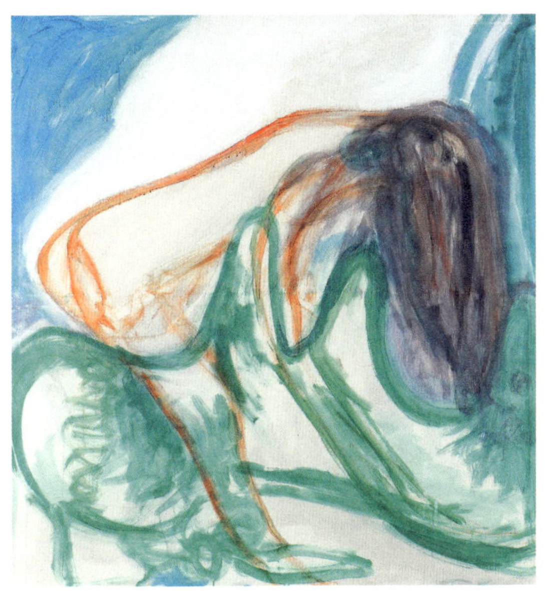

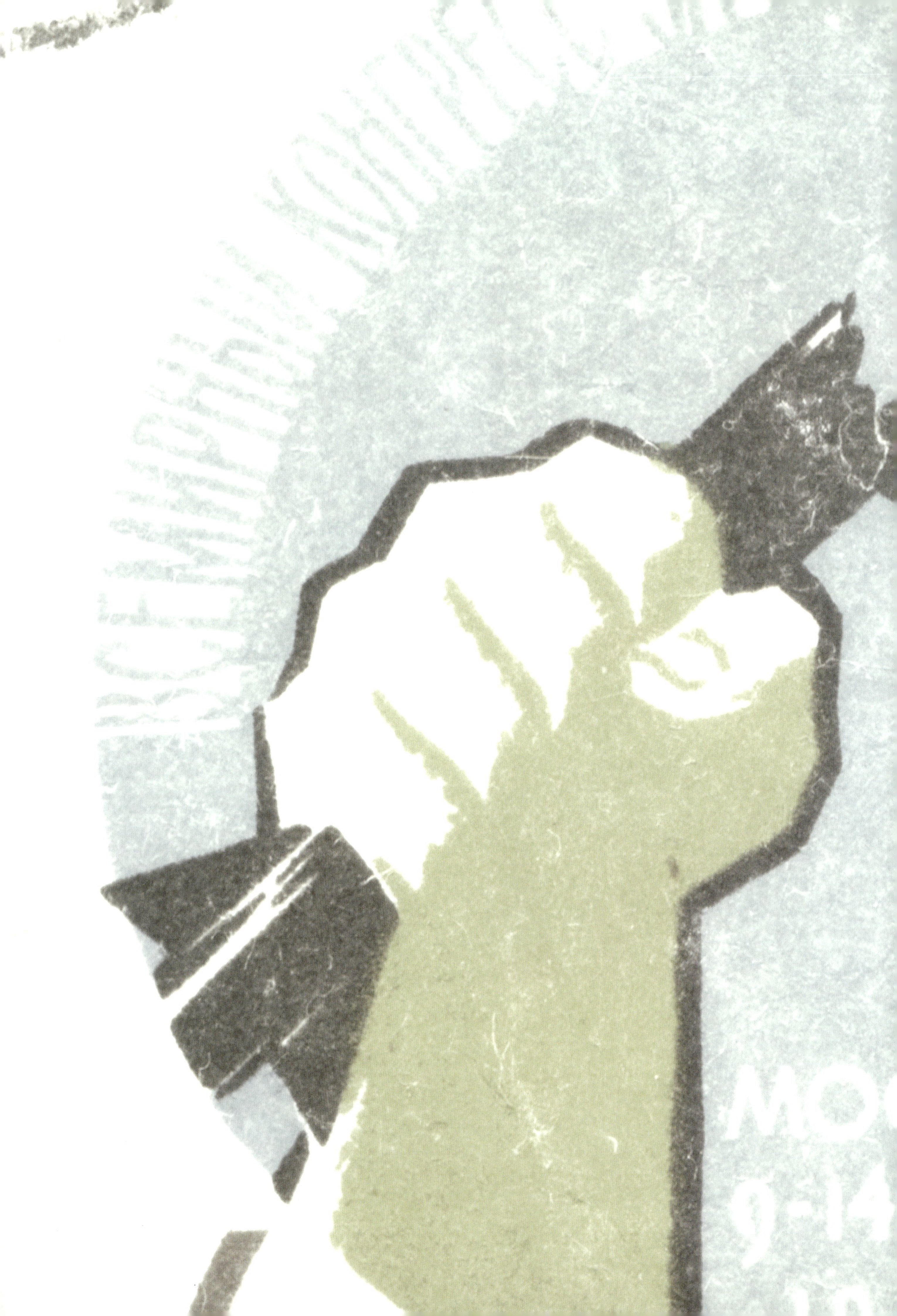

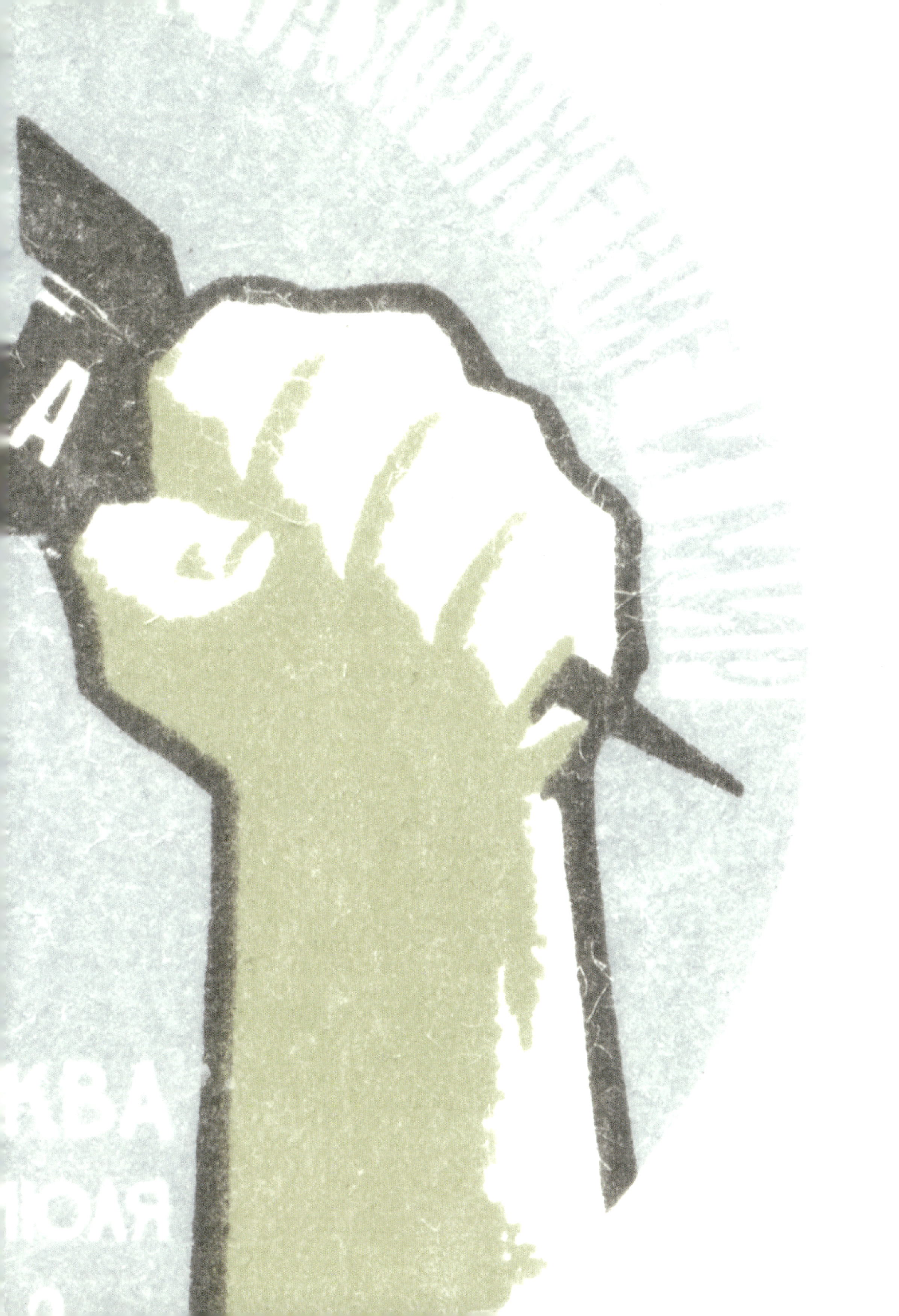

SERGEI VASILIEV

Taken between 1989 and 1993, Sergei Vasiliev's photographs of Soviet prisoners document the secret code language of criminals in the USSR, evidence of a gritty spirit of picaresque resistance within a violently repressive culture.

Vasiliev worked as staff photographer for a newspaper in Chelyabinsk for thirty years, during which time he was also a prison warden. From 1948 onward, a fellow worker, Danzig Baldaev, had begun drawing and cataloguing the extensive range of designs made by prisoners onto their skin. These homemade tattoos, scraped and inked into skin with melted book heels, urine or blood, contained a whole range of coded messages against the Soviet regime and about the prisoners' individual crimes.

Although this kind of tattooing was actually illegal, and Baldaev was initially forbidden from continuing, the KGB realised what a resource it could be for their criminal files and eventually supported his documentary project. Vasiliev was brought in to supply hard evidence of the designs' authenticity. Raunchy, grotesque, filled in with insults against the authorities, the imagery developed its own formulas and conventions; for example, a skull means top criminality, a cat is a thief, and so on. To have no tattoos would have meant the lowest status, a lack of toughness; to have certain tattoos could be the sign of an untouchable.

Thanks to their efforts, the secret police, and us now, know more about the iconography of this underground artistic phenomenon. Far from being isolated illustrations from a catalogue in a tattoo parlour, Vasiliev's photographs are a humanizing record that places the faces and bodies of the owners (at one point one in five of the Soviet population) right at the centre of the project.

SV-01

RUSSIAN CRIMINAL TATTOO
ENCYCLOPAEDIA PRINT NO.12, 2010
Giclée print
165 x 112 cm

SV-08

RUSSIAN CRIMINAL TATTOO
ENCYCLOPAEDIA PRINT NO.8, 2010
Giclée print
165 x 112 cm

SV-02

RUSSIAN CRIMINAL TATTOO
ENCYCLOPAEDIA PRINT NO.9, 2010
Giclée print
165 x 112 cm

SV-09

RUSSIAN CRIMINAL TATTOO
ENCYCLOPAEDIA PRINT NO.13, 2010
Giclée print
165 x 112 cm

SV-03

RUSSIAN CRIMINAL TATTOO
ENCYCLOPAEDIA PRINT NO.17, 2010
Giclée print
165 x 112 cm

SV-10

RUSSIAN CRIMINAL TATTOO
ENCYCLOPAEDIA PRINT NO.19, 2010
Giclée print
165 x 112 cm

SV-04

RUSSIAN CRIMINAL TATTOO
ENCYCLOPAEDIA PRINT NO.10, 2010
Giclée print
165 x 112 cm

SV-11

RUSSIAN CRIMINAL TATTOO
ENCYCLOPAEDIA PRINT NO.20, 2010
Giclée print
112 x 165 cm

SV-05

RUSSIAN CRIMINAL TATTOO
ENCYCLOPAEDIA PRINT NO.5, 2010
Giclée print
165 x 112 cm

SV-12

RUSSIAN CRIMINAL TATTOO
ENCYCLOPAEDIA PRINT NO.4, 2010
Giclée print
112 x 165 cm

SV-06

RUSSIAN CRIMINAL TATTOO
ENCYCLOPAEDIA PRINT NO.7, 2010
Giclée print
165 x 112 cm

SV-13

RUSSIAN CRIMINAL TATTOO
ENCYCLOPAEDIA PRINT NO.18, 2010
Giclée print
112 x 165 cm

SV-07

RUSSIAN CRIMINAL TATTOO
ENCYCLOPAEDIA PRINT NO.15, 2010
Giclée print
165 x 112 cm

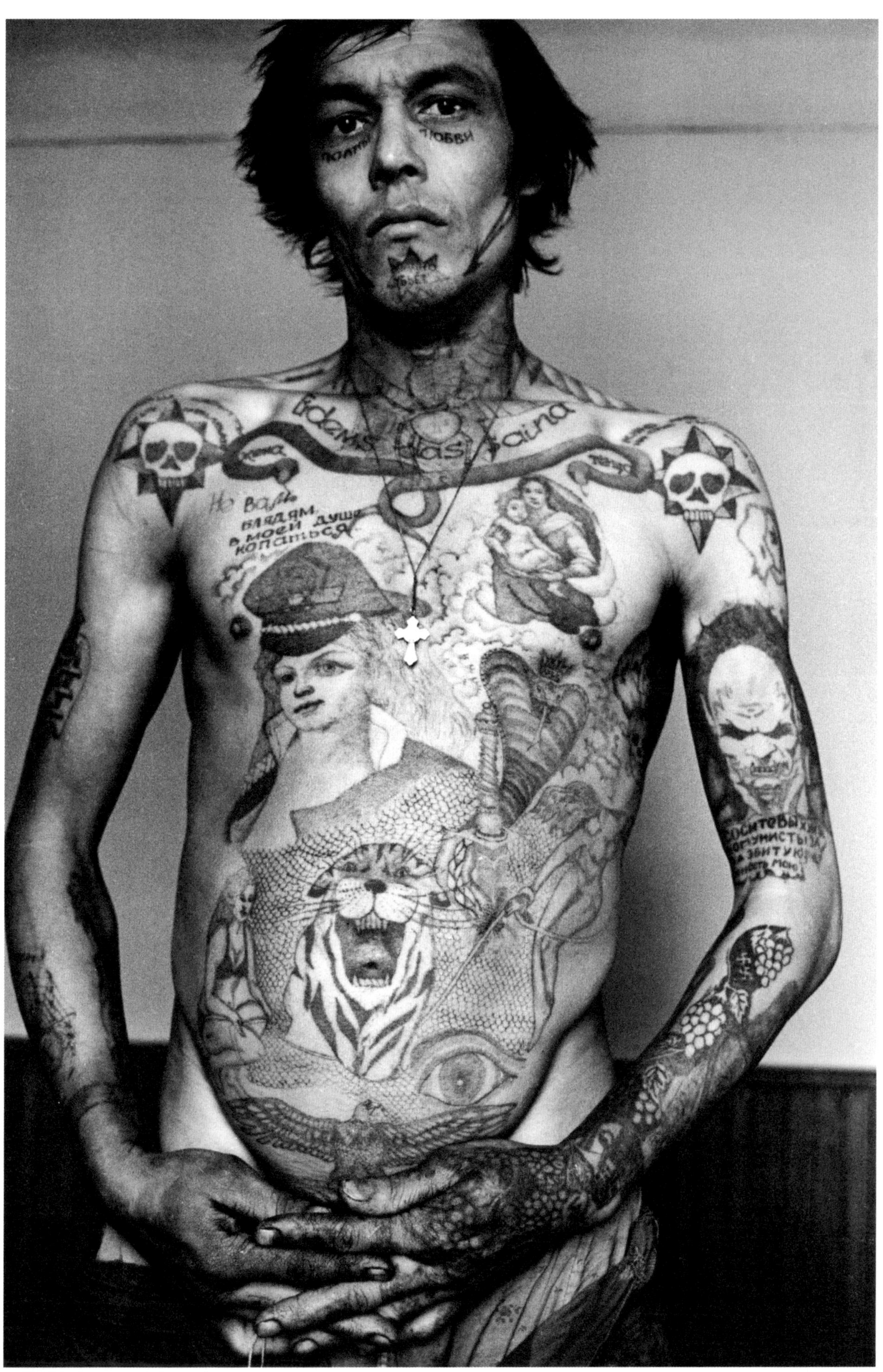

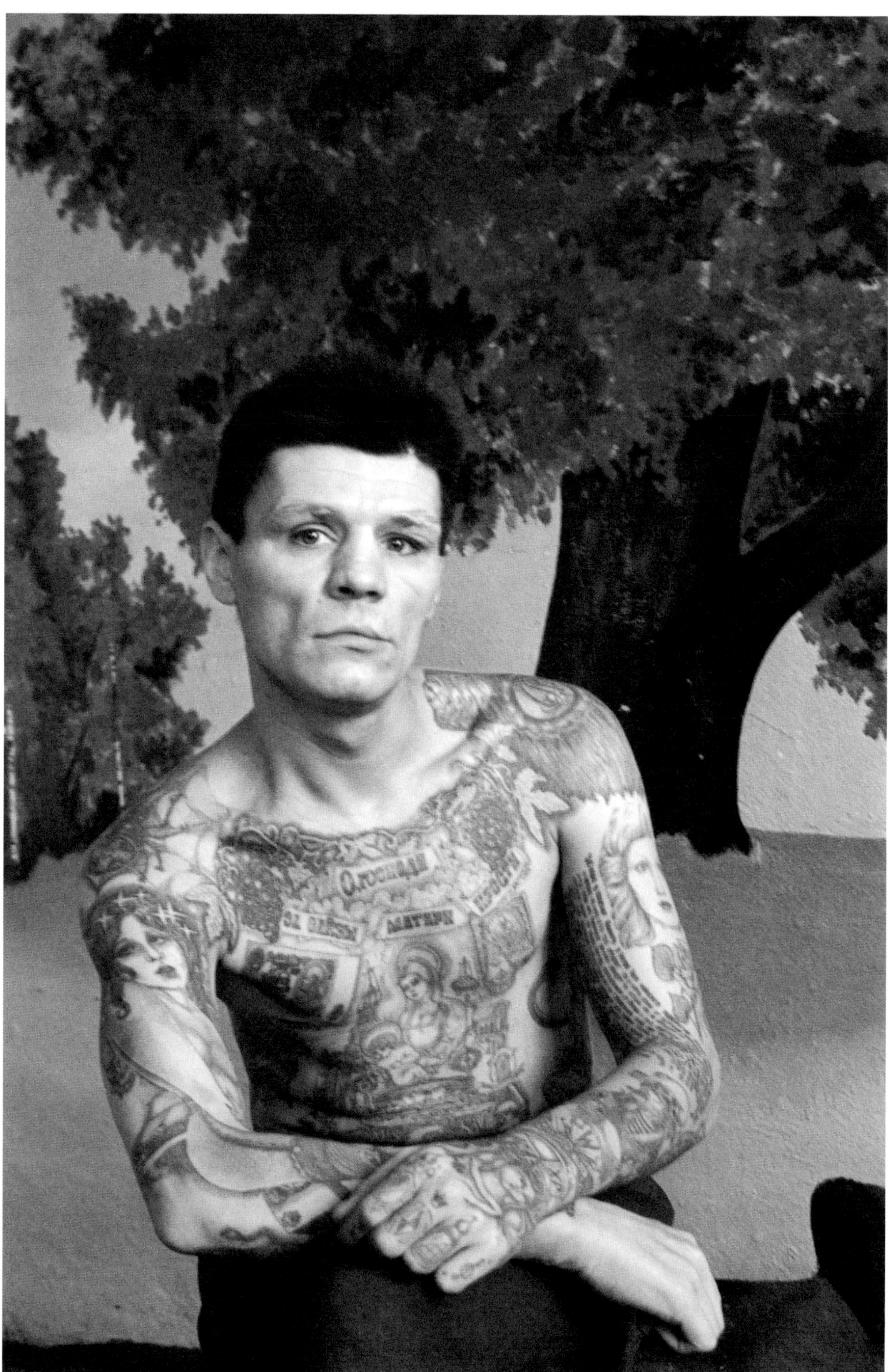

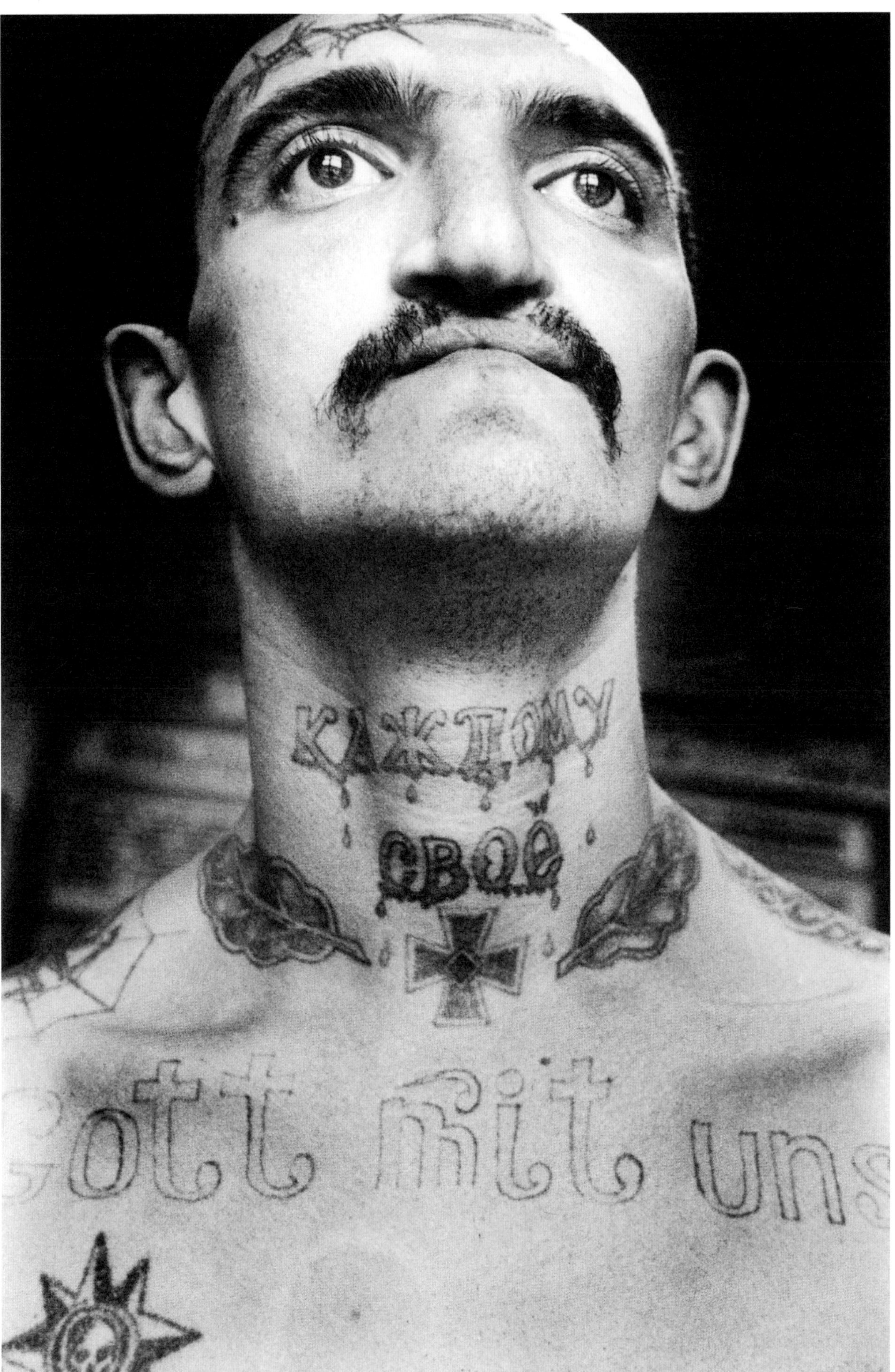

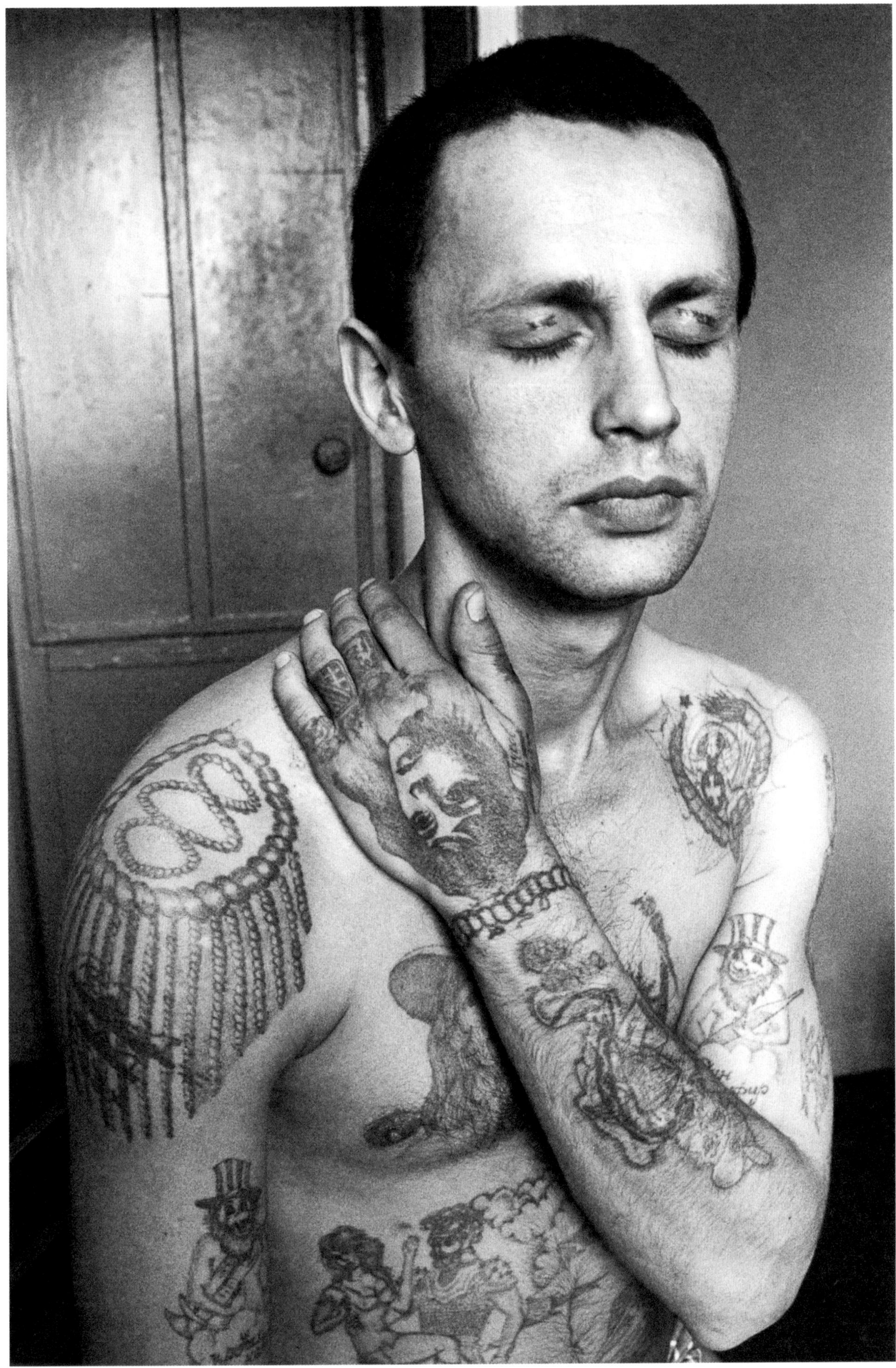

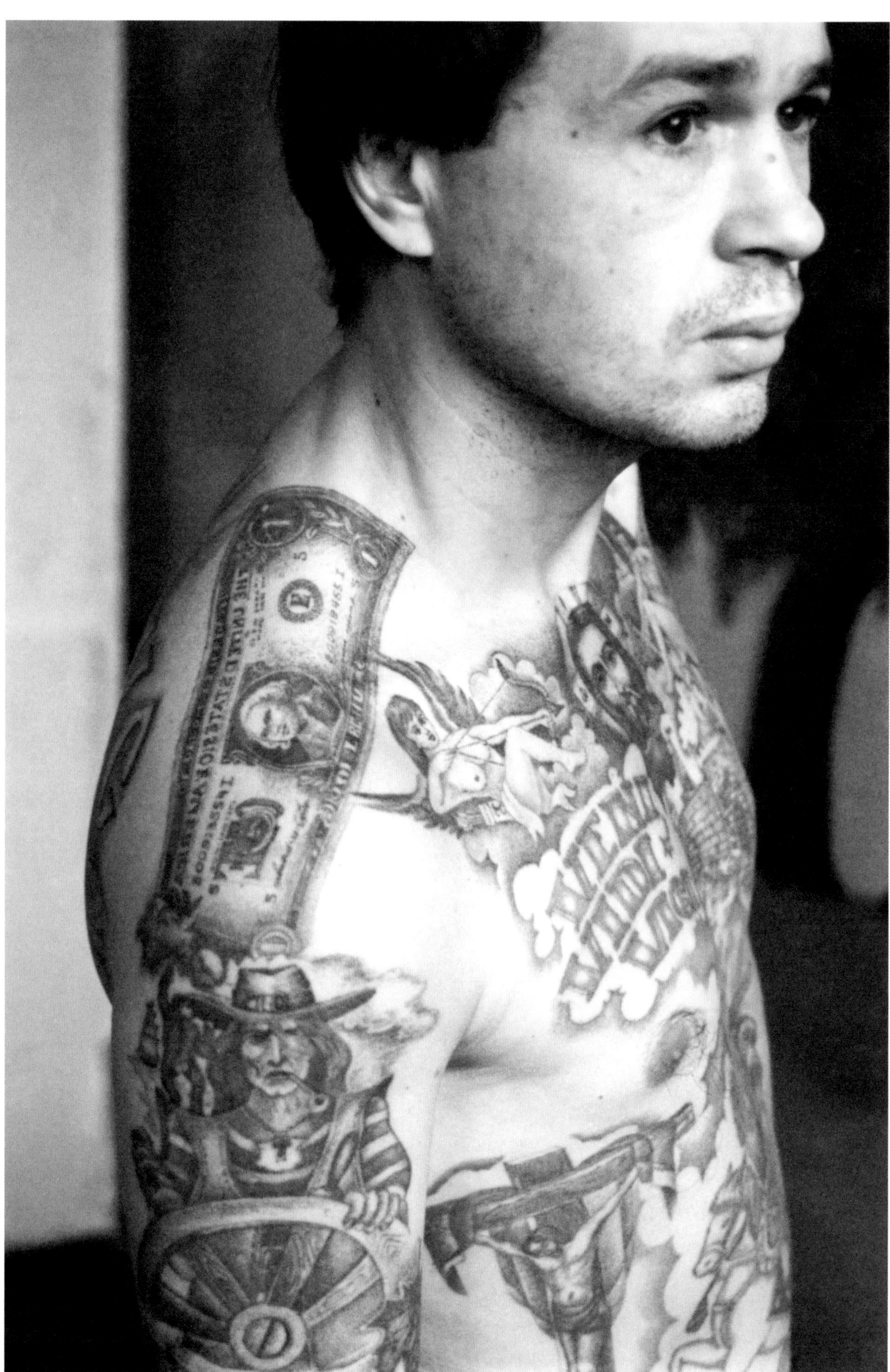

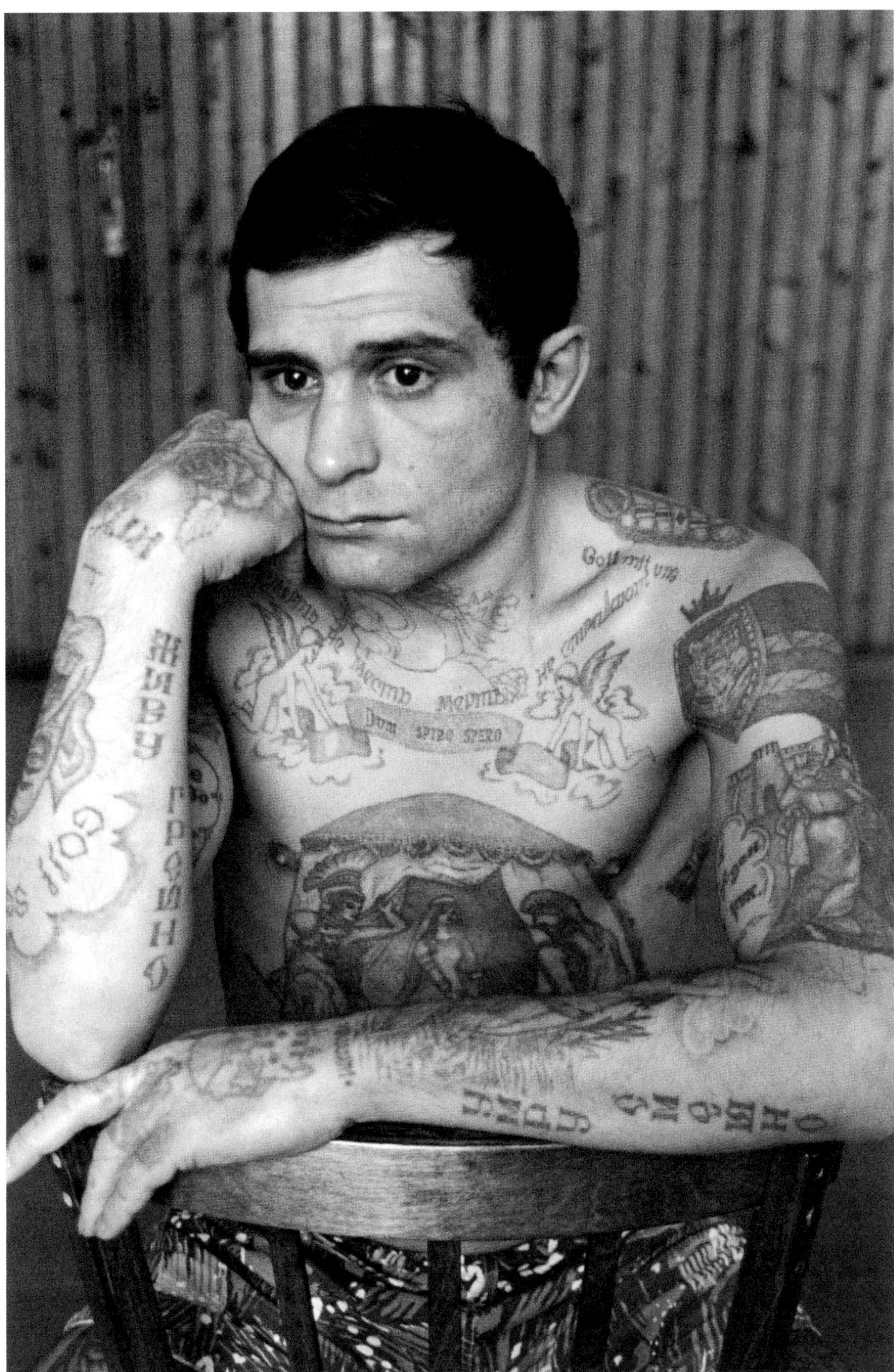

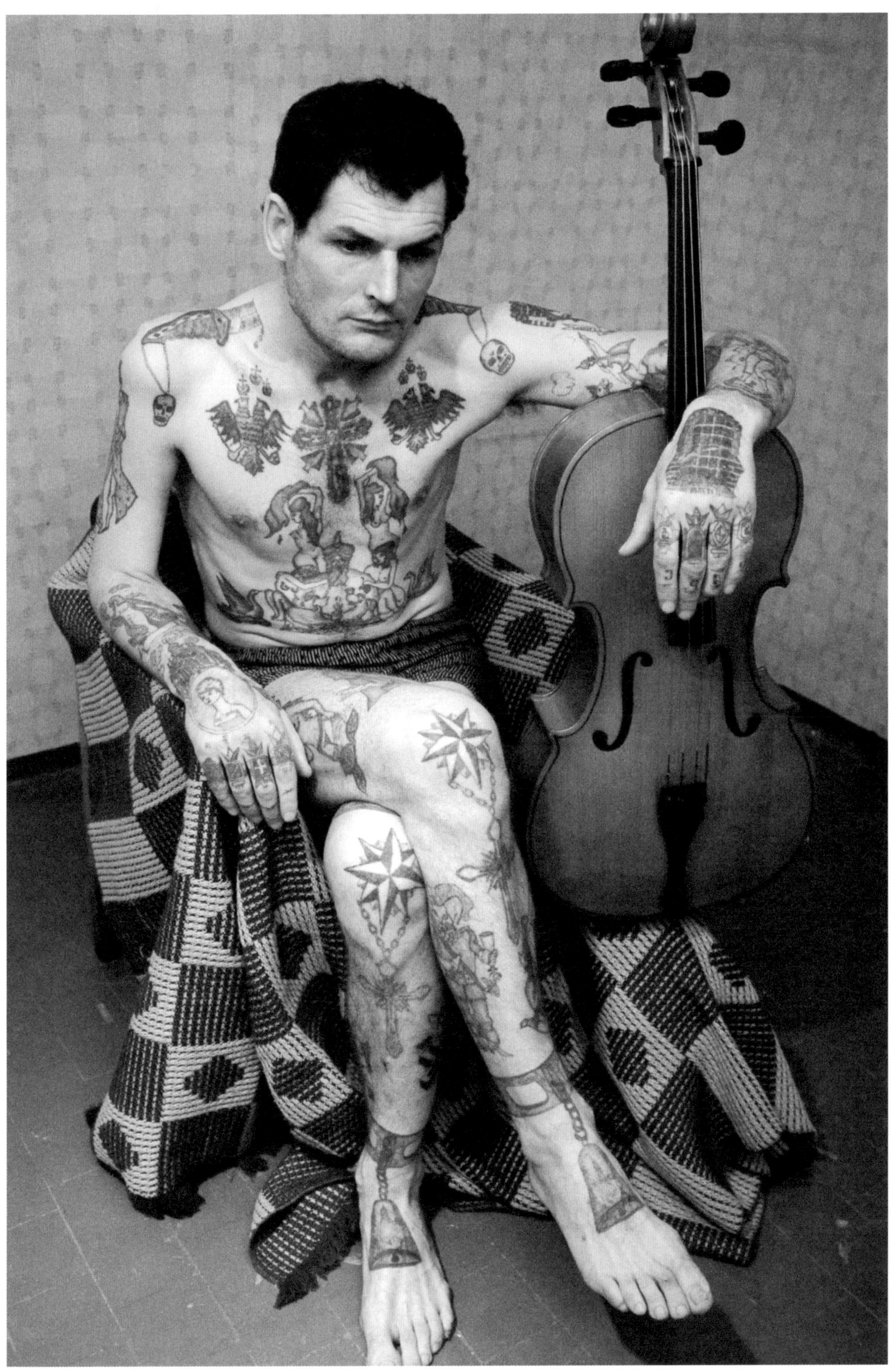

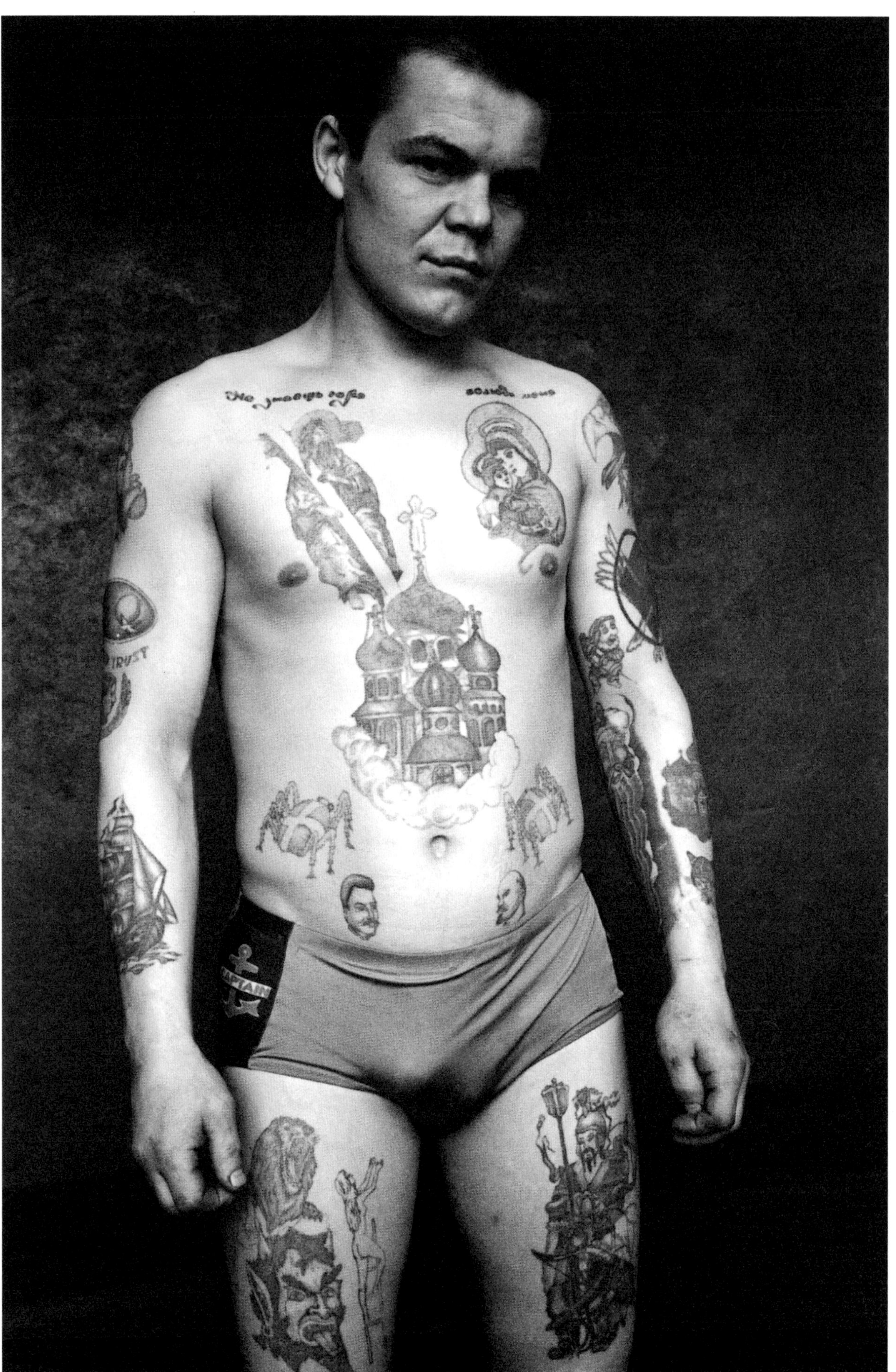

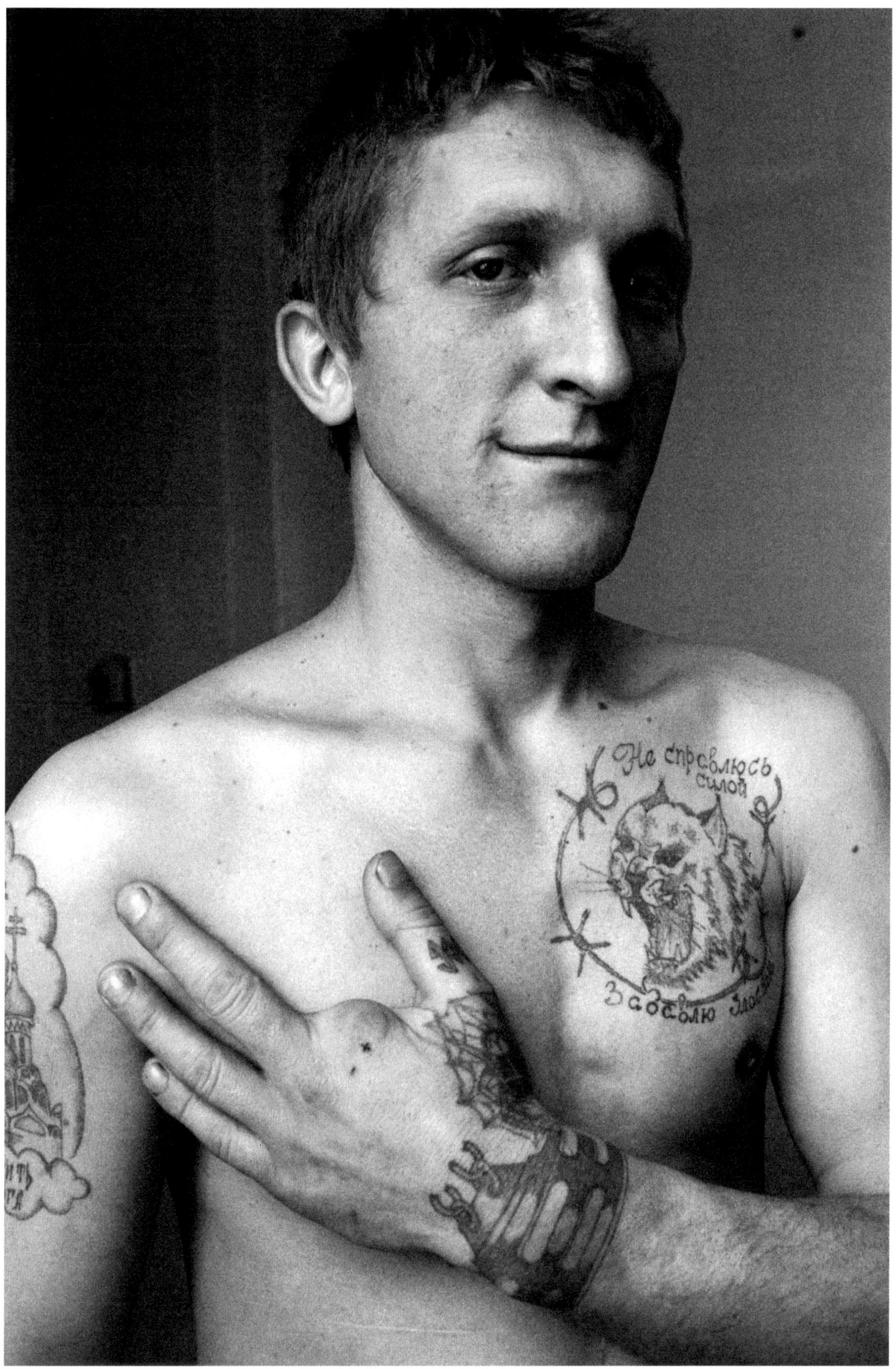
Не справлюсь силой
За волю злобой

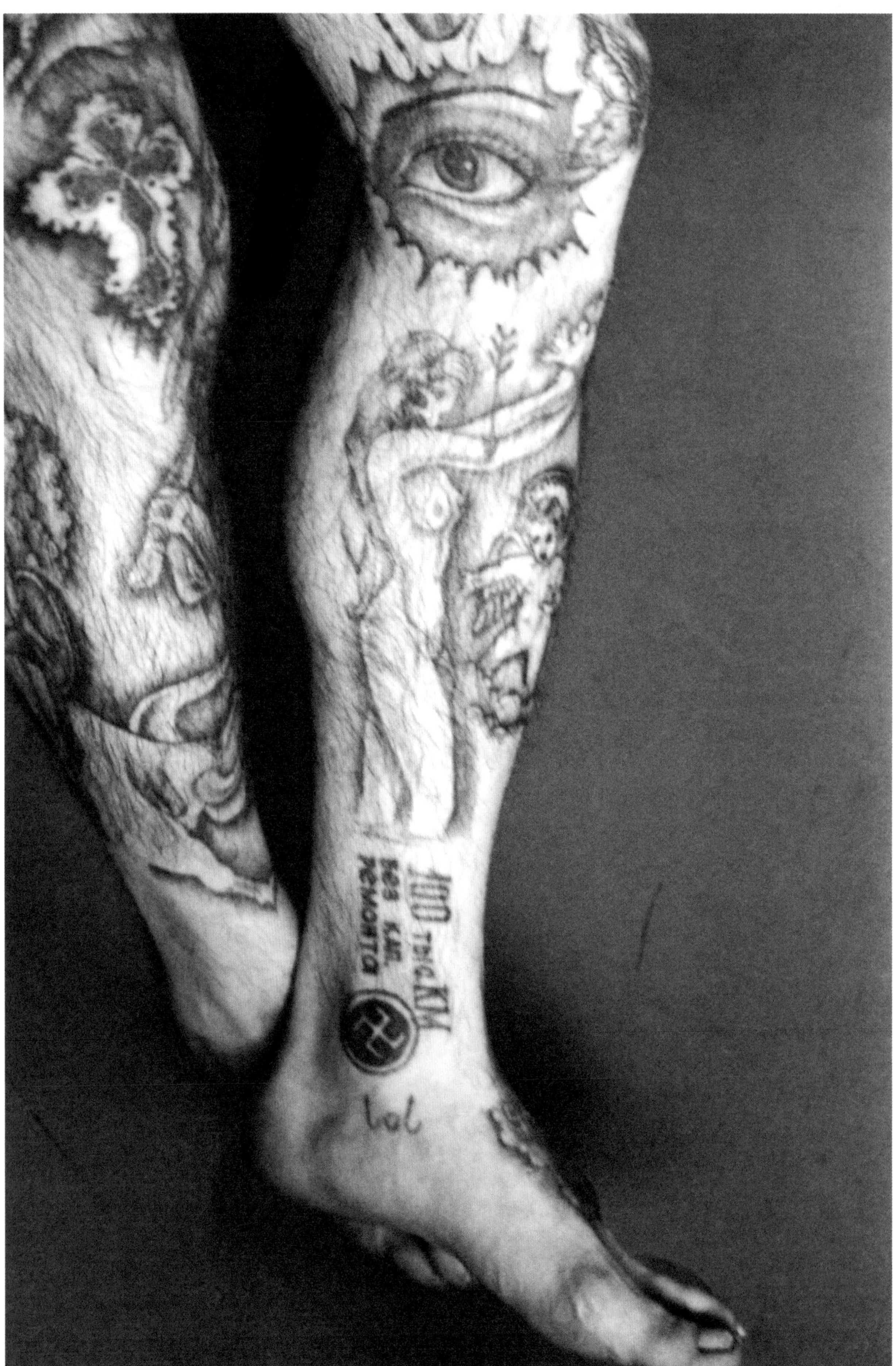

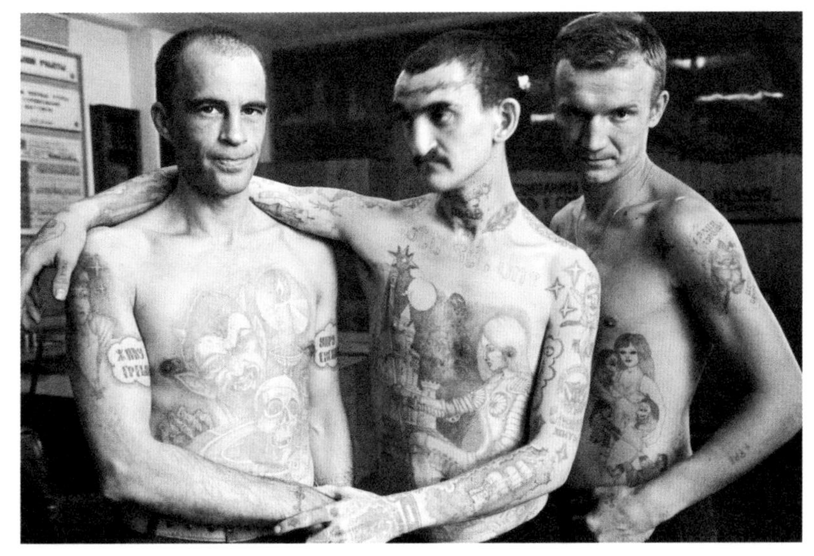

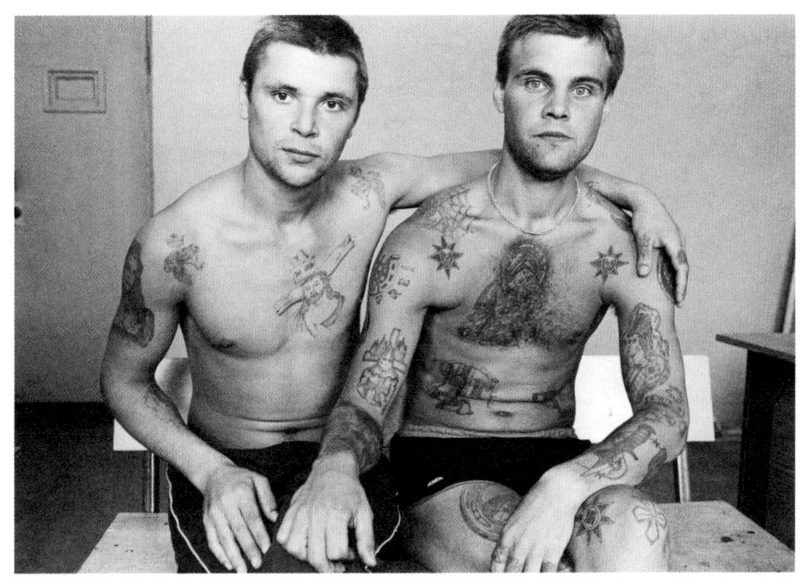

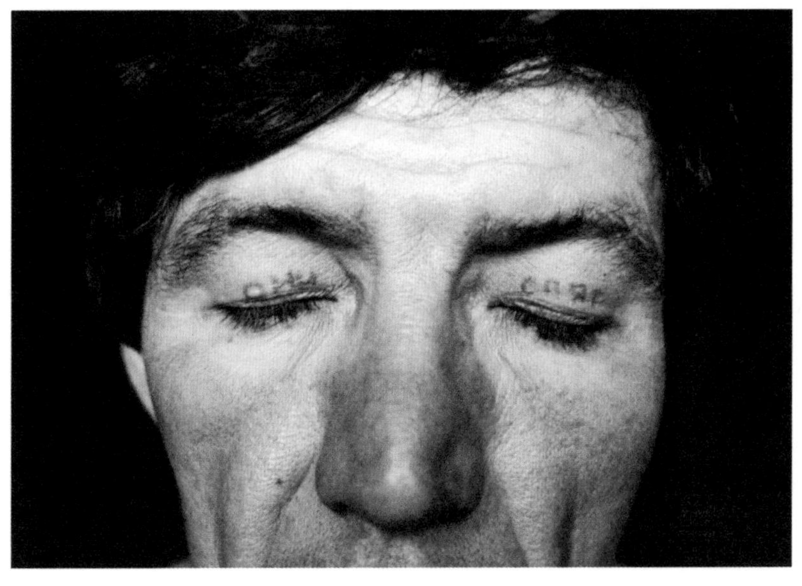

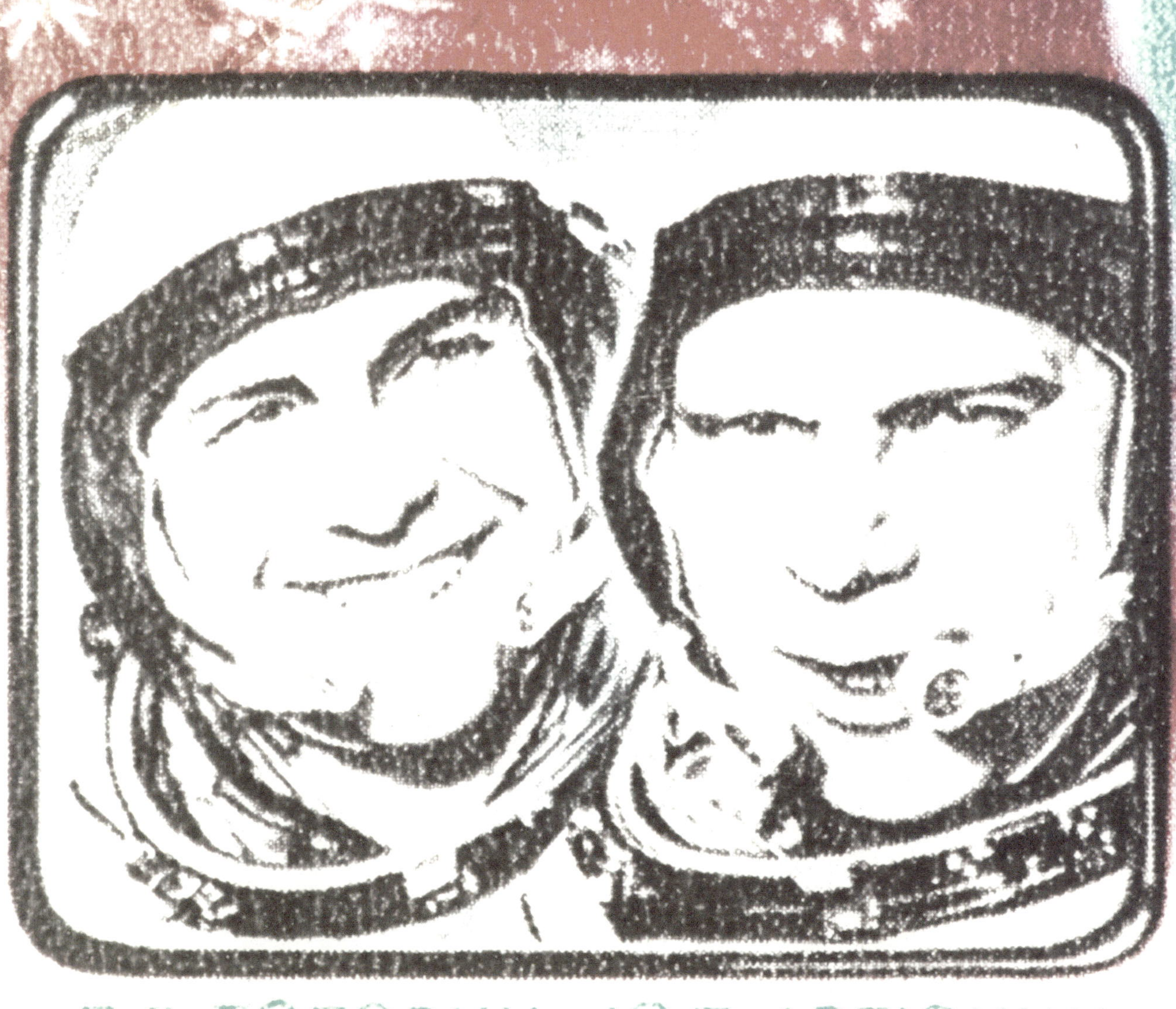

ТРАНСПОРТНЫЙ КОРАБЛЬ „СОЮЗ-14"
3 — 19 ИЮЛЯ
П.Р. ПОПОВИЧ   Ю.П. АРТЮХИН
10 к
1974
ПОЧТА СССР

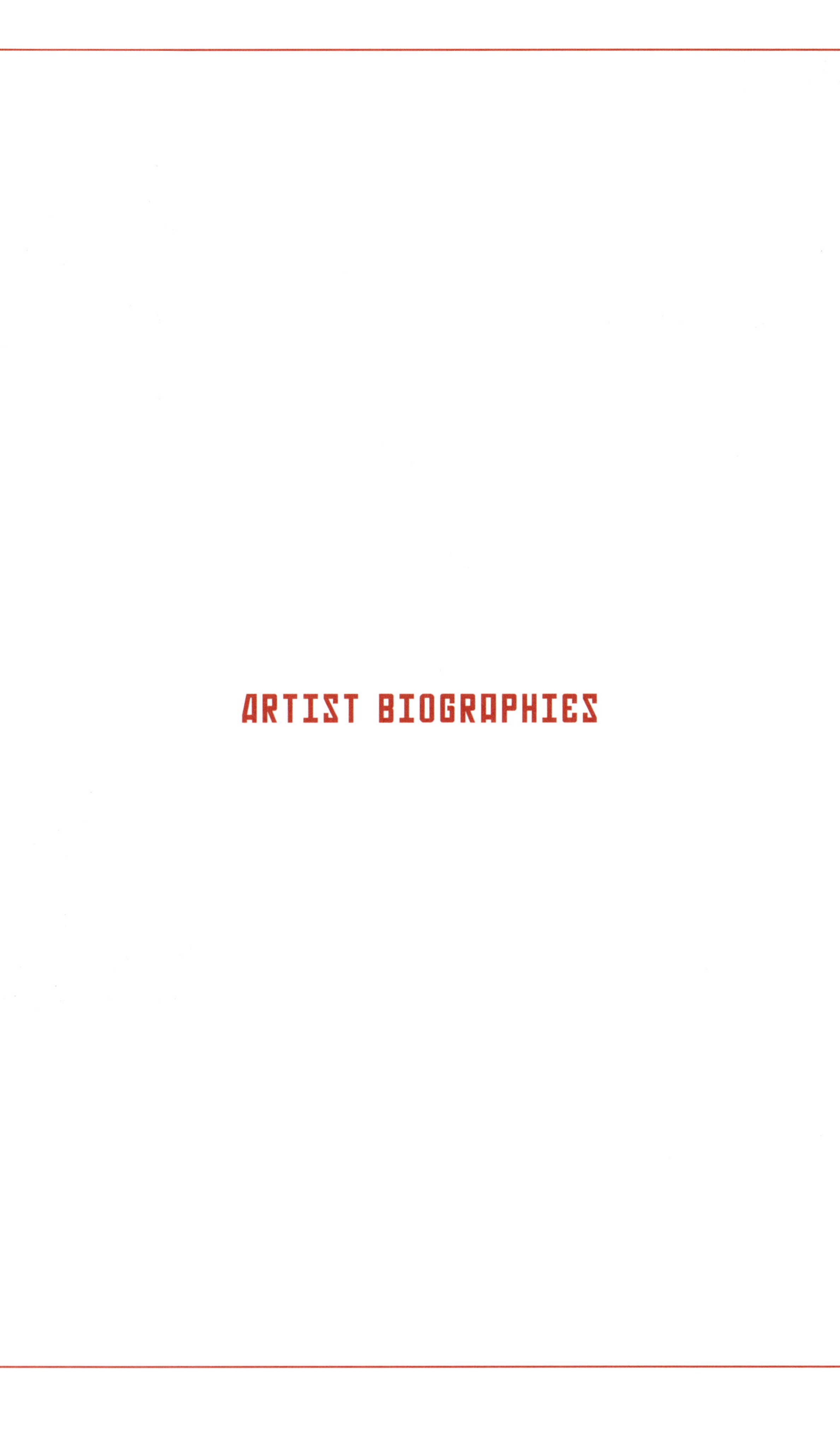

ARTIST BIOGRAPHIES

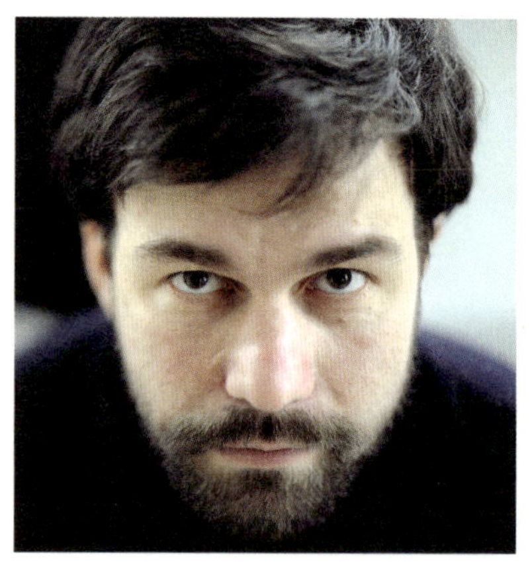

JANIS AVOTINS

Janis Avotins was born in the Soviet Union in 1981. He studied at the Janis Rozentals School of Fine Art, Latvia, and received an MA in Painting from the Latvian Academy of Art in 2003. Avotins has since had solo shows at IBID Projects, London; Rüdiger Schöttle, Munich; Akinci Gallery, Amsterdam; Ludwig Forum in Aachen, Germany; and Johnen Gallery, Berlin. He has exhibited in group shows at the Riga Art Space, Latvia; Hudson Valley Center for Contemporary Art, New York; Remap2, Athens; and Marianne Boesky Gallery, New York. He was selected to exhibit in the second and third Prague Biennales and the 2010 Vilnius Painting Triennale. Avotins lives and works in Riga, Latvia.

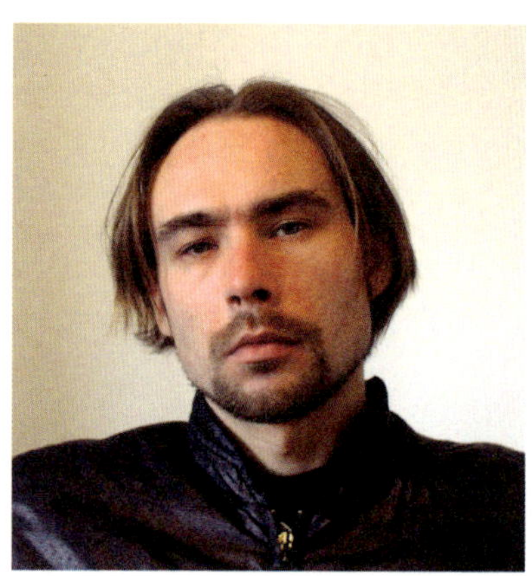

DANIEL BRAGIN

Daniel Bragin was born in Moscow in 1981. He studied in the sculpture department at ArtEZ institute of the Arts, Enschede, The Netherlands, and is currently studying at the Royal College of Art, London. Bragin has recently had his first major solo show at the Closed Gallery, Thessaloniki, Greece, and his work has been exhibited in group shows at Langestraat 56, Enschede; Twente Biennale 2011, Hengelo, The Netherlands; ArtOlive Jong Talent 2011, Amsterdam; and The DeltA Center of Contemporary Art, The Hague. He lives and works in London and Amsterdam.

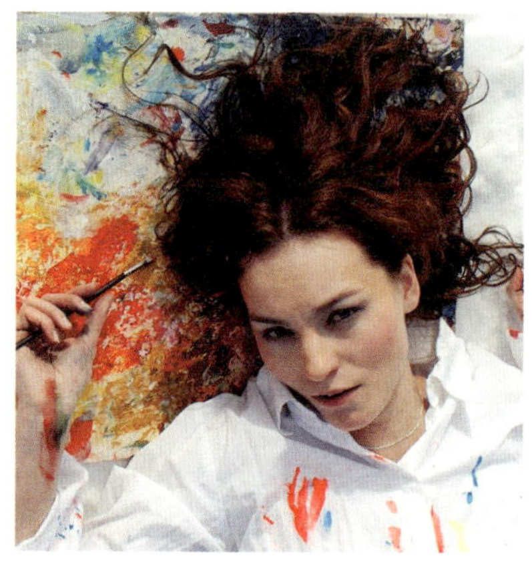

DASHA FURSEY

Dasha Fursey was born in St. Petersburg in 1983, where she studied at the city's Academy of Fine Art. Her work has been exhibited in solo shows at A&C Projects, New York; Schuebbe Projects, Dusseldorf; Galerie Orel Art, Paris; and Freud's Dream Museum, St. Petersburg. She has also exhibited in group shows at the second Ural Industrial Biennale of Contemporary Art, Yekaterinburg; the 53rd Venice Biennale, The State Hermitage Museum, St. Petersburg; Vostochnaya Gallery, Moscow; and the Museum of Modern and Contemporary Art of Trento and Rovereto, Italy. She lives and works in St.Petersburg, London and Paris.

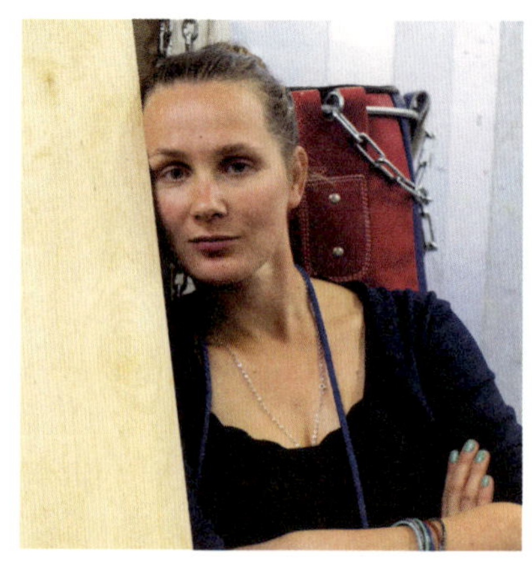

LIUDMILA KONSTANTINOVA

Liudmila Konstantinova was born in Moscow in 1980. She has exhibited in group and solo shows at Sotheby's, the 2011 Moscow Biennale of Contemporary Art; ArtRU Gallery, Lenivka Gallery, M&J Gallery and Centre of Contemporary Art Winzavod, all in Moscow, and at Les Salaisons, Romanville, France, and Kunstvlaai 6, Amsterdam. Konstantinova lives and works in Moscow.

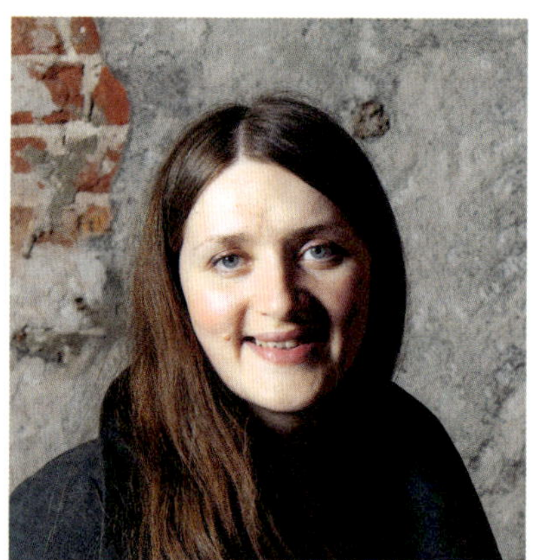

IRINA KORINA

Irina Korina was born in Moscow in 1977. She studied Stage Design at the Russian Theater Academy, Moscow, before studying at Kunstakademie, Vienna. Korina has had solo shows at Scaramouche Gallery, New York; MMCA and XL Gallery, Moscow; and Bloomberg Space, London. Her work has been shown in group exhibitions in Arts Santa Mònica, Barcelona; Galerija SC, Zagreb; PAC,

Milan; Garage CCC and Baibakov Art Projects, Moscow. She was selected to participate in the 2009 X Baltic Triennial of International Art, Vilnius, and in the Russian Pavilion at the 53rd Venice Biennale. Korina lives and works in Moscow.

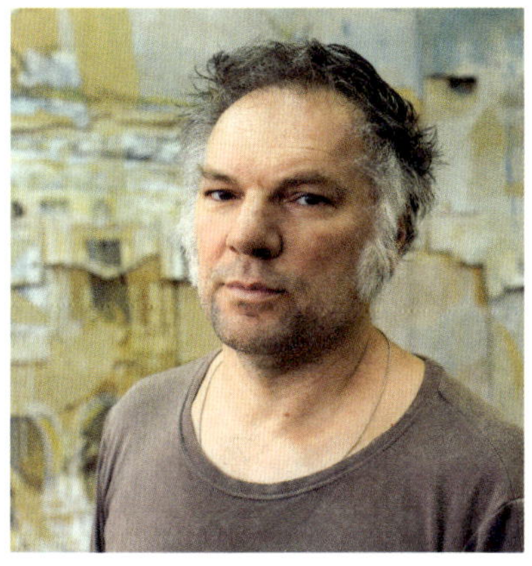

VALERY KOSHLYAKOV

Valery Koshlyakov was born in Salsk, Russia, in 1962. Koshlyakov studied at the Rostov-on-Don Higher Art School, Russia, and became a member of the artistic association Art or Death in 1988. He has had solo shows at Galerie Michael Schultz, Berlin; Nina Lumer Gallery, Milan; Ludwig Galerie Schloss Oberhausen, Oberhausen; Galerie Krinzinger, Vienna; Galerie Orel Art, Paris; and Walter Bischoff Galerie, Berlin. Koshlyakov has exhibited in group shows at the Musée du Louvre, Paris; the Guggenheim Museum, New York; Garage CCC, Moscow; Musée Ingres, Montauban, France; and the Pinchuk Art Centre, Kiev. He was selected for the 3rd Moscow Biennale in 2009. He lives and works in Moscow.

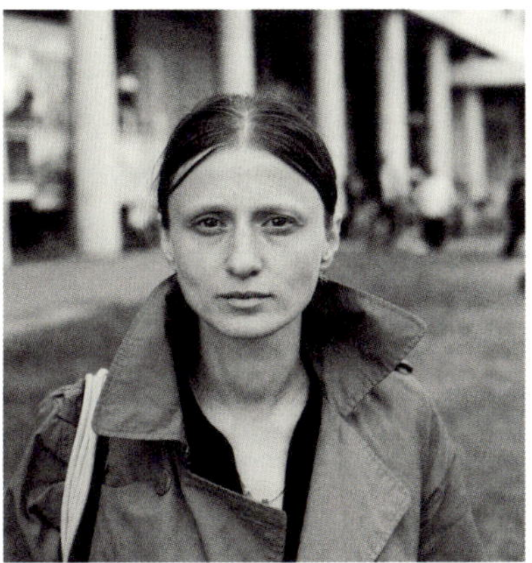

DARIA KROTOVA

Daria Krotova was born in Moscow in 1971. She studied Psychology and History of Art before training in Fine Art in France and Russia. She has had solo shows in Moscow at Galerie Iragui, Garage CCC, V Glaz Gallery, and at Roots Contemporary, Brussels. She has exhibited in group shows at Guelman Gallery, and Baibakov Art Projects, Moscow. Krotova was selected to participate in several special projects at the 2011 Moscow Biennale of Contemporary Art and has exhibited at Art Moscow Fair and Fast Art 2 and 3 in Moscow. She lives and works in France and Moscow.

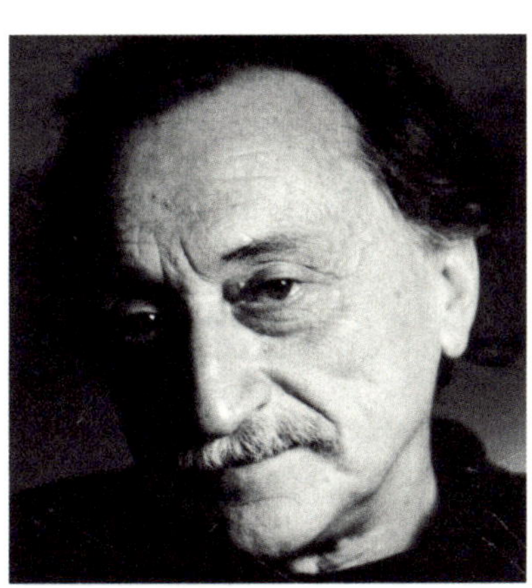

BORIS MIKHAILOV

Boris Mikhailov was born in Kharkov, in the former USSR, in 1938. Mikhailov is a self-taught photographer and has had solo shows at Sprovieri Gallery, London; La criée - centre d'art contemporain, Rennes, France; MoMA, New York; Spregel Museum, Hanover; Deweer Gallery, Belgium; Galerie Barbara Weiss, Berlin; and The Photographers' Gallery, London. He has also been in group shows at Tate Modern, London; Pinchuk Art Centre, Kiev; Fotomuseum Winterthur, Switzerland; Pace/MacGill Gallery, New York; Victoria and Albert Museum, London; Mori Art Museum, Tokyo; and he was selected for the Ukrainian Pavilion at the 52nd Venice Biennale. Mikhailov lives and works in Berlin and Kharkov.

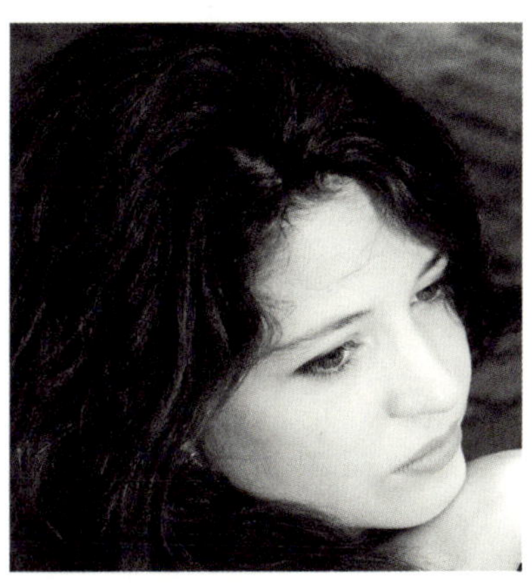

NIKA NEELOVA

Nika Neelova was born in Moscow in 1987. She studied for a BA in Fine Art at the Royal Academy of Fine Art, The Hague, before graduating with an MFA (Sculpture) from the Slade School of Fine Art, London. She has had solo shows at Jarmuschek + Partner, Berlin; Charlie Smith Gallery, London; and Scheltema Center, Leiden, The Netherlands. Neelova has exhibited in group shows at Christie's and Somerset House, London; Federica Schiavo Gallery, Rome; Christus Triumphatorkerk, The Hague; QASIMI Homme, Paris; and Torrance Art Museum, US. She won the 2010 New Sensations Prize. Neelova lives and works in London.

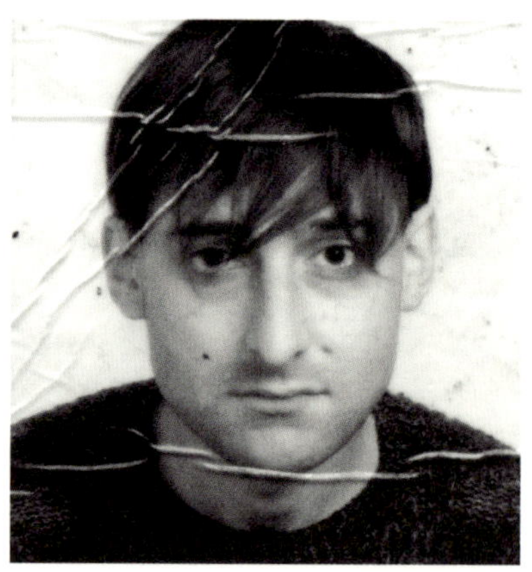

VIKENTI NILIN

Vikenti Nilin was born in 1971 in Moscow. He has had many solo shows in Moscow at European Mission, XL Gallery, State Tretyakov Gallery, DOM Club, and REFLEX Gallery. His work has been exhibited in group shows in Moscow at Central House of Artists, Andrey Sakharov Museum, Gogol Club, XI Project Gallery and Jamez Gallery; and at the Helios Cultural Center, Toyama, Japan. Nilin lives and works in Moscow.

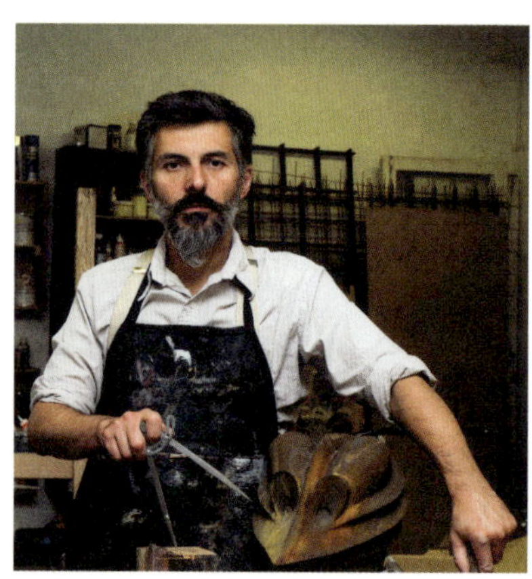

GOSHA OSTRETSOV

Gosha Ostretsov was born in Moscow in 1967. He studied at the Bolshoi Theatre School of Theatre Design, Moscow, and has exhibited in solo shows at Rabouan Moussion Gallery, Paris; Paradise Row, London; Marat Guelman Gallery, Triumph Gallery and Central House of Artists, Moscow. His work has been shown in group exhibitions at TM Project Gallery, Geneva; Baibakov Projects and Centre for Contemporary Art Winzavod, Moscow; and Flowers East, London. He was selected to exhibit in the 2008 Moscow Photo Biennial. Ostretsov lives and works in Moscow.

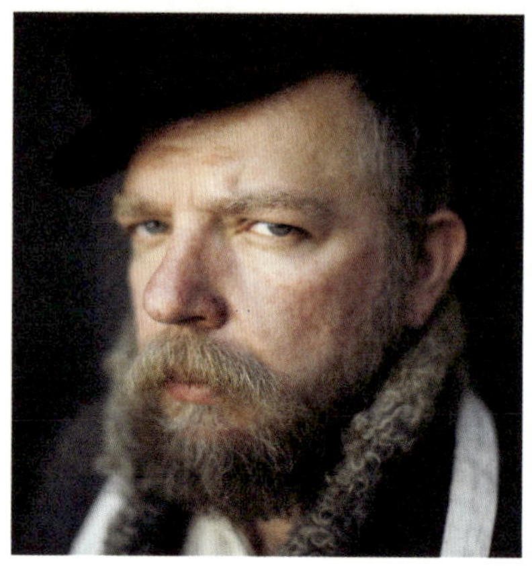

SERGEY PAKHOMOV

Sergey Pakhomov was born in Moscow in 1966. Pakhomov has exhibited in solo shows at Art Raum, Gallery Tseh V and Central House of Artists, Moscow; D137 Gallery, St Petersburg; and KulturKontakt, Austria. He has also exhibited in group shows at Aircraft Gallery, Bratislava; Marat Guelman Gallery, Ruarts Gallery, and Darwin Museum, all in Moscow; and East Side Gallery, Berlin. He was selected to participate in the 4th international Biennial, Königsberg, Russia. Pakhomov lives and works in Moscow.

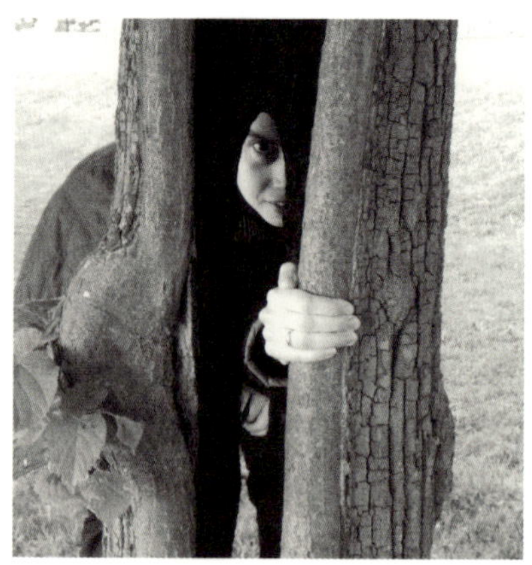

ANNA PARKINA

Anna Parkina was born in Moscow in 1979. She studied at École des Beaux-Arts, Paris and Université Paris 8. Parkina has had solo shows at the San Francisco Museum of Modern Art; Wilkinson Gallery, London; Gladstone Gallery, New York; GMG Gallery, Moscow; COMA and Autocenter, Berlin. She has shown in group exhibitions at Fondazione Sandretto Re Rebaudengo, Turin; KAI 10 Raum Für Kunst, Dusseldorf; CAPC, Bordeaux; and Galerie Eva Winkeler, Frankfurt. She was selected for the 3rd Moscow Biennale and 53rd Venice Biennale in 2009. Parkina lives and works in Moscow.

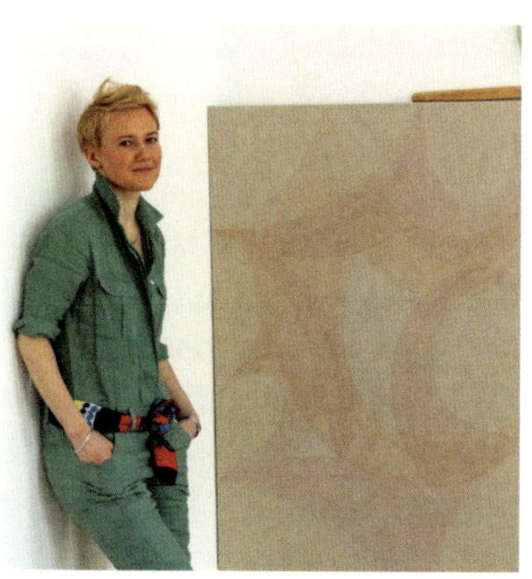

YELENA POPOVA

Yelena Popova was born in Urals, Russia in 1978. She has a BA from Moscow Art Theatre School and an MA from the Royal College of Art, London. Popova has had solo shows at Figge von Rosen Gallery, Berlin; Wallner Gallery, Nottingham; 40 Kvadratov Gallery, Smolensk, Russia; and Hand and Heart Gallery, Nottingham. She has exhibited in group shows at the ICA, London; Project Space, Derby; White Columns Gallery, New York; and Blyth Gallery, Imperial College, London. Popova was shortlisted for the 2011 New Sensations Prize and twice for the Young Artists Biennale, Moscow. Popova lives and works in Nottingham, UK.

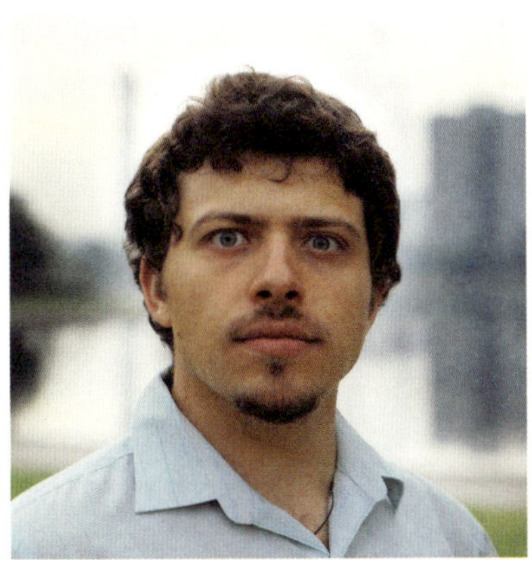

ROMAN SAVCHENKO

Roman Savchenko was born in Moscow in 1983. Savchenko has exhibited in solo and group shows at Project Factory Hall, Artspace, Sputnik Art TSUM, Stella Art Foundation and Marat Guelman Gallery, all in Moscow; Wilkinson Gallery, London; and Museum of Modern Art, Rostov-on-Dov. He was selected to participate in the 3rd Moscow Biennial. Savchenko lives and works in Moscow.

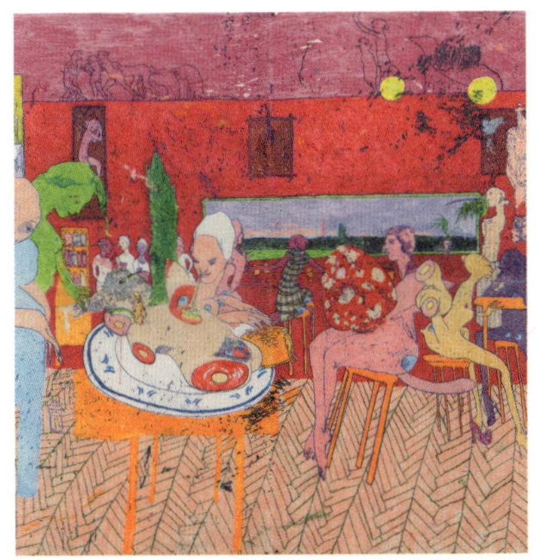

DASHA SHISHKIN

Dasha Shishkin was born in Moscow in 1977. Shishkin holds an MFA from Columbia University, New York, and has exhibited in solo shows at Contemporary Arts Center, Cincinnati; Susanne Vielmetter, Los Angeles; Zach Feuer Gallery, New York and Los Angeles; Gio Marconi, Milan; and Rosenfeld, Munich. She has also exhibited in group shows at Neuberger Museum of Art, Purchase, New York; The Observatory, Dublin; Denver Art Museum, Denver; Museum für Gegenwartskunst, Siegen; Visual Centre of Academy of Art and Design, Tsinghua University, Beijing; and Arndt & Partner, Zurich. Shishkin lives and works in New York.

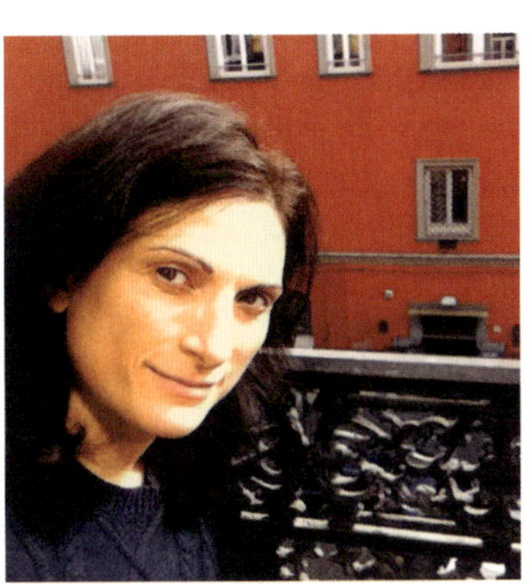

TAMUNA SIRBILADZE

Tamuna Sirbiladze was born in Tbilisi, Georgia, in 1971. Sirbiladze has exhibited in solo and group shows internationally at Galerie Charim Ungar, Berlin; Galerie Niko Vujasin and Galerie Andreas Huber, both in Vienna; A.M.P, Athens; Jonathan Viner, London; Gavin Brown's Enterprise, New York; Galerie ColletPark, Paris; Howard House Contemporary, Seattle; Museum of Modern Art, Tbilisi, and Top Kino, Vienna. Sirbiladze lives and works in Vienna.

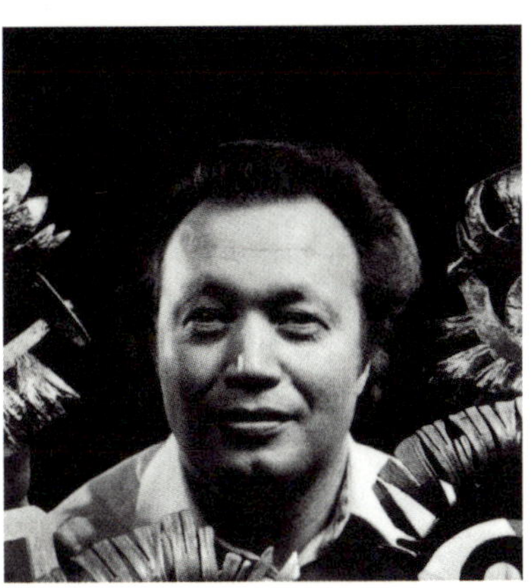

SERGEI VASILIEV

Sergei Vasiliev was born in Chelyabinsk, Russia, in 1937. Vasiliev has exhibited internationally and his work is held in numerous museums' collections. He is the author of more than twenty books, including *Russian Beauty* (1996), and *Zonen* (1994). He has received many honours for his work including International Master of Press Photography from the International Organization of Photo Journalists (Prague, 1985). Vasiliev lives and works in Chelyabinsk.

ACKNOWLEDGEMENTS

The Saatchi Gallery gratefully acknowledges the following who have contributed photographs of the artists and artworks:

Tom Baker, Sam Drake, Dasha Fursey portrait courtesy Dimitry Tolstih, Liudmila Konstantinova portrait courtesy Andrey Bezukladnikov, Valery Koshlyakov artworks and portrait courtesy Vladimir Sichov, Daria Krotova portrait courtesy Vladimir Mishukov, Boris Mikhailov portrait courtesy Sprovieri Gallery, London, Gosha Ostretsov portrait courtesy Andrey Bezukladnikov, Sergey Pakhomov portrait courtesy Danil Golovkin, Yelena Popova portrait courtesy Simon Vogel, Dasha Shishkin, *Not Sad, Just Sighing*, courtesy Susanne Vielmetter Los Angeles Projects and Zach Feuer Gallery, New York, Photo credit: Jason Mandella

The Saatchi Gallery would also like to thank:

FUEL Design, Gosha Ostretsov, Ibid Projects, London, Irena Hochman Fine Art Ltd., Jonathan Viner Gallery, London, Liudmila Konstantinova, Marat Guelman Gallery, Moscow, Olga Golovanova, Olivier Varenne, Sprovieri Gallery, London, Susanne Vielmetter Los Angeles Projects, Wilkinson Gallery, London, Zach Feuer Gallery, New York

Published by the Saatchi Gallery in 2012
© Saatchi Gallery 2012

Edited by Georgina Marling and Rebecca Wilson, Saatchi Gallery

Designed by Alastair Goodbody at Silver Square Studio, London
Printed and bound by MM Artbook printing

In Art We Trust © Dimitri Ozerkov 2012
Winter's Gone, Summer's Here, Thanks To The Party For That © Gosha Ostretsov 2012
Artist texts © Lupe Núñez-Fernández 2012

Front cover: detail from *Case History* by Boris Mikhailov, 1997-1998

Dr Dimitri Ozerkov is director of the Contemporary Art Department of The State Hermitage Museum, St. Petersburg, Russia. He was the curator of the Saatchi Gallery's 'Newspeak: British Art Now' when it premiered at the Hermitage, and 'Dmitri Prigov' at the 54th Venice Biennale.

Lupe Núñez-Fernández is a writer and translator based in London and Madrid. She was formerly deputy editor of ArtReview, an editor at Phaidon Books and on the editorial staff at Modern Painters and LUX.

SPONSORS

GALLERY PATRONS
BNP Paribas
CHANEL
Prudential
Standard Chartered

EDUCATION PATRONS
Deutsche Bank
Google
Lille 3000
Magic of Persia

MEDIA PARTNER
The Sunday Times

SPECIAL PROJECTS PARTNER
HUGO BOSS

FOUNDING PATRON
Dinesen

CORPORATE PATRONS
Allford Hall Monaghan Morris
ARUP
Asahi
ClearChannel
ERCO
Goedhuis & Co
Hyatt Regency London – The Churchill
Martinspeed
Parallel Contemporary Art
Pernod Ricard UK
Pommery
Suntory Whisky
Xirrus

CORPORATE MEMBERS
Crane TV
Doublet
Hallett Independent
Pemberton Greenish
Robert Walters

BENEFACTORS
Gillian & Stuart Corbyn
Patricia & Jon Moynihan
Tsukanov Family Foundation

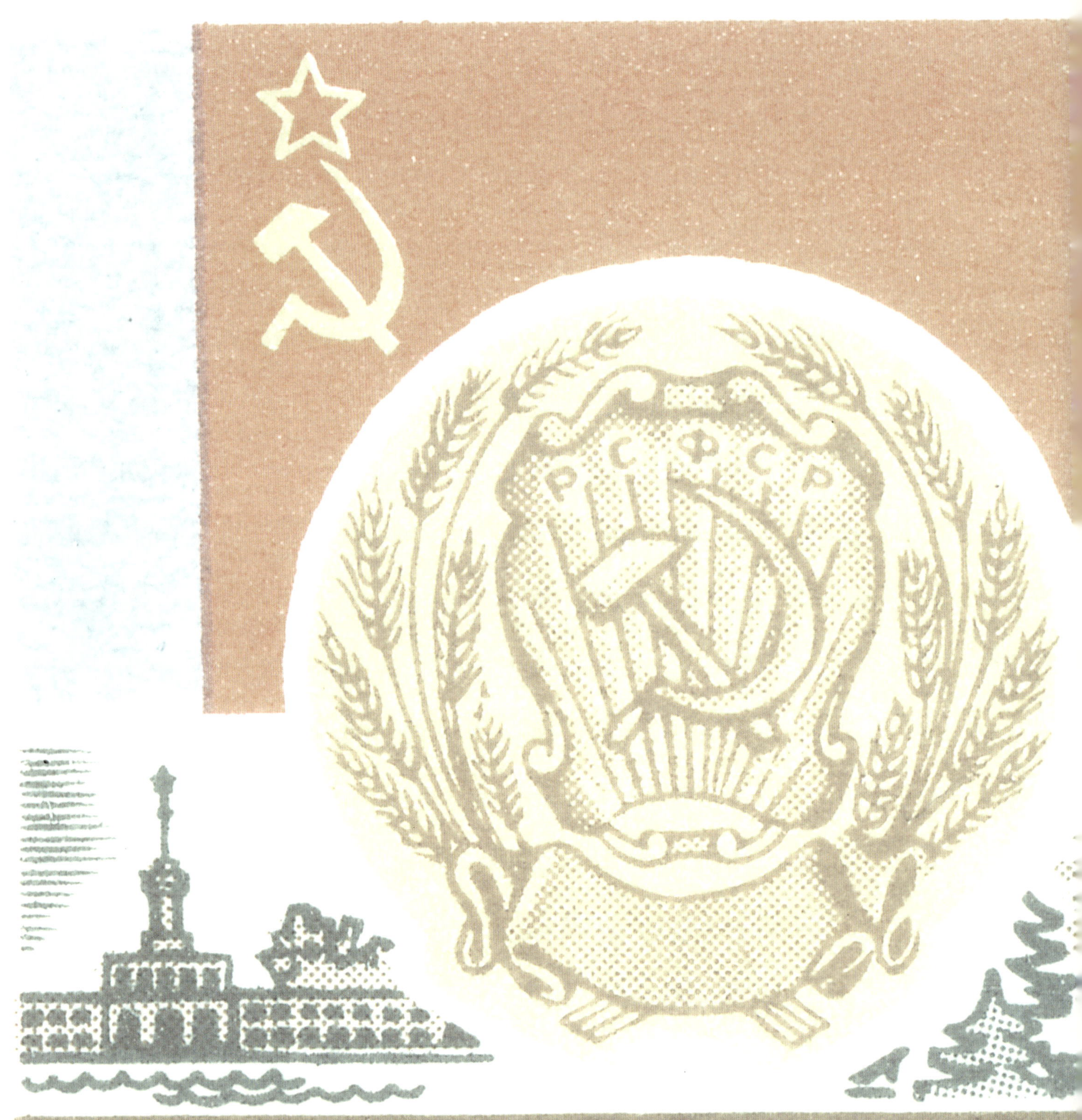
50·ЛЕТИЕ ВЕЛИКО
РСФСР
РОССИЙСКАЯ СОВЕТСК
ФЕДЕРАТИВНАЯ
СОЦИАЛИСТИЧЕСКАЯ РЕСПУБ